The Law of Outer Space

Judge Manfred Lachs
(1914-1993)

The Law of Outer Space

An Experience in Contemporary Law-Making

by

Manfred Lachs

Reissued on the occasion of the 50th anniversary of the International Institute of Space Law

IISL

Edited by

Tanja Masson-Zwaan
Stephan Hobe

MARTINUS NIJHOFF PUBLISHERS

LEIDEN • BOSTON
2010

Printed on acid-free paper.

ISBN: 978 9004 18667 5

The Law of Outer Space by Manfred Lachs was first published in 1972 by A.W. Sijthoff International Publishing Company NV, ISBN 90 286 0212 7.

Frontispiece photograph reproduced courtesy of The Hague Academy of International Law.

PRINTED AND BOUND IN THE NETHERLANDS.

Table of Contents

Preface by the IISL President

Manfred Lachs' 1972 book on the Law of Outer Space was already becoming a rarity when I was at law school. The library had a copy, but it was no longer available for sale in bookstores. Today, in many places only a photocopy remains. Nevertheless, even now, practically every space law student consults this book, which is brilliant for its foresight and its simplicity.

The International Institute of Space Law (IISL) was founded in 1960 (see also "About the International Institute of Space Law" in this book). In 1990, as the IISL turned 30, Judge Manfred Lachs was elected as its 5th President, succeeding Professor Isabella Diederiks-Verschoor. At the same time, I became Secretary of the IISL and thus had the immense pleasure of working closely with Judge Lachs until he passed away in 1993. Again 20 years later, in 2010, the IISL is celebrating its 50th anniversary, like its sister organisation, the International Academy of Astronautics (IAA).

When the IISL Board of Directors started discussions last year on how to commemorate this golden jubilee, I proposed to republish the 1972 book by Manfred Lachs. Ever since I became IISL President in 2008, it has been one of my priorities to involve the younger generation of space lawyers in the work of the Institute, and making essential resources available for them is an important part of that task. Of course there are many good books by excellent scholars that merit to be revisited, but the book by Lachs has a special meaning that led to my proposal. Not only was he President of the IISL, but also this book especially appeals to young space lawyers and making it once again available for them seemed an excellent opportunity to celebrate fifty years of successful activities of the IISL.

We hope that this re-publication of "The Law of Outer Space" will benefit not only young scholars, but 'older' ones as well. Judge Lachs was always able to express in a few simple words the most complex legal issues, and his clear legal mind is a joy for every scholar. He was particularly sensitive to the need of involving bright young scholars, as was also exemplified by the fact that he served on the bench of the very first space law moot court competition organised by the IISL in 1992, which was renamed the "Manfred Lachs Space Law Moot Court Competition" in his honour after his passing in 1993. I believe that he would have enjoyed to know that his book is still motivating students from all over the world to further their knowledge about space law.

It is a remarkable achievement to write a book that almost four decades later has lost virtually none of its relevance, and it is hoped that Manfred Lachs' wisdom and scholarship will continue to inspire us all for a long time to come.

Tanja Masson-Zwaan
President, IISL
On behalf of the IISL Board of Directors
The Hague, June 2010

Introduction by the IISL Directorate of Studies

Manfred Lachs' *The Law of Outer Space* Revisited

I. About the Author

When Manfred Lachs, Judge of the International Court of Justice from 1967 to 1993, wrote his famous treatise on outer space entitled "The Law of Outer Space: An Experience in Contemporary Law-Making", which appeared in 1972 at the then existing publishing house Sijthoff in Leiden, he was already a well known personality in the world of public international law. Born to the Polish attorney Ignacy Lachs and his wife, the English teacher Sophie Lachs, he studied law at the Jagiellonian University in Krakowa and finished his studies in 1937 with the doctoral degree. He then studied in Vienna and Nancy, receiving another doctoral degree of the Université de Nancy in 1939. After this, he changed to the London School of Economics and Political Science, thus escaping the terror of the holocaust years, which extinguished all the members of his family who had remained in Poland.

It was those years in England that particularly influenced the legal thinking of Manfred Lachs. He acquired a very profound knowledge of English law and English legal history. Moreover, this contributed to his extraordinary command of foreign languages like English, French, German and Russian, which he mastered next to his mother tongue Polish not only orally, but also in writing. He joined the Polish Government-in-exile in London, and became a member of the delegation to the United Nations War Crimes Commission. His first book, entitled "War Crimes–An Attempt to Define the Issues", appeared in 1945.

Lachs subsequently joined the Polish Foreign Ministry, but at the same time pursued an academic career, by taking up a Professorship at the Polish Academy of Science in Warsaw and, three years later, as Professor of international law at the University of Warsaw. He was Legal Advisor to the Polish delegation at the Paris Peace Conference in 1946 and present at the Nürnberg trials on behalf of the Polish people. In 1947, he became Director of the Legal Department of the Polish Ministry of Foreign Affairs, and in 1960 Legal Advisor to the then Foreign Minister Adam Rapacki, at the level of ambassador. During this time, he played an instrumental role in the development of the Rapacki Plan, which aimed at declaring Germany, Poland and Czechoslovakia as nuclear free zones. The plan was presented to the United

Nations in 1957 but was rejected by Western countries that considered this a danger to the balance of power in Europe.

As a representative of Poland, Manfred Lachs was also influential in the United Nations Organization. He was the only person to be appointed three times–in 1949, 1951 and 1955–as President of the Legal Committee of the United Nations, an extraordinary achievement. In 1957, he was elected to the International Law Commission, of which he remained a member until 1966. During this time, he became particularly active in the work on the United Nations Convention on the Law of Treaties. Moreover, in 1962 (until 1966) he became the first Chairman of the Legal Subcommittee of the United Nations Committee on the Peaceful Uses of Outer Space. Under his chairmanship, the "Declaration of Legal Principles Governing the Activities of States in the Exploration and Use of Outer Space" was adopted in 1963, which was, of course, the immediate precursor to the United Nations Treaty on Principles Governing the Activities of States in the Exploration and Use of Outer Space, including the Moon and Other Celestial Bodies, the famous Outer Space Treaty. Then, in October 1966, Manfred Lachs was elected a Judge of the International Court of Justice in The Hague and was sworn in on 6 February 1967. He was Judge for more than 16 years, and from 1973 to 1976 he served as President of the Court. In view of his extraordinary contributions to the law of outer space, he became President of the International Institute of Space Law in 1990 until his death in 1993.

II. About the Book

This extraordinary personality had been active not only as a scientist and professor of international law, but also as a practitioner directing both the Legal Subcommittee of the United Nations Committee on the Peaceful Uses of Outer Space and, more broadly, the early development of international space law. There was nobody more appropriate to write a treatise on international space law than him. In fact, at the time of writing this book, in addition to the Declaration on Legal Principles of 1963, the Outer Space Treaty of 1967, the Rescue Agreement of 1968 and the Liability Convention of 1972 had all been adopted.

It is against this background that one is compelled to read the treatise of Manfred Lachs. It is divided into 12 relatively short chapters of about 10 pages including end notes. As the author makes clear already in the introduction, "mankind is only partly aware of the far-reaching consequences of its entry into space". This is as true today as it was in 1972. The author very correctly writes about "the new horizon of international law that was marked by science's entry into outer space" (Chapter I, p. 11-17). He highlights that, throughout its history, international law has been flexible enough to cover humankind's journeys in and to even the most extreme places, such as the High Seas, and the Arctic and Antarctic regions. Another even more challenging endeavor was about to begin with humankind's entry into the new dimension of outer space. Lachs highlights the unique nature of the new laws that were required, although he correctly notes that space law from its beginning was a part of international law (p. 13).

One should take into particular account Lachs' idea that the treaty-based nature of international space law has, especially with regard to the general legal nature of outer space, created a legal system "erga omnes". That rather ambitious conception of "erga omnes" makes it clear that the legal regime of outer space is of a somewhat objective nature, to be respected not only by space-faring nations and States Parties to the Outer Space Treaty, but by all members of the international community. It is important that Lachs highlights this new character of international space law.

In the second chapter entitled "The new chapter of international law" (pp. 19-25), Lachs maintained that an analogy with international air law would not be possible, due to the profoundly different legal nature of outer space (pp. 19, 20). Rather, international space law would be confronted with unknowns in many respects: Can humans live permanently in outer space? Is there extraterrestrial life? (pp. 21, 22). These are extremely important questions, which are all too little asked by many scholars when describing ordinary problems of space law. Moreover, he correctly underlines the cooperative character of international space endeavors in Chapter III (pp. 27-39).

His brief description of the legal regime of outer space, and the celestial bodies in Chapter IV (pp. 41-51) touches upon all of the important questions that are still relevant today, such as: What is meant by national appropriation? (p. 42). Lachs asserts that national appropriation would cover not only sovereign rights but also property rights (p. 43). Although this might be disputable, it is clear that this dispute goes on even today. It is probably necessary that some clarification be given on this issue and a good opportunity would be when the international community is in a position to establish the legal regime for commercial uses of outer space, which was already anticipated in 1979 in the Moon Agreement.

Manfred Lachs succinctly describes the procedural aspects of law-making in a chapter entitled "The law-making process" (pp. 125-134). Obviously, consensus within the law-making procedure is at the core of this and as many believe, international space law has in this respect made a really valuable contribution to the development of international law. What Lachs could not describe in 1972 however - for obvious reasons - is the increasing reluctance of States to enter into legally binding international agreements. This development, which has been described several times, is alarming because States in an increasing way find it more advantageous to resort to instruments of "soft law", like legally non-binding United Nations General Assembly Resolutions, simply because they do not want to enter into legally binding commitments. The spirit of this chapter makes it very evident that

Manfred Lachs would have fought for the strong observance of the rule of law and against any tendencies to dilute this rule of law!

This gives rise to some more general remarks as to the approach Lachs takes with regard to international law. He does certainly not belong to the positivist school of thinking, but his approach might be circumscribed as "legal realism". He looks upon international law and the United Nations Charter as dynamic instruments as long as a dynamic process regulates the interests of the different actors.

There are, moreover, questions that are not yet answered, even though Manfred Lachs has asked them already 40 years ago. What are the frontiers of outer space? (Chapter V, pp. 53-64). Lachs favors drawing an artificial boundary and rightly also favors a right of innocent passage. These are, however, questions that remain as disputed as ever.

The chapter on jurisdiction over objects and astronauts very precisely states the problems of jurisdiction and ownership as they existed in 1972 and still exist today (pp. 66-74). The same is true for the discussion about the assistance with the return of astronauts and space objects (Chapter VII, pp. 75-88), which provides a very accurate short commentary on the Rescue Agreement and all the rights and obligations contained therein. With a short chapter on space telecommunications (Chapter VIII, pp. 89-96), the author sheds a light on some practical applications of outer space, explaining the importance of telecommunications and the regulatory regime established by the International Telecommunication Union.

The next Chapter IX on "Peaceful use–arms and armament" (pp. 97-104) correctly states that outer space legislation does not prevent States from militarizing outer space and celestial bodies. One can even have doubts as to whether Lachs' statement that "the sense of 'peaceful' is thus clearly defined" is completely accurate (p. 98). In any case, nothing has changed since 1972–the problems remain the same.

Chapter X (pp. 105-111) lists some of the important rights and obligations of States, including *inter alia* the obligation of States to inform other States of upcoming dangers, the right to access other countries' space vehicles (p. 106), the duty to consult other States before undertaking experiments (p. 107) and, finally, the complex question as to whether international space law contains a general obligation to promote the weaker members of the international community (p. 108). Although this was one of the determining and crucial questions of the time, Lachs touches upon this only very briefly (p. 108) and without mentioning the famous Article I paragraph 1 of the Outer Space Treaty. Here, we all know that subsequent developments have brought about a relatively clear response of the international community, through the adoption of the Space Benefits Declaration of 1996. In this respect, we can really state that the development of international law in general, as well as international space law in particular, has transcended the fights of the 1970s for a New International Economic Order.

Chapter XI on responsibility (pp. 113-124) broadly portrays the new feature of strict liability as a consequence of ultra-hazardous activities in outer space (p. 115 *et seq.*). In this area as well, nothing has changed, except that more clearly than was the case in the 1970s, the question of the possible liability of private actors, or the question of State or Governmental liability for wrongful acts of private actors comes into play today. It is very interesting that the book does not mention the option contained in Article VI of the Outer Space Treaty, namely that private actors are also entitled to undertake activities in outer space. In fact, Governments were the main space-faring actors when Lachs wrote the book, and it is only over the past 10 years or so that we have begun to seriously discuss the consequences of private space activities, particularly in the form of national space laws.

Lachs' book could only cover the first phase of international space law, involving traditional Governmental space activities. By contrast, we are now confronted with numerous problems of the current second phase, involving increased private space activities. The problems are partly the same, because even when private actors pursue space activities, the question of Governmental liability is at stake since the basic principle of State liability as contained in the Outer Space Treaty and the Liability Convention have not changed at all.

III. In Conclusion

The conclusions drawn by Manfred Lachs in 1972 (pp. 135-138) on the one hand enthusiastically highlight the ever greater speed of technological developments that characterizes our time. On the other hand, however, with great foresight, Lachs points to imminent risks associated with this progress, including dangers both to the environment and to unequal development. Both contribute to an ever increasing instability among States. One cannot but admit that this forecast remains true in our time as well.

This is a truly great and far-sighted book written in 1972 by a wonderfully wise man, whom the International Institute of Space Law was honored to have as its President. Everybody who studies space law must read this compelling book!

Stephan Hobe
Steven Freeland
Ram Jakhu
IISL Directorate of Studies
Cologne/Montreal/Sydney, June 2010

The Law of Outer Space

Foreword

Most of the issues touched upon in the pages that follow have already been dealt with by other jurists, more competent than I. They have also been discussed in my earlier writings. The present study is therefore intended as no more than a brief account of the first developments in law-making for outer space and it has no greater ambitions than to recapitulate events and indicate the trends. At a time when an important stage in this process has been completed I felt that such a summary would serve a useful purpose.

The issues of law concerned are surely fascinating in the horizons we are forced to contemplate, standing on the brink of a new world, or worlds, far beyond anything man has ever reached for. What had seemed mere abstract speculation has taken on real and concrete shape.

From the very day his instruments entered outer space, man was faced with a range of important problems, which have intensified and proliferated with the speedy development of science and technology. The response of law became an urgent necessity. For, though this new sphere of man's activity is apparently remote, it is nevertheless closely linked with what happens on our globe. It is from earth that space objects begin their journey, from here they are controlled. Man's journey into outer space begins on earth and on earth it comes to an end. It also became swiftly apparent that, while phenomena in outer space could be monitored from earth, terrestrial events could also be monitored, or earth's environment influenced, from outer space. This means that the key issues concerning the new dimension can be resolved only within the framework of the overall interdependence of events. Indeed, a feedback has been set in motion, affecting the actions of States and their relations in many areas.

Furthermore, this is a domain in which the great revolution in science has created the urgent need to bring the activities of States within the framework of law, in view of the dangers and risks involved.

Finally, with the further expansion of our knowledge and scientific progress, the need for new rules of international law is rapidly growing in other domains. Here the experience gained in law-making for outer space may play an illustrative, and at the same time, cautionary role. Hence the impact and special importance of this new chapter of law-in-the-making.[1]

These, then, are the reasons which prompted me to draw up this brief survey, with all the imperfections it is bound to have.

The Hague,
March 1972

Note to the Foreword

1 A general outline and preliminary conclusions on the subject were presented in my lectures delivered at the Academy of International Law, The Hague, in 1964: *Recueil des cours*, tome 113, 1964-III, pp. 7-115.

Introduction

The great adventure began when–on 4 October 1957–the first Sputnik sent into orbit circled round the earth and relayed scientific data from outer space. The first passenger animal, the dog Layka, was followed by chimpanzee Eros and others.

Then it was a man, Yuri Gagarin, who–on 12 April 1961–embarked on a journey among the stars.[1] A few weeks later he was followed by Alan B. Shepherd and Virgil Grissom, making short ballistic journeys.[2]

Space vehicles made ever longer journeys and engaged in ever more fascinating exploits. Man took a walk in space: Alexei Leonov (on 18 March 1965), then Edward White (on 3 June 1965). Early in 1966 the Soviet-launched automatic station Luna 9 soft-landed on the moon and transmitted television images and information from the surface.[3] Subsequently the US vehicles Gemini 6 and Gemini 7 performed a rendezvous in space, and Gemini 8 docked with an unmanned Agena Target Vehicle. Further highly important exploits were accomplished with the aid of Geminis 10 and 11, while outside the cabin of Gemini 12 an astronaut conducted a whole series of experiments.

Meanwhile, other experiments had been directed at Venus.[4]

On 16 January 1969, Soyuz 4 and Soyuz 5 linked up in space to create a platform, and two of their crew passed from one vehicle to the other performing experiments.[5]

The launching of Apollo 10, with its lunar module which approached within eight miles' distance of the moon's surface, preceded the mission of Apollo 11, which culminated in the historic message reported to the world from Houston on 20 July 1969: "Man landed on the moon today. Two pioneers from the planet Earth, Neil A. Armstrong and Edwin E. Aldrin, flew their fragile spacecraft to frightening but safe touchdown at 2017 G.M.T.". Thus for the first time men touched the surface of earth's satellite; they walked on it, performed a series of experiments, collected some samples of moonrock, placed on it a number of instruments and, after climbing back into their module, left the moon, docked with the command ship, rejoined their colleague Michael Collins and with him returned to earth.

The mission of Apollo 11 was followed by Apollo 12, on 19 November 1969, when the lunar module (Lem) landed with great precision in the neighbourhood of Surveyor 3, the unmanned craft which had preceded it over two years earlier (19 April 1967).

Meanwhile three spaceships, Soyuz 6, 7 and 8, with seven men aboard, had performed experiments in manoeuvring, navigation and welding, in conditions of weightlessness, and docking.[6]

The year 1970 witnessed the dramatic rescue-operation of the three astronauts aboard Apollo 13 after their craft had suffered an explosion. Though their mission was not carried out, the manoeuvres that led to their successful re-entry were in themselves a great achievement. There followed the spectacular landing of Apollo 14, which returned after the accomplishment of further remarkable exploits. Later the automatic multi-stage device Luna 16 landed on the moon and returned with lunar samples.

On 17 November 1970 the Soviet Union deposited on the moon an eight-wheeled vehicle weighing 1,667 lb. and equipped with *inter alia* a solar battery, an isotype power-source, a soil-analyser and a (French) laser-reflector. This explored the Sea of Rains for over ten months, moving at intervals over the lunar surface and transmitting images and data back to earth. Venera 7, launched in December 1970, has made a soft landing on Venus and is sending back scientific data. Since 1970 there have been further docking experiments, which have led to the creation of the first manned orbital station and laboratory.

Like all perilous ventures, the exploration of space has claimed its victims: Virgil Grissom, Edward White and Roger B. Chaffee died on 27 January 1967 while undergoing tests for an Apollo flight; on 24 April of the same year Vladimir Komarov lost his life through parachute-failure after accomplishing his mission; and on 30 June 1971 the crew of the Soyuz 11 mission, after a smooth return to earth, were found dead in their cabin: Georgy Dobrovolsky, Victor Patsayev and Vladislav Volkov. These seven names remind us with deep poignancy of the unprecedented kind of heroism required to accept the tremendous hazards not only of flight in outer space but of the preparations, the journey to those regions and the return to earth.

There followed the mission of Apollo 15: the landing of David R. Scott and James B. Irwin at the foot of the lunar Apennines on 30 July 1971, while Alfred M. Worden remained in lunar orbit aboard the command ship; they made three excursions on the surface in a four-wheeled battery-powered roving vehicle. After three days of exploration, having travelled 16 miles, installed scientific instruments, collected 228 pounds of rocks and soil samples, photographed and mapped the moon, they started their journey back to earth and concluded it successfully.

These are but a few of the more remarkable exploits illustrating the progress of fourteen years. The work of launching unmanned satellites and probes has also gone on unceasingly.

These objects flung into space have had a varied career. Some, having performed their mission, have returned to earth, some continue to follow their course, others have "decayed" in orbit, still others have burned themselves out in the dense layers of the atmosphere or have disintegrated in space. At present, well over 2,000 continue to move in space, around the earth, the moon or the sun: satellites, fragments of them and of rockets, every so often joined by new companions.[7] Man, then, has embarked on making his own stars, which are "populating" space.

The adventure briefly recounted in the foregoing paragraphs is undoubtedly in large part the fulfilment of fantasies, which have stirred man's imagination throughout history. Beginning in classical civilisation with Cicero's *Somnium Scipionis*, or Lucian of Samosata's *Journey to the Moon*,[8] such (literal) flights of fancy emerge again in Johann Kepler's *Somnium, sive Astronomia lunaris*.[9] Domingo Gonzales's "report" of his travel to and "landing" on the moon in 1599[10] and *L'autre Monde, voyage imaginaire dans le soleil, la lune, etc.*, by Cyrano de Bergerac (1650); then there were Hans Pfaall's adventures, so brilliantly "recorded" by Edgar Allan Poe;[11] Jules Verne's *De la Terre à la Lune* (1865);[12] and H. G. Wells' *First Men on the Moon* (1901).[13] Such fantasies have even been set to music: witness Haydn's opera *Il mondo della luna* and the lunar excursion of *Mr. Brouček* in Janáček's work.

Now, however, utopias have been ousted by reality.[14] Yet there are those who consider that the venture is "merely a more expensive Everest or North Pole".[15] Others see in it the end of an era: "*Finis*, vous nous privez du rêve et du mystère".[16] Then again, that great mathematician and philosopher of our age, Bertrand Russell, urged men "to keep away from the moon" and other planets: "For my part, I should wish to see a little more wisdom in the conduct of affairs on Earth before we extend our strident and deadly disputes to other planets".[17]

Nevertheless it is hard to see the move into space as other than ineluctable, once the necessary technical and economic potential existed. As has been said, the process was inevitable as a "logical stage in the development of civilization. Its advent was prepared not only by numerous scientific and technological achievements underlying spacecraft and carrier-rockets, but was also due to the requirements of natural science today".[18]

Only 44 years ago, a great scientist (Arthur Eddington) could claim: "Not one of the profusion of stars in their physical myriad clusters looks down on scenes comparable to those which are passing beneath the rays of the sun." Today we are aware that the whole solar system is but a small part of the galaxy of the Milky Way, which takes its place among the billions of other galaxies of the Universe. Each of them–like an island–is separated from the others by the vacuum of intergalactic space. Knowledge of space in the past was based on optical observation and more recently on the use of radio-telescopes. The information acquired by these was very limited, owing to the veiling effects of the atmosphere. The advent of satellites and of probing rockets has created new possibilities.

Konstantin E. Tsiolkovsky carried in him the vision of a future when man "would build mobile stations in the sky, would create living rings around the moon, Earth and Sun; would observe Mars from a distance of a score of miles".[19] Then there were Robert Esnault-Pelteri,[20] Hermann Oberth,[21] Robert Goddard:[22] he alone recorded 214 patents in rocket engineering.[23]

Further progress in rockets and satellites has provided precious information concerning earth-magnetism, and shown that many lines of the earth's magnetic field form a closed area (Van Allen belt). Our knowledge of the sun has likewise increased. New perspectives are being opened up in the use of this centre of radiation and matter as a source of light, heat and energy. We have moved closer to our planetary neighbours in the Universe–to our close companion, the elusive, pale-faced wandering moon.

Yet scientists remain torn between several theories concerning the origin of the moon. The existence or non-existence of certain processes, of protobiological material, of an atmosphere, may provide most valuable evidence in this respect.[24] To use the words of a scientist, the moon may be the Rosetta Stone of life.

The first men who landed on the Sea of Tranquillity found its surface pitted and scattered with thousands of rocks and boulders. The samples brought back by automatic devices as well as by men have supplied information as to the age and chemical composition of its surface and certain pointers to the physical history of the moon.[25] Magnetic measurements have provided data not only as to the present of the moon but as to its past–in which, however, mysterious epochs still remain. There may be very little chance of finding life on the moon, yet it may provide greater possibilities than any other celestial body the solution of many unresolved questions concerning the earth itself.[26]

The next target is Mars. Man's conception of this planet, derived from centuries of observation–especially in the years since Francisco Fontana's sketch, of 1636–is now being emended in the light of recent exploits. By the beginning of 1972, eight probing devices had been launched towards Mars. Mariner 9 (USA), after a 167-day journey, went into orbit round the planet on 14 November 1971, while Mars 2 and 3 (USSR), likewise launched in May, went into orbit on 27 November and 2 December 1971 and deposited capsules on the surface. From the signals and images transmitted, arresting, though sometimes apparently conflicting, new data have been added to the scientific picture. Mars shows very distinctive features, unknown elsewhere in the solar system. It used to be assumed that life was possible there, but the atmosphere surrounding the planet had not provided direct evidence of life and the hypothesis had until recently been seriously contested.[27] Yet there are now indications that Mars is a chemically evolved planet; its canals and canyons seem to show at their edges signs of erosion, and some water vapour, and also evidence of volcanic activity have been discovered.

Little was known of Venus, earth's twin, nearest to our globe and of similar dimensions. Clouds and the surrounding atmosphere made observation difficult. Here again space exploration has led the way to the unlocking of many of its secrets and the revision of some long-held exotic ideas. The very high temperature of the surface of Venus raises the question whether this results from a very strong unknown source of heat or from the energy of the sun penetrating the lower atmosphere ("the greenhouse effect"). It has also been found that Venus has much less surface or atmospheric water than the earth.[28] In the light of these and other findings, it has been labelled "a poisonous and hostile planet".

Only yesterday man's knowledge of the universe was extremely limited. Today he has penetrated not a few of the secrets of the cosmos, and it may be that through outer space he will be able to probe its structure and origins, and those of his own planet, more deeply, gaining insight into the origins of life itself.[29] Yet very great uncertainty remains, and many discoveries lead to puzzlement: we are far from understanding.[30] Among the many scientific achievements in space is the discovery of mysterious cosmic objects, powerful radio-sources: quasars.[31] Knowledge of their presence shows that the peaceful void which had seemed to encapsulate the earth was deceptive and that the great cosmological controversy must needs continue.

Mankind is only partly aware of the far-reaching consequences of its entry into space, and in any case the importance of the step, though all may sense it, can so far be fully appreciated only by the initiated few.

Some of the results of the space venture are conspicuous: they have placed the dominating issue of the security and defence of States in a new light. It is also well known that the possibility has been created for satellites to transmit sound and pictures at very high speed to the remotest corners of the earth and that through the use of space great advances have been made in geography, geology, geodesy, cartography, oceanography, hydrology, meteorology and agriculture, to mention but a few of the many fields.[32]

The dawn of space exploration has also coincided with an immense upsurge of apprehension for the environment, which an unbridled technological civilisation is so grievously damaging. Hence there is concern that nothing should be done in or from outer space which could threaten the balance of nature or jeopardize life–on earth or wherever it may exist.

If all the activities connected with outer space are to be conducted for the benefit of all and to the detriment of none, international co-operation is essential, and if all the possibilities opened up are to be used in a responsible manner, the conduct of States in regard to outer space must be submitted to the rule of law. That is the theme of this book, whose aim is to provide a succinct account of the efforts which have been made to meet these desiderata.

Notes to Introduction

1. Gagarin later described his impression on the launching of his spaceship: "My eyes were fixed on the clock. Its hands indicated 7 minutes past 9 ... what I heard was a piercing whistle and later an ever-growing thunderous roar; the gigantic rocket shuddered and slowly, very slowly, it rose from the launching pad. The fight between the rocket and the gravitational force of the earth began . . ."
2. They were succeeded by Herman Titov, travelling aboard Vostok 2 (August 1961) who performed 17.5 orbits round the globe in a 25-hour flight; six months later, on 20 February 1962, John Glenn, with his spaceship Mercury, orbited the earth three times in 5 hours; further successors included the first woman space-traveller, Valentina Tereshkova.
3. Luna 10 entered orbit on 3 April 1966. Two months later Surveyor 1, launched by the United States, landed on the moon surface and sent back thousands of television pictures.
4. On 1 March 1966 the Soviet interplanetary *zond*, Venera 3, reached Venus after a four-month journey, to be followed by Venera 4, which landed on 18 October 1967 after having, during the final descent stage, transmitted back the first close-up scientific information on the planet. The United States launched Mariner 5 passed within 2,580 miles of Venus.
5. In October 1967 two Soviet unmanned satellites, Cosmos 186 and 188, had automatically linked up in space. The following month the United States initiated unmanned test flights for the Apollo manned lunar flight programme. The next stages in the United States programme were the launching on 11 October 1968 of Apollo 7 with three men on board, who returned after a journey of 780 hours and 27 minutes, and, on 21 December, of Apollo 8, whose three astronauts traversed in 147 hours a distance of 250,000 miles, including 10 orbits round the moon.
6. Soyuz 6 departed first (11 October I 969) to be followed after 14 hours by Soyuz 7. To within trifling margins, the two craft circled in the same orbit. Soyuz 8 was launched the following day.
7. The Figure of 2,149 is given in the Satellite Situation Report issued by the Goddard Space Flight Center and covering the period up to 30 April 1970, as reported in *International Herald-Tribune* for 11 June 1970. In 1965, 1,415 man-made objects or parts thereof were identified in space, 613 of them in earth-orbit. The number of objects in such orbit had risen to 1,158 by October 1966, 274 being "intact" and the rest "space-junk" (*Newsweek*, 19 October 1966). With the launching of Apollo 14, 4,900 man-made objects had gone into orbit; of that number, 2,609 had been launched by the United States and 2,220 by the USSR (report of Aerospace Defence Command, 2 February 1971).
8. In Lucian of Samosata's *Vera Historia*, the hero found himself on the moon by accident. Cf. Gautier Languereau: *Quinze Aventures de l'Espace*, Paris, 1969.
9. Cf. Lear, *Johann Kepler's Dream*, Cambridge 1965.
10. Purportedly translated from the Spanish by "Edward Mahin, Gent." (London 1638), the work is couched in autobiographical style as if to convince the reader that the author–generally assumed to have been in fact Bishop Francis Godwin

(1562-1633 or 1634)–had actually visited the moon. French and German translations appeared in 1648 and 1659 respectively.

11. E. A. Poe, "The Unparalleled Adventure of One Hans Pfaall", in the *Southern Literary Messenger*, 1835.
12. One hundred years later, in an introduction to this book in a collected edition of the works of Verne (Paris 1967), Charles-Noël Martin wrote: "Savoir, sentiments, poésie et science sont alliés au rêve d'hier qui est la réalité d'aujourd'hui. Ces pages, nous les avons lues à quinze ans, avec ravissement, et nous pouvons les lire encore, car l'homme a toujours quinze ans devant l'inconnu." "Le grand voyage," writes Albert Ducrocq, "en vérité, commence en 1865 comme un conte. Sous la plume de l'étonnant Jules Verne, qui a confié à un mathématicien ami le calcul de la vitesse nécessaire pour, depuis la Terre, atteindre la lune." "L'homme et la Lune", Paris, 1969. Remarkably enough, in his *Cinq semaines en ballon*, Verne writes with pessimism of his fear that "le dernier jour du monde soit celui où quelque immense chaudière, chauffée à trois milliards d'atmosphères, fera sauter notre planète".
13. Modern science-fiction was the product of the industrial revolution. Its place in literature was rightly anticipated by the Goncourts when they put down in their journal on 16 July 1856: "Quelque chose que le critique n'a pas vu, un monde littéraire nouveau, les signes de la littérature du XXe siècle. Le miraculeux scientifique, la fable par A plus B . . . Plus de poésie, de l'imagination à coup d'analyse."
14. This however, has not spelt the doom of science-fiction, which on the contrary is thriving in alliance with science fact, though it exhibits a marked trend away from fascination with technical marvels towards a skeptical and often cautionary vision of the future. See in particular S. Lem, "Summa technologiae", Cracow (in Polish); M. Crichton, "La Variété Andromède", and F. Herbert, *Dune*, Paris 1970.
15. A. P. Herbert, letter, *The Times*, 18 August 1962.
16. Alain Bosquet in *Adieu à la lune*, a collection of prose, poems, myths, legends and proverbs on the moon, edited by him, Paris 1969: including extracts from Ariosto, Fontenelle, Cyrano de Bergerac, Baudelaire, Poe, Grimm, Lorca and others. Cf. R. J. Cooper, letter to *The Times*, 25 July 1969: "To me, however, the moon's still a mystery, a presence to be felt, a divine pulsation. I'm not out to analyse the moon, but to enjoy it ... That is enough for me."
17. "I cannot see that we have any reason to rejoice in the prospect": "Why man should keep away from the moon", *The Times*, 15 July 1969, p. 9.
18. A. Blagonravov, *Christian Science Monitor*, 7 October 1967.
19. "The Probing of Space by means of jet devices" (in Russian) in *Nauchnoye Obozrenye* No. 5, 1903, and his collected works published by the Academy of Sciences of the USSR, Moscow 1954.
20. *L'Astronautique*, Paris 1930.
21. *Die Rakete zu den Planeten*, Munich 1923; *Wege für Raumschifffahrt* ("Ways towards space-navigation"), Berlin 1929.
22. "A Method of Reaching Extreme Altitudes", Smithsonian Institute, 1919. The same institute published his collected papers in 1969-1970.
23. The early pioneer Casimir Siemičnowicz also deserves a mention. As long ago as 1650 he produced a very interesting study of rocketry in the *pars prima* of

his *Artis Magnae Artilleriae* (Amsterdam), which was reprinted with a Polish translation in 1963 by the Warsaw Institute of Military History.

24. Cf. S. K. Runcorn, "Key to the solar system in the moon's dust", *The Times*, 9 April 1970; J. A. Wood, "The lunar soil" in *Scientific American*, Vol. 223-2, August 1970, pp. 14 ff.; M. Subotowicz, "Isotopic analysis of moon soil and rocks" (in Polish) in *Postępy Fizyki* XXI, v. 4, 1970, pp. 499 ff.; report by G. M. Brown to British Association, *The Times*, 5 September 1970.
25. Cf. deliberations of NASA-sponsored scientific conference at Houston on Apollo 11 results, reported in *International Herald-Tribune*, 10 January 1970, and *The Times*, 26 January 1970. The successive moon-landings have stimulated the revision of some theories and the conception of new ones. In particular, the belief that the layer of surface-dust would seriously hamper movement was rapidly shown to be false. New evidence as to the mineral composition of the moon was produced in a wealth of material for study and analysis. Samples brought back by the Apollo 11 and 12 missions were first found to be 3,300-4,500 million years old and were believed to date back to the time of the formation of the moon. It was soon established, however, that some of these rocks had apparently solidified at a much later stage in lunar history. The samples collected from Fra Mauro were found to be much younger. However, the rock brought back by the latest missions was again found to be the oldest ever discovered, and it was described as containing the "best clues to date for what the initial conditions were on the moon". Until the final answer is found, these and future discoveries can be expected to produce still further revision of theories.
26. Cf. Hess, Korach, Crest and Simmons, "The exploration of the moon" in *Scientific American*, Vol. 221-4, Oct. 1969, pp. 55 ff., and also an interesting proposal for the study of lunar geology and geophysics, of earth from the moon and applied science, put forward as long ago as 1960 by Dr. F. J. Malina in the report of the Lunar International Laboratory Discussion Panel (*Astronautica*, Vol. 11, 1965, No. 2, pp. 123 ff.). N. Kozyrev has also suggested the installation of a laboratory below the lunar surface (*Pravda*, 12 August 1969).
27. Cf. Sagan, "Life Sciences and Space Research", Vol. II, A session of the Fourth International Space Science Symposium, ed. Florkin and Dollfus, Amsterdam 1965; R. Eshelman, "The atmospheres of Mars and Venus" in *Scientific American*, Vol. 220-3, March 1969, p. 88; D. Verguese, "Le vrai visage de Mars" in *Le Monde*, 26 February 1970.
28. Cf. report of the Soviet Academy of Sciences on the results of the Venera 5 and 6 space-probes, published on 3 June 1969; R. Eshelman, *op. cit.*, pp. 78 ff.; B. Lovell, "Some mysteries of Venus resolved" in *The Times*, 30 October 1967; report on the exploration of Venera 4 and Mariner 5 in *Science*, 29 December 1967, p. 158.
29. W. H. Pickering, "Ten years of space exploration", paper read to the 18th International Astronautical Congress, Belgrade 1967, p. 1.
30. The universe may be larger than has been thought: is it finite or infinite? How did it come into being? Through a great explosion, or was it always in a state of constant expansion and continuous evolution? Several theories and models have been advanced, but for a definite reply more information is required: in the words of R. Calder, "a fairly complete inventory of the contents of the universe" (*Man and the Cosmos*, London 1968, pp. 68 f.). Cf. M. J. Rees and J. Silk, "The origin of galaxies" in *Scientific American*, Vol. 222-6, June 1970, p. 35, and

the earlier theories of the Soviet mathematician A.A. Friedman and the discoveries of the astrophysicist V. Ambartsumian.

31. W. Zonn, "Quasars", lecture delivered to the Polish Astronomical Society in October 1967, in *Postępy Astronomii*, Vol. XVI, fasc. 3, 1968. Cf. P. Véron, *Les Quasars*, Paris 1968.

32. Photographs taken from satellites indicate the possibility of detecting oil and other subterranean or submarine resources, observing the condition of soil and crops and collecting worldwide ecological data. Orbiting satellites could even, it has been suggested, relay information on fish-concentrations to trawlers. They also enable cartography to make great strides, for there are still areas of the globe which require proper mapping. Meteorology owes a breakthrough to satellites, which have made it possible to discover cloud patterns, follow tropical storms and forecast more reliably. They can provide a weather pattern for the whole globe. Navigation satellites are certain to prove of the highest importance, especially for the new supersonic aircraft. Synchronized with the earth's rotation, they warn of intensive radiation at particular stages of an aircraft's flight or of icebergs near the paths of ships. Space-research has also made an outstanding contribution to medicine. One need only mention the experience gathered as to the effects on human beings of the so-called "biological clock".

All these and related problems were dealt with in a series of papers at the United Nations Conference on the Exploration and Peaceful Uses of Outer Space, Vienna, 14-27 August 1968. Cf. *Report* of United Nations Committee on the Peaceful Uses of Outer Space, 1968, pp. 102 ff.; *Space Science and Technology: Benefits to Developing Countries*, United Nations, New York 1968; *La Grande Aventure de l'Espace*, a 2-volume collective work by scientists from France, the USA and the USSR, Paris 1968.

Chapter I

The New Horizon of International Law

Space is obviously a basic dimension, a constitutive element of any legal system; the subjects of law perform acts achieved in space, it is within space that the events law is concerned with take place, that the consequences of compliance with or violation of the rules of law materialize.

Conversely, as the activities of States expanded, law began to cover new areas. Taking cognizance of ever new chapters of human activity beyond the frontiers of States, international law has been constantly acquiring new dimensions. It has followed man throughout his journey in time and space, for this is its function and destiny as reflected by history. Special stations on this journey are marked by scientific and technological development.

Thus law moved with man when he embarked on his great adventures on land, water and in the air. The development of transport by road and on rail gave birth to new rules, first bilateral and later multilateral, extending the protection of the law over men and goods crossing the frontiers of many States. Law followed man in his exploration when he crossed oceans and landed on new shores.

Starting from Europe, after the first Catalan and Andalusian expeditions to the Canary Islands, the great sea-routes were opened; by the Vikings and Gaspar Corte-Real in the North–by Columbus through the Canary Islands in one direction and the Azores in the other direction; in the South by Vasco da Gama and Cabral. The route between Europe and Asia around Africa to the Indian Ocean was established. These obviously were difficult beginnings: a journey from Lisbon to Macabar and back took 18 months; from Malacca to Bab el-Mandeb took 50 days.

Of course the law which followed in the wake of the ships was the *jus gentium* of Europe. But the explorers and those who followed them came into contact with alien civilisations, some of them very ancient and at a very advanced stage of development. There was thus a confrontation, and in it the European undoubtedly derived great strength not only from superior technical resources but also from his being inured by the exclusive nature of the law of nations, seen through his eyes. The mainly seaborne exploration of the post-renaissance era was a competition in which the attempt was made to acquire lands regarded as *res nullius* by the securest means at hand. These ranged from the planting of a flag to full-scale occupation. The "law of nations" which evolved against that background was not universal, for its makers and beneficiaries were European, and the "heathen without the pale" were not considered to be entitled to benefit from it as equals.

Undeterred by obstacles, Europeans pursued their efforts, placing greater and greater emphasis on navigation. Did not Tomé Pires claim as far back as in 1514, that a kingdom without harbours was like a house without windows? The seas became ever more populated and ships crossed them with ever greater facility. Very early the need to establish generally binding principles and rules of navigation became manifest. They evolved slowly and not without great difficulty. National claims to exclusive domination of the seas were bound to result in rivalry. To open them to all was therefore a great advance, and it connoted the eventual necessity of co-operation. Thus the expanding *corpus juris gentium* gave birth to a new chapter.

Centuries later man entered a new dimension. His venture into the air is, of course, of much more recent origin. So, obviously, is the law which governs aerial navigation.

In the process of further development international law was obliged to evolve special régimes and rules for other parts of our globe. Since the expeditions of the first decade of this century, great strides have been made in the process of penetrating the polar regions. Law has been faced with the need to work out the status of the Arctic and the Antarctic.[1] Gradually it has embraced the whole of our globe, the atmosphere surrounding it, the depth of continents and oceans.[2] It has expanded in the endeavour to keep pace with the quest of man to extend control over nature and make it serve his needs.

It may now be said that a universal law obtains between nations in all their contacts and wherever–into whatever dimensions–their activities extend.

The era of space-exploration has thus begun, with immense advantages for all humanity, at a time when international law has become truly universal. This universality is closely linked with the principle of equality, which, as history has shown, could not remain indefinitely suppressed. The necessity of international law thus being true to itself has been learned the hard way, and the lesson offers a telling paradigm for man's venture into outer space.

The new dimension, like those which man penetrated earlier, could not remain a legal vacuum. From a purely theoretical point of view it was, of course, possible to subject outer space to a completely novel set of principles and rules, a legal system different from any to which States are submitted elsewhere. However, there was no basis for such a proposition, nor was there any need for it. In fact it would have conflicted with the very nature of international law.

It was therefore aptly declared that States shall carry on activities in the exploration and use of outer space and within it of all celestial bodies, "in accordance with international law, including the Charter of the United Nations, in the interest of maintaining international peace and security and promoting international co-operation and understanding".[3]

Some comments may be called for on the meaning and implications of the extension of international law to–what the relevant instruments describe as–"outer space, including the moon and other celestial bodies". This obviously implies that in all their activities in regard to and within outer space and on celestial bodies States are subject to the rule of international law. The term thus used refers to the worldwide legal system which is binding on States in all other areas of their mutual relations. It includes its basic principles and rules as they have evolved in their historical development, as well as its most recent acquisitions.

Special reference is made to the Charter of the United Nations. This is not surprising, as the Charter as such has also acquired a new dimension. More important, however, is the fact that it is specifically mentioned as part of international law ("international law, including the Charter of the United Nations"). The reason for this results from the character of its most important provisions. These are–as is well known–of two types: the first confirming established principles and rules of international law,[4] the second consisting of those by which pre-existing law was modernized or given more precision, offering States greater protection by the law.[5]

Both made the Charter, as I suggested some years ago, into a Magna Carta of international relations of the year 1945, and thus an integral part of international law.[6]

However, one should not limit oneself to the text of the Charter. During the quarter of a century since its entry into force many of its provisions have further evolved through practice and interpretation. They have been adapted to the rapidly changing conditions of contemporary life. By accepting the Charter as part of contemporary law applicable to outer space and celestial bodies, one has to accept it as it is today, including all the progress made during the years it has been in operation. Thus the obligation to conform with the Charter of the United Nations implies not only the application of provisions of international law as defined by it but also all those that have grown as a result of the further development of the United Nations and subjected to a new and more up-to-date interpretation.

None of this, however, implies an automatic extension to outer space and celestial bodies of "international law, including the Charter of the United Nations" *in toto.* Many parts of their chapters are destined for specific environments and thus do not lend themselves to application in other areas. Some rules cannot be applied to outer space *ex definitione.* Some others are of the nature of *lex specialis* for specific environments. Others still require adaptation to the needs and characteristics of the new dimension, thus modification is needed.[7] In fact the extension of international law to outer space and celestial bodies is only a first step, forming a basis for further development, the creation of special and specific rules which already have or will become necessary in the future.

The scope of application of some international instruments, both bi- and multi-lateral, has been extended to the new dimension.[8] Other important instruments expressly cover outer space.[9] On the other hand, some instruments covering various domains of international relations and concluded before the "space era" will require a more extensive interpretation.

As to future treaties, in the process of their preparation it will become necessary to consider if and to what extent the opening up of the new dimension may affect their sphere of operation, the rights and duties of States parties to them. It is not likely that many such problems will arise in the very near future. However, with the growth of activities in outer space, negotiators will have to bear this possibility in mind.

Finally one special consideration of a teleological nature. There is little doubt that the main object and purpose of the basic principles of contemporary international law is to safeguard peaceful relations amongst States. This is particularly reflected in the Charter of the United Nations. This very same aim is confirmed with regard to outer space; for it has been laid down that the activities of States should be carried on in the interest not only of "maintaining international peace and security", but also of "promoting international co-operation and understanding". The attainment of these goals is not only closely linked with the need to carry out all obligations imposed on States by international law, and the respect of the rights it guarantees–it is in fact conditioned by them.

Thus the premise and directives of the first and basic principle concerning outer space and the celestial bodies leave no room for doubt. They are essential not only for the proper interpretation of rules of law already in existence but also as guides for the future legislative process in this field.

It is thus evident that the provision stipulating that the activities of States in outer space had to be carried out "in accordance with international law including the Charter of the United Nations" created no new rule of law: it was not one of a law-making character. It confirmed only what was the obvious consequence of the nature and functions of international law.

Was it then at all necessary? History records many cases of treaties confirming either principles of law or rules, shaped by established practice and binding States prior to the birth of contractual ties.[10] Sometimes provisions set forth in treaties become binding on States as customary rules of international law, with all the consequences flowing from this.[11]

Thus, treaty stipulations may either confirm existing rules or alternatively initiate a process that leads to their universal acceptance. In the case before us there need be no mystery as to the intrinsic value of the principle in question. It goes much further, for it is not a mere principle or a rule, it reflects the very essence of international law and is the natural consequence of its development and growth.[12] Yet its declaratory character does not reduce its value. Whatever doubt may have existed has been removed, greater clarity and precision have been given to it.

It is binding not only on those who are parties to the instruments in which the principle is contained, but on all States. Its validity extends *erga omnes*. These conclusions must be seen as the point of departure for further considerations, on the threshold of the new chapter of law.

Notes to Chapter I

1. Cf. Smedal, *Acquisition of Sovereignty over Polar Areas*, 1931; M. W. Mouton, "The International Regime of the Polar Regions", 107 *R.C.A.D.I.* 1962, t. III, pp. 175. An important step concerning Antarctica, its utilization for peaceful purposes and the establishment of a régime of co-operation was taken in the conclusion of the Antarctic Treaty, Washington, 1 December 1959.
2. Cf. action of the UN concerning the Sea-Bed and Ocean Floor; General Assembly resolutions 2340 (XXII) of 18 December 1967, 2467 (XXIII) of 21 December 1968, 2574 (XXIV) of 15 December 1969, and 2749 (XXV) of 17 December 1970.
3. Article III of the Treaty governing the Activities of States in the Exploration and Use of Outer Space, including the Moon and Other Celestial bodies, commended by the General Assembly of the UN on 19 December 1966; cf. the earlier Declaration of Legal Principles Governing the Activities of States in the Exploration and Use of Outer Space, General Assembly resolution 1962 (XVIII), 13 December 1963, para. 4: "The activities of States in the exploration and use of outer space shall be carried on in accordance with international law, including the Charter of the United Nations, in the interest of maintaining international peace and security and promoting international co-operation and understanding." This resolution was preceded by resolution 1721 (XVI), adopted on 20 December 1961, which: "1. Commends to States for their guidance in the exploration and use of outer space the following principles: (*a*) international law, including the Charter of the United Nations, applies to outer space and celestial bodies." Cf. also the resolution adopted by the Institut de Droit International, Brussels, 11 September 1963, paragraph 14: "In all matters not provided for in the preceding paragraphs, States are bound by general international law, including the principles of the Charter of the United Nations". Cf. also The Draft Principles prepared by the David Davies Memorial Institute of International Studies: "2.3 In the exploration and use of outer space and celestial bodies States and international bodies (*a*) are bound by international law and by the provisions of the United Nations Charter and other international agreements, which may be applicable."
4. Cf. Mateescu, M., "Interpretation juridique du Traité de 27 janvier 1967", *Revue générale de l'air et de l'espace*, XXXI, No. 1, 1968, pp. 20-22.
5. In addition to the two categories of provision mentioned the Charter contains of course many others which constitute *lex ex contractu* only.
6. Cf. M. Lachs, "Le Problème de la révision de la Charte des Nations Unies", *R.G.D.I.P.*, XXVIII, No. 1, 1957, pp. 55-59.
7. This view is shared by J. Dutheil de la Rochère: "La Convention sur l'internationalisation de l'espace", *Annuaire français de droit international*, XIII, 1967, pp. 628-629. Cf. also the statement of the representative of Argentina, in the Legal Sub-Committee of the UN Committee for the Peaceful Uses of Outer Space: Document A/AC. 105/C.2, SR.80, 6 July 1967, p. 17.
8. On 3 November 1947 the UN General Assembly adopted resolution 110 (II); as mentioned in Chapter VIII, below, the Assembly's 1963 Declaration of Legal Principles specifically relates this to outer space (preamble, sixth paragraph:

"*Considering* that the aforementioned resolution is applicable to outer space") and so does the 1967 Space Treaty (preamble, eighth paragraph).

9. Cf. The Treaty Banning Nuclear Weapon Tests in the Atmosphere, in Outer Space and Under Water, signed in Moscow on 5 August 1963.
10. Cf. M. Lachs. "Les développements et fonctions des traités multi-latéraux", 92 *R.C.A.D.I.* 1957, t. II, p. 330.
11. Article 38 of the Vienna Convention on the Law of Treaties, 1969. Cf. Article 34 of the Draft Articles on the Law of Treaties prepared by the International Law Commission, Reports of the International Law Commission: G.A., *Official Records*, XXI, Suppl. No. 9 (A/6309/Rev. 1), p. 15, and the commentary to it, p. 61. Cf. also Article 40 of the draft and commentary thereon.
12. This view is confirmed by several writers; cf., in particular, D. Goedhuis, "Reflections on the Evolution of Space Law" in *Netherlands International Law Review*, 1966, No. 2, pp. 117 ff.; cf. also resolution adopted by the International Law Association at its 53rd Conference, Buenos Aires, 1968.

Chapter II

The New Chapter of International Law

The extension of the realm of international law to outer space was but a preliminary. In its wake a host of issues was bound to arise. As indicated earlier, it was not simply a question of applying existing principles and rules within and in regard to the new environment: very many of them required adaptation, in many situations new ones, destined for it only, had to be created.

On the other hand, owing to the great and speedy progress made in the exploration of outer space there are many key issues which call for solution.

Thus the law-makers have had continuously to size up the possibility or advisability of resorting to analogies with other branches of international law, and they have also had to contend with darkness on issues important for the legislative process.

Analogy

It is well known that when new rules are drafted, the comparative method is frequently resorted to, familiar experience being relied upon and similarities sought with situations already resolved. Thus law-makers lean towards analogical solutions.[1] However, in following this course one must bear in mind the idiosyncracies of the environment for which the rules are destined, keep in sight the objective the law is intended to serve, and beware of repeating the mistakes made in kindred fields.

The temptation to draw on experiences of the past is always great. And so it proved in the present instance. The great discoveries of the 15th and 16th centuries were called to mind.[2] Yet one obviously cannot ignore the many fundamental changes which have occurred since in many spheres and, more especially, in international relations. What analogy can subsist today with the mission of the Genoese Columbus when he embarked upon his historic voyage and was given by Ferdinand and Isabella, on 30 April 1492 the commission to "discover and subdue some islands and continent in the ocean"? To invest him with this power, reliance was placed on the famous *Inter Caetera* of Alexander VI, one of the Bulls which claimed the right to grant to Christian kingdoms dominion beyond the "old" continent over lands "in possession of heathens and infidels". What comparison can there be with the mission of a Magellan (a Portuguese), acting for Spain, or of Giovanni de Verrazzano (a Florentine) for King Francis I, or with the part played in this field by corporations vested with patents or charters of their respective States, like that granted by Henry VII in the year 1501: "To sail East, West, North and South and discover lands of Gentiles, Infidels and take possession of them as the King's vassals"?[3] Or with the Treaty of Tordesillas (of 7 June 1494), by which Spain and Portugal agreed to alter the line dividing what they considered their exclusive rights to the New World.

Need one recall how frequently the practices of dividing and disposing of lands and whole continents led to conflict and strife? The lesson should have been learnt.

An ostensibly more promising course was to draw analogies with another chapter of international law: the law of the sea. This offers an illustration of how principles evolved through the confrontation between the doctrines of *mare clausum* and *mare liberum.* The present régime of the high seas is clearly the outcome of their role in trade and transport and reflects their relationship to the continents they surround and link: *natura maris.*[4] To that extent it is *lex specialis.*

Nevertheless, when–typically, under the pressure of new inventions–it became necessary to devise a régime for another medium and environment, the air, many jurists, casting around, naturally felt prompted to suggest that airspace be assimilated to the sea for legal purpose: complete freedom of air-navigation was proposed or, alternatively, a structural dualism like that subsisting between the high seas and the territorial sea. This was, however, to ignore the crucial factors peculiar to the physical relationship between air and earth, and the way in which this created an entirely fresh series of security considerations. When issue was joined between the various solutions proposed in the first decade of our century, victory went to the doctrine of each State's complete sovereignty over the airspace above its territory.[5]

But although analogy here proved unhelpful, to compare the results achieved respectively in regard to the sea and the air is an instructive exercise. For it is *as if* in regard to airspace a doctrine corresponding, not to that of the territorial sea (with its connotation of limits), but to that of *mare clausum* had prevailed, as if the existence of anything corresponding in the air to *mare liberum*, the high seas, had been denied. One may surmise, however, that if the invention of orbiting satellites had been contemporaneous with that of the aeroplane, different and more far reaching solutions would then have been devised; possibly with the result of exposing the dangers of analogical procedures still further.

For present purposes, the foregoing may serve to illustrate the fact that the "mechanical transfer" of institutions from one environment to another is of little avail:[6] it may lead to distortions and even seriously stunt the development of the new branch of law.

Yet despite Lord Mansfield's warning ("There is nothing in law so misleading as a metaphor or an analogy") or Einstein's caveat that analogies have been "a source not only of the most fruitful theories, but also of the most misleading fallacies", the analogical method cannot utterly be discarded. One has simply to beware of its pitfalls and seek to grasp reality as comprehensively as possible in proceeding from tried systems to the construction of new ones. The usefulness of an analogy is of course conditioned by the experience acquired in operating a given rule or institution. But, just as obviously, it is only when it really fits the new situation that it offers assistance–sometimes in the application of an existing rule *mutatis mutandis*, more often in pointing the way to a new rule. It is in any case a serious mistake to employ analogy for the purpose of bringing a new developing branch of international law within the purview of traditional systems inseparable from institutions whose own transmutation is in progress. Analogy must be used creatively.

Thus the new branch known as the law of outer space must reflect the most progressive tendencies of international law. It must be directed towards the future, not to a world that has been left behind. Hence, when resorting to analogies, account must be taken of the most recent developments in international law as a whole.

The Unknowns of Outer Space

By his venture into outer space, man has uncovered some of nature's secrets, but there are very many questions that he still cannot answer. These unknowns present many difficulties in the law-making process. Can man live permanently in outer space? Earlier experiments have demonstrated the harmful biological effects of cosmic radiation, reduced gravity and weightlessness, which thus expose astronauts to peculiar hazards. Preliminary conclusions have indicated that these phenomena might constitute "the main obstacle in man's penetration into outer space".[7] More recently it has been shown that, while the human body possesses a remarkable capacity for physiological adaptation, there remain serious problems requiring solution should much longer journeys be envisaged.[8]

It still remains uncertain whether man can establish himself on the moon or on one of the planets of the solar system.

No real answer has been given to the question whether extraterrestrial life exists. If one accepts the view that life appears at a determined stage of cosmological development, then the possibility of its existence beyond our planet should not be ruled out.[9] It may therefore well be that life is "a pervasive constituent of the universe"; in different environments it may exist in different forms.[10] If so, the uniqueness and centrality of man can be questioned and it may turn out that he is not a Robinson Crusoe in the universe. However, the acceptance of the view of the universality of life does not exclude the possibility that it may have come to an end on other planets.

And indeed many scientists question the existence of life beyond our globe.[11] Meanwhile, on this subject, the universe retains its secret.

While we are acting within the frontiers of present knowledge, and ruling out speculation, the law of outer space must be anthropocentric, as is international law in general. Will it remain so? To this question a jurist is the least qualified to reply. As we proceed with the formulation of this law, it will remain a law made by man and destined for him, whether he extends his presence beyond the earth for only short periods of time or is able to establish himself in space permanently. It cannot be otherwise. The anthropocentric character of the law of outer space is the obvious result of man's being its sole architect. Far from reducing, this increases his responsibilities. Not only must he see to it that the law be established in the interest of mankind as a whole, and prevent whatever dangers human action in outer space may produce to life and security on our globe, but he is also bound to provide adequate safeguards to ensure that nothing be done to upset the balance of nature or possibly jeopardize non-terrestrial life whether or in whatever the form in which it may exist.

Despite the many remaining unknowns, the knowledge already acquired has created an adequate basis for the laying-down of a number of principles and specific rules for this new sphere of human activity.[12]

This is how the new chapter on the law of outer space has begun to be written.[13] It is international co-operation that has enabled this process to get under way.

Notes to Chapter II

1. Cf. F. Castberg, "La méthodologie du droit international public", *43 Recueil des cours*, 1933-1, p. 353.
2. Cf. F. W. Rauchhaupt, "A Light from the Past to Show up the Legal Problems of our Age of Space", *Colloquium on the Law of Outer Space*, 1958, Vienna 1959, pp. 1 f.
3. Cf. M. F. Lindley, *The Acquisition and Government of Backward Territory in International Law*, London 1926, p. 92; cf. also p. 28.
4. "The shrinkage of maritime sovereignty may be traced primarily to changed concepts of the value of the sea to the world community" : A. T. Mahan, *The Influence of Sea Power upon History*, Boston 1980, ed. London 1965, pp. 1, 25 and 27; cf. also: Regime of the High Seas, Memorandum U.N. Secretariat Doc. A/CN.4/32, in *Yearbook* International Law Commission, 1950, v. II, pp. 67 ff., G. Gidel, "Explosions nucléaires et Liberté de la haute mer", *Festschrift für J. Spiropoulos*, Bonn 1957, pp. 181 ff. "National Sovereignty of Outer Space", 74 *Harvard Law Review*, 1961, No. 6, p. 1161, also J. P. A. François, "Réflexions sur l'Occupation", *Mélanges Guggenheim*, Geneva, l958, pp. 795 ff. Cf. R. Bierzanek, "La nature juridique de la haute mer", *R.G.D.I.P.*, LXV, 1961, pp. 233 ff.
5. Fauchille's proposals in 1902 and 1910 (Projet de règlement, Institut de droit international, Brussels 1902; *Annuaire de l'Institut de droit international*, XXI, 1906, pp. 293 and 327. *Rapport à l'Institut de droit international*, Paris 1910.) Cf. also the Resolution of the Institute adopted in Madrid (*Annuaire de l'Institut de droit international*, XXIV, 1911, pp. 23 and 303.) Cf. Article 1 of the 1919 Paris Convention for the Regulation of Aerial Navigation: "... every Power has complete and exclusive sovereignty over the air space above its territory"; 11 *League of Nations Treaty Series*, p. 173; Article 1 of the 1928 Havana Convention, *US Treaty Series*, Vol. 4, p. 4729; Article 1 of the 1944 Chicago Convention on International Civil Aviation, 15, *UN Treaty Series*, p. 295.
6. Cf. S. V. Molodtzov, *The International Legal Régime of the Open Seas and the Continental Shelf* (in Russian), Moscow 1960, p. 185. See also M. Cohen, *Law and Politics in Space*, Montreal 1964, p. 13. US Supreme Court in *Chicago and Southern Air Lines* v. *Waterman Steamship Corporation*, 333 US 103, 107 (1948); "Only very limited analogies may be derived from the corpus of maritime and air law": A. G. Haley, "Law of Outer Space–A Problem for International Agreement", 7 *The American University Law Review*, No. 2, 1958, p. 71.
7. Cf. early comments by N. M. Sisakiyan, O. G. Gazenko, V. V. Antipov; Satellite Biological Experiments, Academy of Sciences of the USSR, *COSPAR Symposium* Florence, May 1964. Cf. also a series of interesting reports submitted to the fifteenth International Astronautical Congress, Warsaw, 7-12 September 1964. W. I. Yazdorsky, "Basic Scientific Trends of Space Biology in the Exploration of Outer Space", *Problems of Space Biology*, No. 1 (in Russian), Moscow 1964, p. 5; also D. Verguese, "L'homme s'adapte bien à l'espace", *Le Monde*, 28 December 1968, p. 2. It is claimed by scientists that weightlessness causes a higher tendency to motion-sickness, changes in biological rhythms and physiological functions: T. Nicholson, "Space: Problem of Weightlessness", *The Times*, 26 June 1970. The experience of Apollo flights suggests that cosmic rays are likely to damage the eyes or brain of man, and destroy a number of cells: *Interna-*

tional Herald-Tribune, 27 May 1970. More recently two cosmonauts have lost weight and developed "instability" of the cardiovascular system. Though these were said not to be serious, "the process of re-adaptation to earth" took some time. Cf. *Tass* report, 23 June 1970, and *International Herald-Tribune*, 24 June 1970.

8. "Unusual gravitational environments and changes which occur in man during space flight reduce work capacity and could impair the physical abilities of astronauts for some time after landing on another planet ..."; astronauts are reported to have experienced dizziness and trouble in controlling their movements; particular difficulties were encountered by Leonov (Voskhod 2) and White (Gemini 4) during the time spent outside the spacecraft; growing fatigue and other negative phenomena were recorded in the case of the astronauts who worked on the moon: cf. T. Nicholson, "Medical Hazards of the Astronauts", *The Times*, 30 January 1971.
Prolonged subjection to weightlessness may produce basic change in the muscular tissue, hence there have been repeated suggestions that artificial gravity should be created in space-stations (cf. P. Wright, "Unknown Dangers of Prolonged Weightlessness", *The Times*, 1 July 1971). On the technical obstacles to the realization of this idea, cf. *Aviation and Cosmonautics*, Moscow, July 1971.
9. Cf. N. M. Sissakian, "On the way to inhabited space", *Impact of Science on Society*, Vol. XV, Unesco 1965, N. 3, pp. 137 ff.; P.H.A. Sneath, *Planets and Life*, London 1970; J. Needham (editor), *The Chemistry of Life*, Cambridge 1970; G. Niss, *The Molecules of Life* (trans. from German), London 1970. Cf. also R. Calder, *Man and the Cosmos*, London 1968, pp. 182-194.
10. See M. W. Ovenden, *Life in the Universe*, New York 1962, p. 55. H. Shapley, *The View from a Distant Star: Man's Future in the Universe*, New York 1963 p. 57: G. Wold in a collection of essays on *The Physics and Chemistry of Life*, New York 1965, p. 36. Cf. the findings of J. S. Shklovsky and C. Sagan in *Intelligent Life in the Universe*, San Francisco 1966; some do not exclude the possibility of the lowest forms of life (J. Ruffié, in *Le Monde* of 8 August 1969). Cf. also J. Brooks and G. Shaw, *Nature*, 16 August 1969, pp. 223, 756. However, the traces of hydrocarbons originally detected in lunar specimens brought back by the Apollo 11 astronauts have been contaminants from the containers, and the conclusion is that "no living, dead or even fossilized organisms" were detected (*International Herald Tribune*, 8 August and 9-10 September 1969).
11. "Mon sentiment", writes A. Lwoff, "est qu'il n'y a pas de vie en dehors de la Terre" (*Le Monde*, 24 July 1969).
12. It is worth recalling that the first works on the subject were published long before man's entry into outer space. V. Mandl, *Das Weltraumrecht: Ein Problem der Raumfahrt*, Berlin 1932; E. Korovine, "La conquête de la stratosphère et le droit international". *Revue générale de droit international public*, No. 6, 1934, pp. 675-686.
13. Many suggestions have been made as to the name it should bear, most of them derived from the environment which is to be its realm. Some call it the law of space (*droit de l'espace*). Cf. Ch. Chaumont, *Le Droit de l'espace*, Paris 1960, p. 5; E. Pepin, "Les problèmes juridiques de l'espace", *Revue française de droit aérien*, No. 4, 1959, p. 4. The resolution adopted by the Institut de Droit International, Brussels 1963, is headed: "Le régime juridique de l'espace". Others call it the law of inter-planetary space: N. H. Jacob, "Droit interplanétaire", 15 *Revue*

générale de l'Air, 1952, p 287. H. Valadão, "The Law of Interplanetary Space" (*Second Colloquium of the International Institute of Space Law*, 1959), Vienna 1960, p. 156. E. Danier, "Les voyages interplanétaires et le droit", 15 *Revue générale de l'Air*, 1952, p. 423; *droit astronautique:* J. Kroell, "Eléments créateurs d'un droit astronautique". 16 *Revue générale de l'Air*, 1953, p. 222; *kosmicheskoye pravo*: this term has been accepted generally by jurists in the Soviet Union: cf. the writtings of Korovin, Osnitzkaya, Zhukov and others. It has also been suggested that there should be two branches: (*a*) *droit astronautique* and (*b*) *droit interplanétaire*. The first is to concern itself with "la circulation interplanétaire et intersidérale", the second with "la prise de possession elle-même des lieux sans maîtres extraterrestres et à l'exploitation des corps solides". J. Kroell, *op. cit.*, p. 232. Proposals have also been made to merge the new rules with the law of the air in order to create a unified system covering all human activities in what may become one environment above the earth. Cooper has called this "aerospace". Cf. J. C. Cooper, "Aerospace Law, Subject Matter and Terminology", 29 *Journal of Air Law and Commerce*, 1963, p. 89. Even more far-reaching suggestions have been made, aiming at the creation of "metalaw", the law which is to regulate the whole of the universe. Cf. A. G. Haley, *Space Law and Government*, New York 1963, pp. 394-421.
While giving these suggestions all the attention they deserve, it should be recalled that the official documents and, more particularly, the first instruments dealing with the subject employ the terms: "legal principles" or "principles governing the activities of States in the exploration and use of outer space ..."; non-English terms corresponding to outer space are: *espace extra-atmosphérique; kosmicheskoye prostranstvo; espacio ultra-terrestre*; these may be viewed therefore as *verba legis*.

Chapter III

First Stages of International Co-Operation

The very notion of law-making in international relations implies the co-operation of States. Once they approach their common task, the existing international law is placed under test and, where it makes inadequate or insufficiently express provision for the reconcilement of the interests brought into contact, new rules of law have to be elicited. Not only is this process necessary for the purpose of regulating situations having arisen, or on the point of arising, in the sphere of co-operative activity concerned, but it may also prove essential, and will certainly be advisable, with a view to enabling concurrent national activities to continue or to advance to new stages. Thus law calls for co-operation, and co-operation calls for law.

Given the scale and seriousness of the ventures into the new dimension, it was inevitable that States should realize the urgent necessity of bringing them within the framework of law. By so doing they made a conscious contribution to the development of international law, under the aegis of the world community. This is how the gradual movement towards the legal regulation of international co-operation has taken place.

In man's venture into space a pioneering role was obviously played by the scientists and technicians who devised and constructed the first satellites; great have been the achievements of the astronauts. However, the road has been a long one, and men of many lands helped pave the way.

The first steps towards co-operation were taken in the early 1950's with the establishment of the International Astronautical Federation.[1] This Federation was founded with the objectives of fostering the development of astronautics for peaceful purposes, encouraging research in sciences relating to astronautics, and promoting international co-operation in these fields. The International Academy of Astronautics, founded by the Federation in 1960, has become a rallying-centre for leading scientists in many fields related to space research.[2] A great landmark was the International Geophysical Year of 1957-1958 (whose predecessors had been the two Polar Years of 1882-1883 and 1932-1933) the collaboration of 66 nations in national and international scientific bodies, unions and inter-governmental organizations enabled a uniquely ambitious venture in international scientific co-operation to be carried out with success.[3]

About 50,000 scientists and technicians, at about 4,000 stations, situated in various parts of the globe, engaged in data-gathering experiments and observations ranging from measurements of solar activity, study of the physics of the upper atmosphere, meteorology and geomagnetism, to seismology and investigation of the ocean and of the structure and interior of the earth.

It was at that very time that the first satellites and space vehicles were launched–some of them outside the IGY programme.

The International Geophysical Year was continued by International Geophysical Co-operation,[4] and followed by another important venture. While the IGY had been organized at a time of very high solar activity, the highest since systematic observations began two hundred years ago, the new venture was to cover a contrasting period of minimum solar activity: 1964 and 1965, the years of the "Quiet Sun", a phenomenon occurring every eleven years. Again, thousands of specialists in sixty-five countries, engaged in a common effort covering meteorology, aeronomy, geomagnetism, research into the aurora borealis, atmospherics and radio-atmospherics of the ionosphere, cosmic rays and the activity of the sun. In the field of biology the work has been carried further by the International Biological Programme, which commenced on 1 July 1967 and was planned to continue for five years.

New developments marked by the launching of satellites underlined the need for co-operation in, and the co-ordination of space research. "To provide the world scientific community with the means whereby it may exploit the possibilities of satellites and space probes of all kinds for scientific purposes, and exchange all the resulting data on a co-operative basis" a special Committee for Space Research was called into being in 1958.[5]

The number of institutions engaged in research and co-ordination has been continuously growing. Existing intergovernmental organizations have extended their activities into this new field. The United Nations Educational, Scientific and Cultural Organization (Unesco) has been promoting an exchange of information, giving assistance to member States and non-governmental organizations in the training of astronomers and geo-physicists, and promoting scientific projects.[6] One of these programmes, in which 101 nations are now co-operating, has as its purpose to study the world water-balance, to collect and acquire much greater knowledge of the hydrological cycle, and to envisage more effective means of coping with the world's water problems. The vital urgency of ensuring an adequate supply of water for agriculture, industry and even the daily life of man have lent this programme impetus. It has further been realized that space technology and the use of satellites may acquire great importance for its implementation and the future of hydrology altogether.[7]

The International Civil Aviation Organization (ICAO) (whose activities concern an area that is the closest neighbour of outer space) concentrates on telecommunication and meteorology, and on all those problems of space activity which have repercussions on aviation.[8]

The World Meteorological Organization (WMO) has taken up problems concerning weather-forecasting, observation-posts and telecommunication. To this end it has created a special Advisory Committee and established technical commissions. It has also set up a World Weather Watch.[9]

The International Telecommunication Union (ITU), entrusted as it is with the task of "Maintaining and extending international co-operation for the improvement and rational use of telegraphy or telephone communication of signs, writings, images, and sounds of nature by wire, radio or other systems or processes of electric or visual (semaphore) signalling", has initiated and carried out important work in the field of communication with and between space vehicles and more particularly a new allocation of wavelengths in communication between earth and space, in space and through space.[10]

Other international organizations have also been involved. Special tasks already face the World Health Organization in the fields of biology, physiology and psychology, the effects of radiation on astronauts and also the pollution of space. In another sphere, closely related to its main functions, action has been undertaken by the International Atomic Energy Agency.[11]

Concurrently, co-operation has also been developing on less universal bases. Special organizations have been set up by countries of Western Europe[12] and of Latin America.[13] Common plans and programmes are being elaborated by socialist States.[14]

New forms of co-operation are moreover evolving on the multi- and bilateral levels. Arrangements are made for tracking facilities and in the field of telecommunications.[15]

Programmes of co-operation have to be shaped in the many avenues opened up by the new science and technology.[16] An impressive display in this field was the United Nations Conference on the Exploration and Peaceful Uses of Outer Space held in Vienna in 1968. It was attended by representatives of 78 States and nine specialized agencies, three inter-governmental organizations and one non-governmental organization.[17]

Above and beyond these are issues of a more fundamental nature which have arisen; they concern the key problems of the law for outer space.

Inevitably, the impetus towards their solution had to come from the United Nations, the organization which has been established "to maintain international peace and security" and constitutes the main centre of worldwide co-operation. Need one recall that its Charter has entrusted one of its principal organs, the General Assembly, to "initiate studies and make recommendations for the purpose of ... promoting international co-operation in the political field and encouraging the progressive development of international law and its codification".[18]

Small wonder, therefore, that, on the morrow of the successful launching of the first satellites, problems of outer space entered the agenda of the United Nations. They made their first appearance in 1957, in the context of the debate on disarmament. A year later a special item on outer space was placed before the General Assembly.[19]

It was then that an *Ad Hoc* Committee on the Peaceful Uses of Outer Space was set up;[20] the General Assembly returned to the issue a year later. This time, it established the membership of the Committee at 24, elected for a period of two years. The Committee's terms of reference were specifically defined. Two years later in 1961, it was made permanent and enlarged by four member States.[21] It was also instructed henceforth to maintain close contact with all governmental and non-governmental organizations dealing with related issues as well as to collect data on the activities of member States in the field of the exploration and use of outer space.[22]

The United Nations Committee for the Peaceful Uses of Outer Space embarked on its real substantive work only in 1962. This was also the starting point for the deliberations of the Scientific and Technical and the Legal Sub-Committees.[23]

Since then the Committee has become the main centre of international co-operation and co-ordination in the field of the exploration and peaceful uses of outer space.[24]

The Scientific and Technical Sub-Committee dealt mainly with the exchange and dissemination of information; the encouragement of international programmes of space research and making the results of exploration accessible to countries which are not engaged in it; education and training in the field of space; and the evaluation of the work done by the specialized agencies engaged in space research.

The important problem of the dangerous effects of some experiments in outer space was taken up.[25] The Sub-Committee recommended in 1962 that the United Nations take under its auspices the establishment and use of equatorial sounding and launching bases.[26]

The Legal Sub-Committee was entrusted with the task "to study legal problems which may arise from the exploration and use of outer space".

At its successive sessions it has dealt with general and specific issues of space law.[27] It has been faced with the need of and proposals for the elaboration of a set of basic principles which, once accepted, could form the point of departure for detailed rules and provisions in this field.

The results of these labours are reflected in two important documents: the first was the Declaration of Legal Principles Governing the Activities of States in the Exploration and Use of Outer Space, unanimously adopted by the General Assembly of the United Nations on 13 December 1963.[28] The other is the Treaty on Legal Principles Governing the Activities of States in the Exploration and Use of Outer Space, including the Moon and Other Celestial Bodies, commended by the General Assembly of the United Nations on 19 December 1966.[29]

The way to these basic documents was paved by a series of resolutions of the General Assembly.[30]

Simultaneously, the United Nations was engaged in the elaboration of two specific instruments. One was on the Assistance to and Return of Astronauts and Space Objects. The Agreement on the Rescue of Astronauts, Return of Astronauts and the Return of Objects launched into Outer Space was finally agreed upon and commended by the General Assembly on 19 December 1967.[31]

The other concerned liability for damage caused by space objects. After long deliberations the Convention on International Liability for Damage caused by Space Objects was completed, and was commended by the General Assembly on 29 November 1971.[32]

The records of the deliberations of the United Nations Committee on the Peaceful Uses of Outer Space, and particularly of its Legal Sub-Committee, during these years, offer a wealth of interesting material. They reflect the many, sometimes conflicting, proposals, long debates and difficult negotiations, they mirror the first stages of the law-making process.

Finally, mention should be made of the work of non-governmental organizations, in particular the Institut de Droit International and also the International Law Association and International Institute of Space Law made an important contribution on the subject.[33]

A closer analysis of facts and developments would reveal that in this so essential sphere, where science and technology have made such giant strides, modest yet important progress in co-operation has been recorded within a relatively short time.

Does anyone need reminding that law-making is always a complex and laborious process? In this domain it has been particularly so. There is no mystery about this. The difficulties were obvious; the venture into space was developing, in a complicated international situation. Yet notwithstanding these difficulties, international law has succeeded in truly establishing itself in the new dimension.

Notes to Chapter III

1. Membership of the Federation is composed of national societies. It holds annual congresses at which the results of space missions, experiments and research are discussed.
2. The Academy has three sections: basic sciences, engineering sciences and life sciences. It thus provides a platform for an interchange of views and knowledge in widely different fields and has a truly interdisciplinary character. It elects its honorary members, ordinary members and corresponding members, and publishes *Astronautica Acta*. Cf. *The International Academy of Astronautics, The First Decade*, Paris 1970.
3. The programme was carried out under the auspices of the International Council of Scientific Unions (ICSU), the origin of which dates back to 1919 and which was established "to co-ordinate and facilitate the activities of international scientific unions in the field of natural sciences and to act as co-ordinating centre for the national organizations adhering to the Council". It is an international non-governmental organization bringing together academies of science, national research councils, scientific organizations and unions of scientists, and international scientific unions, among them the International Astronomical Union, the International Mathematical Union and the International Union of Geodesy and Geophysics.
4. In 1959 ICSU formed the International Committee for Geophysics with the purpose "to develop and to co-ordinate international plans for the furtherance of co-operation in geophysics and related sciences, especially those of an interdisciplinary nature".
5. Known as Cospar, this committee was set up by ICSU with a programme carried out by working groups on a continuous basis. Its annual scientific symposia are of special importance. At the 13th Plenary Session held in Leningrad on 20-29 May 1970, the impressive results of over 12 years' space research were reviewed, the subjects including high energy cosmic rays, the upper atmosphere of the earth, the ionosphere, rocket and satellite meteorology and lunar and Venus research. On Cospar in general, see L. E. Schwartz, *International Organizations and Space Co-operation*, Durham (North Carolina) 1962, pp. 32 ff., N. Roy, on Cospar in the *ICSU Review of World Science*, April 1963, and Cospar *Bulletins*.
6. Cf. Resolution 2.41 adopted by the General Conference of Unesco, Tenth Session, 1958: It established a working group on meteorites (1964) and a group of experts in the field of space communications (1965) and pursued studies concerning the use of space communications for education and cultural research.
7. It is estimated that "more than 90% of the world's people have less than the minimum standard of piped or bottled water delivered to the household. Probably one out of four persons suffers in some way from debilitating waterborne disease". Cf. *A Study Submitted to the United Nations Conference on the Exploration and Peaceful Uses of Outer Space: Satellites, Hydrology and International Hydrological Decade:* A/CONF.34/IV.11 of 25 June 1968, pp. 1 and 6-10.
8. Of particular importance is the allocation of radio waves, the use of communication satellites for communication with aircraft and air radio navigation service. ICAO has also outlined the scope of its participation in programmes

for the exploration and use of outer space. Cf. Resolution A15-11 adopted at the 15th Session of the Assembly of ICAO, 1965, which provided for the study "of those technical aspects of space activities that affect international air navigation". In the field of meteorology it is co-operating with the World Meteorological Organization. It has been taking a special interest in the application of communications satellites in aeronautical mobile service and their possible use for surveillance of air traffic, to ensure greater safety for air-transport.

9. A series of resolutions adopted by the General Assembly of the United Nations has entrusted the World Meteorological Organization with special tasks: *inter alia* resolutions 1721 (XVI), 1802 (XVIII), 1963 (XVIII). Cf. subsequent action taken by the World Meteorological Congresses held in Geneva in 1963 and 1967, also *Second Report on the Advancement of Atmospheric Sciences and Their Application in the Light of Developments in Outer Space*, Geneva, June 1963; *World Weather Watch*, publication of the WMO, No. 183, TP. 92, Geneva 1966. Cf. also statement made by the representative of the World Meteorological Organization in the Political Committee of the 22nd Session of the General Assembly of the United Nations, 19 October 1967, UN Document A/C.1/PV.1500, pp. 2-15. Cf. also successive progress reports by WMO to the General Assembly of the United Nations.

10. A special chapter is devoted below to the problem of telecommunication in space, in view of its special importance.

11. Being primarily concerned with the peaceful uses of nuclear energy, it concentrates its interests in the field of cosmic rays and the study of the harmful consequences of the use of nuclear materials in space and the utilization of nuclear power in space.

12. (*a*) European Organization for the Development and Construction of Space Vehicle Launchers (ELDO)–cf. The Convention was signed in London, 29 March-30 April 1962 (*UN Treaty Series* 507, pp. 178 ff.) and ratified by Australia, Belgium, Federal Republic of Germany, France, Italy, Netherlands and the United Kingdom. Its initial programme provided for the development and construction of three stage space vehicle launchers and satellite test vehicles, and for placing a satellite in orbit. One of ELDO's members (United Kingdom) having decided to withdraw and not to take part in any other programme following the development of two Europa space vehicles, alternative projects were envisaged for the ten-year European Space Programme.

(*b*) European Space Research Organization (ESRO). A convention and the protocols establishing this organization were signed in Paris on 14 June 1962. Its objects are scientific research in outer space, and the design, construction and launching of sounding rockets, satellites and space probes: Parties: Belgium, Denmark, Federal Republic of Germany, France, Italy, Netherlands, Spain, Sweden, Switzerland and the United Kingdom (*UN Treaty Series*, 528, pp. 33 ff.). Cf. also an agreement concerning the sounding rocket base at Kiruna, concluded between ESRO and Sweden in Paris on 29 July 1964 (which base is to be taken over by Sweden on 1 July 1972), the agreement signed with Italy on 15 June 1964 with regard to two series of experiments in Sardinia and similar agreements. The programme of ESRO envisaged the launching of 250 sounding rockets and nine satellites within eight years, but the financial implications and the withdrawal of one of the members, necessitated a revision of the programme in 1968. At its meeting at Noordwijk on 12-14 July 1971, the Council of ESRO decided to continue the scientific satellite programme and its participation in NASA's small astronomical satellite project (SAS-d). It was further agreed to carry out projects in telecommunication and other applications of satellites, *inter alia* an aeronautic and meteorological programme. (Sounding rockets are to be abandoned after 1973.)

(*c*) European Organization for Astronomical Research in the Southern Hemisphere established by a Convention signed in Paris on 5 October 1962 by Belgium, France, the Federal Republic of Germany, the Netherlands and Sweden. This Convention (*UN Treaty Series*, Vol. 502, pp. 226 ff.) entered into force on 24 December 1963 after the deposit of instruments of ratification by the above-named countries.

13. At a conference held in Buenos Aires, 28 November-3 December 1960, the Inter-American Committee for Space Research was established with the purpose of promoting space research and assisting the creation of national organizations to encourage and co-ordinate space activities in Latin America (UN Doc. A/AC.105/L.29, p. 48). The provisional committee included representatives of Argentina, Bolivia, Brazil, Chile, Peru, Uruguay and the United States. It organizes meetings and symposia on space research, and engages in teaching and related activities.

14. At a conference held in Moscow, 15-20 November 1965, with the participation of Bulgaria, Czechoslovakia, Cuba, Mongolia, the German Democratic Republic, Poland, Romania, Hungary, and the USSR, the problems concerning "the most useful forms and directives in the field of co-operation concerning research and peaceful uses of outer space with consideration of the scientific and technical possibilities and resources of the particular socialist States" were discussed. Further concrete forms of co-operation were established at a conference of experts on Co-operation in the Peaceful Exploration and Use of Outer Space, held in Moscow, 5-13 April 1967. Agreements and protocols were drafted concerning a series of experiments and projects relating to the study of the physical properties of outer space, space meteorology and space biology and medicine; a programme for a joint launching of satellites and rockets was mapped out; and the establishment of an international satellite communication system envisaged. Cf. UN A/6668, 10 May 1967. The Academy of Sciences in the USSR has been entrusted with the co-ordination of this work, which now includes 100 institutes, observatories and other scientific bodies, with the participation of about 2,000 scientists. A special co-ordinating body, Interkosmos, has been set up and within its framework two satellites (Interkosmos I and II) were launched in 1969. Annual conferences of scientists and experts review the implementation of common programmes and plan further projects. At a conference held in Wroclaw (15-20 June 1970) the programme of joint experiments in launching rockets and satellites, and of observations, was adopted for a period of five years. Cf. also Chapter VIII below.

15. For a list of the earlier agreements concluded in this respect see *Yearbook of Air and Space Law*, Institute of Air and Space Law, McGill University, Montreal 1967, pp. 415-421.

16. Cf. for instance the Agreements between the Comité de Recherches Spatiales (France) and the National Aeronautics and Space Administration (USA) of 29

March 1961; between the Centre National d'Etudes Spatiales (France) and the National Space Investigation Commission (Argentina) of 12 October 1962; between the Soviet Academy of Sciences and NASA of 8 June 1962, providing for co-operation in some areas of telecommunications, meteorology and geomagnetic survey; of 8 October 1965, for an exchange of information in weather satellite programmes and for co-operation in space biology and medicine; of 21 January 1971 on the exchange of lunar samples; that on 26 June 1971, for further exchanges of information and for the development of a compatible docking system and studies on the link-up of American and Soviet space craft: "the first such experiment might be the docking of an Apollo (US) spacecraft with a manned orbital scientific station of the Salyut type (USSR). A subsequent experiment might be the docking of a manned spacecraft of the Soyuz type (USSR) with an orbital scientific station of the Skylab type (US)" (Statement issued after a conference held in Houston from 21-25 June 1971: *Tass* report and *International Herald Tribune*, 28 June 1972). Cf. an agreement between France and the USSR, providing for co-operation in telecommunication, weather observation and scientific experiments in space (Decree of 14 January 1967, *Journal Officiel*, No. 17, 20 January 1967, p. 793); a further Agreement on specific joint ventures was concluded between the last two countries on 17 October 1969.

17. Cf. Documentation (referred to in the last footnote to the Introduction, above) on the United Nations 1968 Conference on the Exploration and Peaceful Uses of Outer Space in *Report of the Committee on the Peaceful Uses of Outer Space*, Twenty-third Session of the General Assembly, Official Records, A/7285, Annex II, pp. 13-123. In his note preceding the Report on the Conference, the Secretary-General of the United Nations U Thant stated: "The success of these efforts encourages us to believe that we can now press forward to greater levels of co-operation to harness the practical benefits that can accrue to man from the vast technological and scientific advances made through space exploration."
18. Article 13 of the Charter which states that "the General Assembly shall initiate studies and make recommendations for the purpose of: (*a*) promoting international co-operation in the political field and encouraging the progressive development of international law and its codification; (*b*) promoting international co-operation in the economic, social, cultural, educational and health fields …". Cf. also Article 58.
19. Cf. proposal by the United States: Doc. A/3902, of 2 September 1958; cf. also Doc. A/3818, presented earlier by the USSR, 17 March 1958.
20. The draft resolution for the setting-up of such a committee was approved by the Political Committee of the General Assembly by 54 votes to 9 with 18 abstentions, and subsequently adopted by the plenary session of the General Assembly (resolution 1348 (XIII) of 13 December 1958). The Committee was to be composed of representatives of Argentina, Australia, Belgium, Brazil, Canada, Czechoslovakia, France, India, Iran, Italy, Japan, Mexico, Poland, Sweden, USSR, UAR, the United Kingdom and the USA. This composition gave rise to objections from socialist States which voted against the resolution on the ground that it did not afford them adequate representation.
    The Committee was requested to report on:

"(*a*) The activities and resources of the United Nations, of its specialized agencies and of other international bodies relating to the peaceful uses of outer space;
(*b*) The area of international cooperation and programs in the peaceful uses of outer space which could appropriately be undertaken under United Nations auspices to the benefit of States irrespective of the state of their economic or scientific development, taking into account the following proposals, among others:
  (i) Continuation on a permanent basis of the outer space research now being carried on within the framework of the International Geophysical Year;
  (ii) Organisation of the mutual exchange and dissemination of information on outer space research; and
  (iii) Coordination of national research programs for the study of outer space, and the rendering of all possible assistance and help towards their realization;
(*c*) The future organisational arrangements to facilitate international cooperation in this field within the framework of the United Nations;
(*d*) The nature of legal problems which may arise in the carrying out of programs to explore outer space."

The *Ad Hoc* Committee under the Chairmanship of Mr. Matsushima (Japan) set up two Committees of the whole: one a technical and the other a legal one. They held 25 meetings (6 May-25 June 1959) in which, however, Czechoslovakia, India, Poland, UAR and USSR did not take part. The Committee submitted a report to the 14th Session of the General Assembly: A/4141 of 14 July 1959. The Committee divided the legal problems entrusted to it (paragraph 1 (*d*) above) into two groups: "Legal Problems Susceptible of Priority Treatment" and "Other Problems" (Part III of the report, pp. 22-25).

21. Resolution 1472 (XIV) of 12 December 1959, which established a Committee consisting of representatives of Albania, Argentina, Australia, Austria, Belgium, Brazil, Bulgaria, Canada, Czechoslovakia, France, Hungary, India, Iran, Italy, Japan, Lebanon, Mexico, Poland, Romania, Sweden, USSR, United Arab Republic, United Kingdom and United States. The Committee was entrusted with the following tasks:

"(*a*) To review as appropriate the area of international co-operation, and to study practical and feasible means for giving effect to programmes in the peaceful uses of outer space which could appropriately be undertaken under United Nations auspices, including *inter alia:*
  (i) Assistance for the continuation on a permanent basis of the research on outer space carried on within the framework of the International Geophysical Year;
  (ii) Organization of the mutual exchange and dissemination of information on outer space research;
  (iii) Encouragement of national research programmes for the study of outer space, and the rendering of all possible assistance and help towards their realization;
(*b*) To study the nature of legal problems which may arise from the exploration of outer space."

However, owing to differences of view concerning its methods of work and voting procedure, the Committee did not in fact begin its task. It was only in 1961 that a new resolution was adopted by the General Assembly (resolution 1721 (XVI) of 20 December 1961) and the membership of the Committee was further increased (part E of the resolution). Henceforth the Committee was to include the following States: Albania, Argentina, Australia, Austria, Belgium, Brazil, Bulgaria, Canada, Chad, Czechoslovakia, France, Hungary, India, Iran,

Italy, Japan, Lebanon, Morocco, Mexico, Mongolia, Poland, Romania, Sierra Leone, Sweden, UAR, United Kingdom, United States and the USSR.

22. Consequently reports have been submitted annually to the Committee by member States and international organizations and collected in a series of United Nations documents under the titles *Review of National and Co-operative International Space Activities* and *Review of the Activities and Resources of the United Nations, of its Specialized Agencies and other Competent International Bodies relating to Peaceful Uses of Outer Space.* It was also decided that representatives of Cospar, the international Telecommunication Union, the World Health Organization, ICAO and Unesco would take part as observers in the meetings of the Committee and of the two Sub-Committees.

23. The Committee first met between 19 and 20 March 1962. The first Chairman was F. Matsch (Austria); later, the Chair was occupied successively by K. Waldheim, H. Haymerle (Austria) and again by K. Waldheim (until his election as Secretary-General of the United Nations). The Sub-Committees met in Geneva on 28 May 1962. D. F. Martyn (Australia) was elected Chairman of the Scientific and Technical Sub-Committee, and M. Lachs (Poland) Chairman of the Legal Sub-Committee.

24. At the same time a special section has been set up in the Secretariat of the United Nations–the Outer Space Affairs Group–which is the administrative arm of the Committee for the Peaceful Uses of Outer Space. It is headed by Mr. A.H. Abdel-Ghani and performs very useful functions in this respect.

25. Cf. the early *Report of the United Nations Committee on the Peaceful Uses of Outer Space,* Part II: recommendations based on the report of the Scientific and Technical Sub-Committee and the reports prepared by the ITU and WMO; UN Document A/5549, 24 September 1963, pp. 3-8.

26. Cf. resolution 1802 (XVII) of 14 December 1962, Part B, 4; Memorandum of the Government of India concerning the Establishment of an International Equatorial Sounding Rocket Facility, A/AC.105/8, 22 January 1963; *Report of the Committee on the Peaceful Uses of Outer Space,* A/5549, 24 September 1963, Part II, p. 6, para. 16; General Assembly resolution 1963 (XVIII) of 13 December 1963, Part II (*e*); *Report of the Scientific Group Established at the Request of the Government of India to Visit the Rocket Launching Site at Thumba.* A/AC.105/17, 20 February 1964; cf. also progress reports on the work of the Thumba Equatorial Rocket Launching Station (TERIS), A/AC.105/C.1/L.15 and those which followed. With the assistance of the United Nations Development Programme the construction of an Experimental Satellite Communication Earth Station in Ahmedabad (India) as a centre for research and training has been realized: cf. A/AC.105/C.1/L.19 of 6 June 1967.

Cf. also letters of the Permanent Representative of Italy to the United Nations concerning the programmes of the San Marco research station (A/AC.105/4 of 22 May 1962 and A/AC.105/18 of 26 March 1964).

27. On the agenda of the first session of the Sub-Committee were the following items: proposals for (1) a declaration of legal principles concerning the activities of States and the exploration and use of outer space; (2) international agreement on assistance to cosmonauts and space vehicles in case of emergency landing; (3) liability for damage caused by space vehicles. In the course of further deliberations suggestions were submitted on: (i) the establishment of a frontier between outer space and atmospheric space; (ii) jurisdiction over man

in outer space and manned space platforms on celestial bodies; (iii) measures to be taken in order to prevent interference in the implementation of space projects, scientific experiments and other space activities; (iv) the prevention of pollution of outer space and celestial bodies; (v) the control of launching and placing into orbit of space vehicles and artificial satellites; (vi) control by the United Nations of radio and television programmes broadcast through outer space: *Report of the Legal Sub-Committee* on the work of its first session, 28 May-20 June 1962, A/AC.105/6, 9 July 1962, pp. 3-9.

Cf. *Report of the Legal Sub-Committee* (second session, New York, 16 April-3 May 1963) A/AC.105/12, 6 May 1963; *Additional Report* of a special meeting of the Committee on 22 November 1963, at which the Declaration of Legal Principles Governing the Activities of States in the Exploration and Peaceful Uses of Outer Space was adopted: A/5549/Add. 1 of 27 November 1963; *Report* on the third session (first part), Geneva, 9-26 March 1964, A/AC.105/19, 26 March 1964; *idem* (second part), New York, 5-23 October 1964, A/AC.10/21, 23 October 1964; *Report* on the fourth session, New York, 20 September-1 October 1965, A/AC.105/29; *Interim Report by the Chairman* upon the suspension of the fifth session (12 July-4 August 1966), Document AA/AC.105/C.2/L.16; *Report* on the fifth session, A/AC.105/35. (Since 1967 the Legal Sub-Committee has been very ably presided over by Mr. E. Wyzner.) Cf. further the *Reports* on the sixth session (19 June-14 July 1967), A/AC.105/37; the seventh session (4-28 June 1968), A/AC.105/45; the eighth session (9 June-4 July 1969), A/AC.105/58; the ninth session (8 June-3 July 1970), A/AC.105/85; and the tenth session (7 June-2 July 1971), A/AC.105/94, 8 July 1971.

28. General Assembly resolution 1962 (XVIII).
29. General Assembly resolution 2222 (XXI). The Treaty was opened for signature in London, Moscow and Washington on 27 January 1967, and entered into force on 10 October 1967.
30. Cf. in particular resolutions 1721 (XVI) of 20 December 1961, 1802 (XVII) of 14 December 1962, 1963 (XVIII) of 13 December 1963 and 2130 (XX) of 21 December 1965. See also Ecosoc resolution 913 (XXXIV) of 2 August 1962.
31. General Assembly resolution 2345 (XXIII). The Agreement was opened for signature on 22 April 1968 and entered into force on 3 December 1968.
32. General Assembly resolution 2777 (XXVI).
33. Cf. the resolution of the Institut de Droit International, Brussels, 11 September 1963; it was preceded by a Report of G. W. Jenks, 50 *Annuaire de l'Institut de Droit International*, t. I, 1963, pp. 128-496; and t. II, pp. 361-364; cf. also the interesting debate which led up to the adoption of the resolution.

The International Law Association adopted a series of resolutions at its sessions in Hamburg 1960, Brussels 1962, Tokyo 1964, Helsinki 1966, Buenos Aires 1968 and The Hague 1970. Cf. in particular Memorandum of the Chairman of the Air Law Committee; Report of Dr. D. Goedhuis; Report of the 49th Conference, Hamburg, 1960, pp. 271-289, Annexes I and II; debate at the Conference, pp. 245-269; Report of the Sub-Committee of the Air and Space Law Committee on Air Sovereignty and the Legal Status of Outer Space; Report of the 50th Conference, Brussels 1962, pp. 72-100, Annexes, and debate pp. 31-68; Report of the 51st Conference, Tokyo, 1964, pp. 652-750; Annexes, pp. 751-776 and debate pp. 623-647; Report of the 52nd Conference, Helsinki, 1966, pp. 186-191; Annexes, pp. 191 ff.; and debates, pp. 143-159; Report of the 53rd Conference,

Buenos Aires, 1968, pp. 157-190; and debate, pp. 81-101; Report of the 54th Conference, The Hague, 1970. Cf. also the Proceedings of the Annual Colloquium of the International Institute of Space Law.

Chapter IV

The Legal Regime of Outer Space and Celestial Bodies

Space, it has been said, is a basic dimension of any legal system. In this respect, outer space represents a new category; this is obviously due to many factors: in particular its vastness, infinitely outreaching everything that has ever been gathered within the framework of law, and its physical relationship to Earth.

Cuius est solum eius est usque ad coelum et ad sidera: this principle, inherited from Roman Law, was accepted by international law and adapted to its needs.[1] For centuries States faced no practical questions concerning the control over their airspace nor the height to which their sovereignty extended.[2] (One of the earliest to speak on the subject was Grotius, when he claimed "freedom of space at an altitude beyond the range of the hunter's weapon".) Only the first journey of a man-made satellite reopened the issue: what was *coelum*? Can sovereignty extend *ad infinitum*?[3] If so, how could a State assert the resultant rights and discharge the resultant obligations? *Ad infinitum*–would it not be tantamount to sovereignty *ad absurdum*?[4] Moreover, taking into account the movements of the Earth, the sun and the planets, this could lead to strange and most unrealistic situations. The purview of a State's sovereignty would be subjected to continuous changes, its boundaries constantly shifted. Finally, the physical extent of a State's sovereignty would be in striking disproportion to its land territory, so that a claim to jurisdiction over the Atlantic based on sovereignty over the island of St. Helena would form but a mild analogy.[5]

1. It has been laid down that "outer space, including the moon and other celestial bodies, is not subject to national appropriation by claim of sovereignty, by means of use or occupation, or by any other means".[6] Thus States have been barred from extending to them, and exercising within them, those rights which constitute attributes of territorial sovereignty.[7]

The rule in question mentions specifically two terms: "use" and "occupation". The first does not belong to the catalogue of traditional titles to territory known in international law. It is closest to the "continuous and peaceful display of State authority",[8] the satisfaction of which dual condition has been held equivalent to a title to sovereignty.[9]

If adapted to outer space, this notion would betoken rather the utilization of that space by man and man-made instruments than the continuous display of authority.[10]

The other title referred to is "occupation", so frequently invoked by States in the past. As eventually evolved, it postulated the reality of the exercise of power, a notion shaped by practice at successive stages of history.[11]

There is no need, however, to enter into further theoretical analysis on the subject: neither use, nor occupation, can constitute legal titles justifying the extension of sovereign rights by any States over outer space, over the moon and other celestial bodies. The exclusion of such claims, having been cited *exempli gratia,* is supplemented by that of appropriation "by any other means". What other means could these be? One might mention the oldest of them–discovery. However, this has long been reduced in international law to an inchoate title, requiring to be supplemented by a more valid one.

Some other possible titles may be thought of, among them those advanced with regard to parts of our globe. Contiguity is one. The occupation of a small part of land, or of a shore was once held to justify claims to large areas. Analogously, claim might hypothetically be laid to parts of outer space by virtue of their bordering on airspace. However, while our globe was being subjected to gradual apportionment, this title lost its validity and has for a long time been an anachronism in all other environments.[12]

Thus, whatever criteria one adopts, such claims are bound to be considered as devoid of legal foundation.

This glance at some titles to territory in international law may appear a digression from the main theme, especially as many of them are today mere historical curiosities of limited interest. The intention of confronting them with the new environment was, however, precisely to illustrate the unreality of their application to it. It was *ex abundante cautela* that these titles were indicated and at once discarded.

Non-appropriation, then, is the rule. It could hardly be claimed that, as reflecting the will of States incorporated in a treaty provision, it is a rule of conventional character, with all the consequences thereof. For the basic rules defining the status of outer space–of which this is one–are rules of general international law. This conclusion is based on the whole complex of States' rights and obligations, written and unwritten. Thus it is scarcely conceivable that by withdrawing from the treaty a State could acquire freedom of action or the right to extend its sovereignty to outer space.[13]

The law uses the term "national appropriation", thus the question arises–is this to be understood as including not only sovereign rights but also property rights.[14] It is submitted that it should be read as covering both. "Appropriation" in the wider sense is involved. States are thus also barred from establishing proprietary links in regard to the new dimension.[15] Property being the legal expression of a basic form of "appropriation", it confers the right to use or dispose of an object and exclude all others from doing so. The question of property rights concerning objects introduced into outer space is, of course, an entirely distinct matter. What we are concerned with here are areas of nature. No such exclusive status is admitted in regard to them on the part of any State, as would prevent others from exercising equal rights to which they are entitled. These general principles apply to outer space as a whole and to any part of it. The term "part", theoretically speaking, would mean any of the volumes into which this great void, as a whole, might be divided. But distinct from this, more important, and of real practical value, are certain of the constituent physical phenomena, the harnessing of which modern science has already made possible, or may soon do so. Among these are solar radiation, cosmic and electromagnetic rays as sources of energy, or interstellar gases.[16]

2. "Outer space, including the Moon and other celestial bodies, shall be free for exploration and use by all States without discrimination of any kind and on a basis of equality and in accordance with international law ...".[17] Thus, laying down freedom of action for States, the law specifies conditions of its use by three elements of the definition: (*a*) the prohibition of discrimination; (*b*) the recognition of the equality of all States; (*c*) the requirement that the activities be conducted in accordance with international law.

These three elements can be said to be complementary: equality bars discrimination and so does international law, which also requires equality. However it should be borne in mind that at present only a very few States are engaged in the exploration of outer space. This is a fact which cannot be altered by law; what the latter can do, however, is to refuse to sanction situations which may close the door to equal rights and benefits for all States in the future.

Even for today the principles involved are of practical importance. While the use of outer space may be limited to a very small number of Powers, there are many more who carry out space experiments and explore certain of its areas. Their rights are thus protected. This is further stressed by the provision laying down that States "shall conduct all their activities in outer space, including the Moon and other celestial bodies, with due regard to the corresponding interests of all other States ...".[18] These interests are consequent upon the recognition of the rights of other States, and are to be construed on a basis of a reasonable interpretation of those rights. They constitute the limits of the freedom of action of States in outer space.

Special attention should be paid to the provision that "the exploration and use of outer space, including the Moon and other celestial bodies, shall be carried out for the benefit and in the interests of all countries, irrespective of their degree of economic or scientific development, and shall be the province of all mankind".[19] All countries are beneficiaries of the rights thus laid down.[20]

The complex of rights and obligations is further strengthened by the provision that the activities in question shall be carried on "in the interest of maintaining international peace and security and promoting international co-operation and understanding".[21]

Finally, mention should be made of the problem of investigation. A specific provision lays down that: "There shall be freedom of scientific investigation in outer space, including the Moon and other celestial bodies, and States shall facilitate and encourage international co-operation in such investigation".[22] This indicates an intention to extend to it special legal protection. While the term "use" still awaits more detailed definition,[23] "exploration" and "investigation" have specific meanings. Indeed, at this stage they constitute the main centre of activities in outer space. Yet even these formulae will require further elaboration in detail.[24]

Now something more may be said on those objects which, to use the words of a dictionary "can be observed in the sky beyond the atmospheric envelope of the earth". What are they? We know but a few of them: comets, stars, asteroids, meteorites of most varied shapes and sizes–which "populate" outer space. In the language of the first rules of the law of outer space they have been described by a generic term as "celestial bodies" or "the Moon and other celestial bodies".[25] Do these terms cover all natural objects so different not only in size but also in structure and following different paths in the universe? At the early stages of law-making it was suggested that they be endowed with status different from that of outer space proper;[26] that they be subject to appropriation as *terra nullius* and that occupation as title to sovereignty over them be recognized.[27] There were also attempts to apply to them different legal criteria.[28]

There are, of course, myriads of celestial bodies–from giants to micrometeorites, yet size could not be accepted as a test for their legal status: for how could one establish the minimum size below which an object would cease to be a "celestial body"? It is submitted that in the present state of man's knowledge there is little that can serve as a basis for any distinction between a natural or physical definition of a celestial body, on the one hand, and a legal definition on the other.

For the present, the term "celestial bodies" as employed in the relevant instruments should therefore be viewed as the largest common denominator of all "land areas" in outer space.

Their juridical situation having been assimilated to that of outer space *sensu largo,* they:

(i) are not subject to national appropriation by claim to sovereignty by means of use or occupation or by any other means, and therefore States cannot extend sovereignty over them and that they cannot be subjects of proprietary rights;

(ii) are free for exploration and use by all States without discrimination of any kind, on a basis of equality and in accordance with international law;
(iii) are free for scientific investigation, and States shall facilitate and encourage international co-operation in such investigation;
(iv) are to be explored, for the benefit and in the interest of all countries, irrespective of their degree of economic or scientific development, and shall be the province of all mankind.

This, however, concerns the general premises of the law only. For one cannot ignore the fact that celestial bodies by their very nature pose specific problems which require specific solutions. In fact this is reflected in some of the rules already adopted.

The freedom of exploration and use of "the Moon and other celestial bodies" includes the right of "free access to all areas of celestial bodies".[29] Here is a logical consequence of that freedom. It should therefore be given the widest possible interpretation. The term "access" should be understood as including the landing of space objects and of man, the placing of manned or unmanned equipment, and the establishment of direct or indirect contact between man and the celestial body. States are barred from preventing the free access of other States or from creating difficulties in this respect.

It has been suggested that this guarantee of access on the basis of equality could be viewed as an application of what has been known as the "open door" principle. However, it is doubtful whether this analogy with an institution of the past–one with such specific connotations–is called for. Apart from the general caution to be exercised in this respect, it is the institution itself which requires a new approach.

Freedom of access to all areas of celestial bodies confers on all States the right to establish stations and installations, to conduct experiments and make use of the celestial body as a whole and any part of it.[30] Equality requires that this right be exercised only to an extent compatible with due regard for the corresponding rights and interests of other States.

Within the framework of these considerations special mention should be made of the eventual use and exploitation of natural wealth and resources. Neither priority in discovery nor the mastery of technical facilities could constitute a title to exclusive rights in this field. Those who command these special possibilities may no doubt be entitled to claim that their efforts leading to the discovery and use of the facilities or resources should duly be taken into account. This could not, however, affect the basic principles: that the Moon and celestial bodies are "not subject to national appropriation", and that the exploration and use of outer space and celestial bodies "shall be carried out for the benefit and in the interest of all countries".[31]

Thus the law has determined the status of outer space and celestial bodies in a number of principles and rules. Their implementation, however, will require the elaboration of more detailed provisions if a conflict of interpretations is to be avoided.

Can these considerations lead to some conclusions of a general nature? It has been suggested that outer space and celestial bodies be considered as *res extra commercium, res communis* or *res communis omnium.*[32] It is true that some of these definitions have been accepted in other areas of international law. However, their application to outer space and celestial bodies is conditioned by a reply to a basic question: "Is outer space with the celestial bodies a 'thing'–*res* within the meaning of the law?" It is this which raises serious doubts. The term itself has many meanings. Municipal law qualifies *res* in the context of its institutions–in particular of the real rights established. Though the notion has also been adopted by international law, one can hardly argue that outer space and celestial bodies, though physically the latter may be reminiscent of some parts of our globe, can be encompassed by this term. None of them being a *res,* they cannot in fact become *res extra commercium* or *communis.*

Outer space and'celestial bodies are to be viewed as spheres of States' activities; as an environment subjected to a special legal régime and enjoying the particular protection of the law. This determines the relationship between States and the new dimension.

Notes to Chapter IV

1. Cf. J. C. Cooper, "Roman Law and the Maxim *Cuius Est Solum* in International Law", 1 *McGill Law Journal*, 1952, p. 23; A. de la Pradelle, "De l'origine de la maxime *cuius solum eius coelum*", *Revue générale de droit aérien*, 1932, pp. 294 ff.; "Cuius est solum eius est summitas usque ad coelum" (Bury *v.* Pope, 1, Cro. Eliz. 118 (1586). Temp. Ed. I., Blackstone *Commentaries*, 4 ed. 1770, Vol. II, p. 18). Cf. J. F. Lycklama à Nijeholt, *Air Sovereignty*, The Hague, 1910, p. 34; Ch. Hyde, *International Law*, Boston 1947, Vol. I, p. 590. Cf. McNair, who suggested that the maxim "has merely been used either to darken counsel or to afford a short cut and an excuse for not thinking the matter upon a basis of principles": *The Law of the Air*, London 1953, p. 297.
2. Cf. E. Giraud, "La notion d'espace dans les relations internationales", *Zeitschrift für ausländisches öffentliches Recht und Völkerrecht*, Vol. 19, 1958, p. 1'9. Cf. however Ming Min Peng, "Le vol à haute altitude et l'article 1er de la Convention de Chicago", 1944, *Revue française de droit aérien*, No. 4, 1952.
3. Cf. the earlier comments of D. Saporta, "Les satellites artificiels", 18 *Revue général' de l'air*, 1955, pp. 297-300; R. C. Hingorani, "La Souveraineté sur l'espace extra-atmosphérique", 20 *Revue générale de l'air*, 1957, No. 3, pp. 248-252; G. Dahm, *Völkerrecht*, Stuttgart 1958, Vol. I, p. 730; cf. O. Schachter, "Who owns the Universe?", in *Across the Space Frontier*, ed. Ch. Ryan, 1952, pp. 130 ff.
4. "The sky as understood by the traditional word *coelum* simply does not go that high": G. G. Fenwick, "How High is the Sky?", 52 *American Journal of International Law*, No. 1, 1958, p. 98. Cf. R. Quadri, "Droit international cosmique", 98 *R.C.A.D.I.*, 1959, pp. 505 ff. at p. 531; J. L. Brierly, *The Law of Nations*, ed. H. Waldock, Oxford 1963, pp. 219-220; also the earlier view of Schönborn, "La nature juridique du territoire", 30 *R.C.A.D.I.*, 1929, pp. 85 ff., at p. 158.
5. Cf. C. W. Jenks, "International Law and Activities in Space", 5 *I.C.L.Q.*, 1956, pp. 99 ff., at p. 103; B. Cheng, "From Air Law to Space Law", 13 *Current Legal Problems*, 1960, pp. 232-233.
6. Article II of the Treaty on Principles Governing the Activities of States in the Exploration and Use of Outer Space, Including the Moon and Other Celestial Bodies: cf. paragraph 3 of the Declaration of Legal Principles Governing the Activities of States in the Exploration and Use of Outer Space, 1963; cf. Part A, 1 (*b*), of the earlier General Assembly resolution 1721 (XVI) of 20 December 1961. Cf. explicit statements made prior to the adoption of the rule in question: the declaration of the USSR, *Pravda*, 18 November 1959, and in the United Nations, 22 September 1960 (Official Records, p. 48, para. 58, which renounced all claims to this effect). Cf. also the statements of the representative of the United States: "We have rejected the concept of national sovereignty in outer space. No Moon, no planet shall ever fly a single nation's flag" (Committee on the Peaceful Uses of Outer Space, 19 March 1962. A/AC.105/PV.2, pp. 13-15); of the representative of the USSR; "No human activity on the Moon or any other celestial body could be taken as justification for national appropriation" (Legal Sub-Committee, 20 October 1966, A/AC.105/C.2/SR.63, p. 10). Cf. Art. 2 of the Geneva Convention on the High Seas 1958: "The high seas being open to all nations, no State may validly purport to subject any part of them to its sovereignty."

7. Cf. *North Atlantic Coast Fisheries* arbitration (1910), P.C.A., VII, p. 114. A. Galina, "On the Question of Interplanetary Law" (in Russian), *Sovietskoye Gosudarstvoye Pravo,* No. 7, July 1958, pp. 52-58.
8. Cf. *Palmas* arbitration, *UNRIAA,* II, pp. 839 and 867 f.; earlier *Grisbadarna* case (1909), P.C.A., VI, 1909; *UNRIAA,* XI, p. 161.
9. *Palmas, op. cit.*, p. 839.
10. *Ibid.*, p. 840.
11. Established in practice and developed by theory, occupation consisted of the three well-known elements: (*a*) the *animus occupandi* of a State vis-à-vis an area which constituted (*b*) *terra nullius,* and (*c*) "the taking of possession" with a clear manifestation of the will permanently to exercise authority within the area. Cf. *Clipperton* Award of 28 January 1931, *UNRIAA,* II, p. 1110. The interpretation of the term "occupation" aroused serious and continuous controversy, and sometimes legal fictions were resorted to (cf. Ullman, *Völkerrecht,* Freiburg im Breisgau 1898, p. 195), cf. Holtzendorff, *Handbuch des Völkerrechts,* Vol. II, Berlin 1885, p. 256; J. C. Bluntschli, *Le Droit international codifié,* 4th ed., Paris 1886, paras. 278 and 280; Ghirardini: "Delle cosidette 'occupazione qualificate' nel diritto internazionale", *Rivista di diritto internazionale,* 1912, p. 46. See further Bonfils, *Manuel de droit international public,* 2nd ed., Paris 1898, p. 279; Foignet, *Manuel élémentaire de droit international public,* 4th ed., Paris 1902, pp. 101 ff.
12. It was invoked in various forms: cf. *Aves Island Arbitration,* Lapradelle et Politis, *Recueil des Arbitrages Internationaux,* II, pp. 404 ff. at pp. 410-411. But "The title of contiguity, understood as a basis of territorial sovereignty has no foundation in international law" (*Palmas, loc. cit.*, p. 869).
13. Cf. Goedhuis (*ILA Report,* 53rd Conference, Buenos Aires 1969, p. 159) who reiterates his earlier view that the principles in question have become generally binding (while suggesting that the language of the Treaty is not very clear). Sauer claimed that a State having renounced its rights could also withdraw its renunciation "Die völkerrechtliche Bedeutung der Sputniks", 8 *Jahrbuch für internationales Recht,* No. 1/2, 1959, pp. 37-41. This thesis is scarcely acceptable. Cf. also Chapter XII below.
14. Cf. the statement of the representative of France in the Legal Sub-Committee, 19 September 1966.
15. Cf. the statement of the representative of Belgium in the Legal Sub-Committee, 4 August 1966. He took note of the "interpretation of the term 'non-appropriation' advanced by several delegations–apparently without contradiction–as covering both the establishment of sovereignty and the creation of titles to property in private law". Speaking in the Political Committee of the General Assembly on the Space Treaty, the representative of France expressed satisfaction that the Treaty affirmed "three basic principles". As first among them he mentioned "the prohibition of the proclaiming of rights of sovereignty or ownership in outer space". General Assembly, First Committee, 17 December 1966. Cf. however a different view by S. Gorove: "Interpreting Article II of the Outer Space Treaty", *Fordham Law Review,* March 1969, pp. 351-353. Cf. Ortolan's reasoning concerning the high seas: "La mer n'est pas susceptible de tomber dans la propriété des hommes parce que la mer ne peut être possédée" (*Règles internationales et diplomatie de la mer,* Paris, 3rd ed., 1856, p. 127).

16. Cf. M. S. McDougal, H. D. Lasswell and I. A. Vlasic, *Law and Public Order in Space*, New Haven 1963, pp. 750 ff. In this respect an analogy may be drawn with the situation of the high seas, the resources of which can be used within what is recognized as freedom of the seas. Cf. B. Cheng, "Le traité de 1967 sur l'espace", 95 *Journal du droit international*, No. 3, 1968, p. 574. Again a distinction may be required between exhaustible and inexhaustible resources. Cf. Gorove, *op. cit.*, p. 350.
17. Article I, paragraph 2, of the Treaty of 1967. Cf. also the Declaration of Legal Principles of 1963, para. 2, and resolution 1721 (XVI) of 1961, part A, para. 1 (*b*).
18. Cf. Article IX of the Treaty of 1967, and paragraph 6 of the Declaration of Legal Principles of 1963; cf. also Article 2 in fine of the 1958 Geneva Convention on the High Seas.
19. Article I, paragraph 1, of the Treaty of 1967; cf. paragraph 3 of the preamble and paragraph 1 of the Declaration of Legal Principles of 1963. Cf. also the second paragraph of the preamble to resolution 1721 (XVI) of 1961. This is further stressed by the words of the preamble to the Treaty of 1967: "Recognizing the common interest of all mankind in the progress of the exploration and use of outer space for peaceful purposes" (second paragraph).
20. The expression "all countries" should be read in the light of the third paragraph of the preamble and Article I as a whole: it reflects the universality of the law on the subject.
21. Article III of the Treaty of 1967, *in fine*; paragraph 4 of the 1963 Declaration of Legal Principles.
22. Article I, paragraph 3, of the Treaty of 1967. It is worth recalling that in regard to the Antarctic the following definition was used: "Freedom of scientific investigations in Antarctica and co-operation towards that end, as applied during the International Geophysical Year, shall continue, subject to the provisions of the present Treaty." (Article II, Antarctic Treaty, Washington, 1959.)
23. Cf. Article II of the 1958 Geneva Convention on the High Seas. Cf. initiative of France to this effect: statement in the Legal Sub-Committee, 5 July 1967, A/AC.105/C.2/SR.80, pp. 6-12, also 19 June 1968, A/AC.105/C.2/SR.102, pp. 4-6; cf. report of Legal Sub-Committee on the work of its seventh session: paras. 14-16. The issue was placed on the agenda of its eighth session as item 3 (*b*), "The utilization of outer space and celestial bodies, including the various implications of space communications" and there were proposals by Poland, Argentina, Canada, Belgium and Czechoslovakia; cf. the resolutions adopted: Report, 8th session, paras. 9-13 and Annex I, pp. 4, 6-7. At the ninth session, priority having been given to the draft convention on liability, the issue was reserved for later: Report, 9th session 1970, paras. 29 and 30. Cf. General Assembly resolution 2733 (XXV) and the recommendation adopted at the tenth session to include the issue among the important subjects to be considered at a further session: Report, 10th session, 1971, para. 28. Cf. also the draft treaty concerning the Moon submitted by the USSR on 4 June 1971: A/8391 (in particular Articles IV, V and VIII).
24. Cf. the more precise formulations of the Antarctic Treaty, Article III.
25. Cf. successive resolutions of the General Assembly of the United Nations, in particular the Declaration of Legal Principles of 1963, and the terms used by the Treaty of 1967.

26. A list of these proposals was recorded by C. W. Jenks in his *Rapport préliminaire,* Institut du droit international, pp. 109-201; cf. also M. G. Markov, "Moon Landing and International Law", III *Rivista di diritto Aéreo,* 1964, No. 9, pp. 9 ff.
27. At the 49th Conference of the International Law Association the chairman of the Space Law Committee stated that only a minority had spoken in favour of applying to celestial bodies the principles of international law governing the acquisition of territory on earth (*Report,* Hamburg 1960, pp. 70 ff.).
28. Thus it has been argued that they should be divided into two groups: those which may and those which may not be subjected to occupation. Particular interest was displayed in regard to the moon. "The Sun and all planets and the moon" were to be "not appropriable", not so "meteorites ... any rock in space, which can really be used and controlled" (E. L. Fasan, "Law and Peace for Celestial Bodies", *Proceedings,* Fifth Colloquium on the Law of Outer Space, 23-29 September 1962, pp. 8 f.). Cf. also his *Weltraumrecht,* Mainz 1965, pp. 107-111. Cf. also A. A. Cocca: "... planets are the only celestial bodies considered such from a legal viewpoint; i.e., bodies admitting occupation if they are vacant" ("Basic Statute for the Moon and Celestial Bodies", *Rivista di Diritto Aéreo,* No. 6, 1963, 2nd quarter, para. V (*b*); also his *Tratamiento Legal de la Meteoria Extraterrestre,* Buenos Aires, 1967). On meteorites cf. McDougall, Lasswell and Vlasic, *op. cit.,* p. 755; also J. Machowski, "The Legal Status of Meteors and Meteorites", 39 *Yearbook A.A.A.,* 1969, pp. 101 ff.
29. Article I, paragraph 2 *(in fine),* of the 1967 Space Treaty.
30. It is in this context that doubts were expressed whether proprietary rights are really barred on celestial bodies. It was suggested that movable objects "attached to celestial bodies become immovables", which "grants the State to which they belong a right to the 'soil' of celestial bodies or at least a right to the surface". Thus it is contended that "we arrive at an ownership ... by technical and industrial occupation, without giving it a name" (N. M. Matte, *Aerospace Law,* London 1969, pp. 313 f.). Cf. also Mankiewicz, "Interventions with respect to permanent stations on the Moon", *Proceedings,* Eleventh Colloquium on the Law of Outer Space, New York, 1968. For different views see G. P. Zhukov, *The Law of Outer Space* (in Russian), Moscow 1966, pp. 238-240 and Fawcett, "The Politics of the Moon", 25 *The World To-day,* No. 8, 1969, p. 359.
It was also suggested that the establishment of permanent stations of which States made exclusive use would be incompatible with the existing law. Cf. Mankiewicz, *op. cit.* However, there is no convincing reason why the establishment of stations or installations on celestial bodies should be viewed as implying that "national appropriation" does not include proprietary rights. Cf. "Some Legal Problems arising from the Utilization of Outer Space", report by the chairman of the Space Committee of the ILA (D. Goedhuis) to the 54th Conference, The Hague 1970, p. 9. Cf. further, F. Vallat, "The Outer Space Treaty", 73 *The Aeronautical Journal,* No. 705, 1969, p. 754, and S. Bhatt, "Legal Controls of the Exploration and Use of the Moon and Celestial Bodies", 8 *Indian Journal of International Law,* No. 1, 1968, pp. 42 f. and 46 f.
31. See the early study on the subject by A. J. W. Rozelear, "Extra-terrestrial Mining", 15 *Journal of the British Interplanetary Society,* Nov./Dec. 1955, pp. 308-313. Here again, the distinction between "appropriation" on the one hand and "use and exploration" on the other should be made clear. Cf. M. McDougal in *Law and Politics in Space,* McGill, p. 121, and ILA Space Law Committee

Report 1970, *op. cit.*, pp. 11-13; also C. Kiss, "Le régime juridique applicable aux matériaux provenant de la lune et des autres corps célestes": Report of CNRS outer-space law working-group, containing a series of proposals on research and exploitation of the moon and other celestial bodies, in XVI *Annuaire français de droit international*, 1970, pp. 764-767. In this connection it is worth recalling the proposal made by France in the Legal Sub-Committee for the study of the compatibility of the non-appropriation principle with the possible exploration and exploitation of celestial bodies: A/AC.105/C.2/SR.57, p. 16 (20 October 1965). Cf. also the suggestion of Poland that "in the elaboration of treaty rules governing the exploration and use of outer space, it is necessary to prepare such rules relating specifically to man's activities on the surface of the moon and other celestial bodies" (working paper submitted to the Legal Sub-Committee: A/AC.105/C.2/L.53 of 13 June 1969). This was later combined with a proposal by Argentina. Cf. a Draft Agreement on the Principles Governing the Use of the Natural Resources of the Moon and Other Celestial Bodies, submitted by Argentina on 23 June 1970 (A/AC.105/C.2/L.71 and Corr. 1), Report of Legal Sub-Committee, 9th session, Annex II (Art. 2: "All substances originating in the Moon or other celestial bodies shall be regarded as natural resources"; Art. 4: "The benefits obtained from the use of the natural resources of the Moon and other celestial bodies shall be made available to all peoples without discrimination of any kind"). In the context of these proposals cf. footnote 23 above. The issues involved are in future to be considered under a more extensive heading. "Matters relating to the legal régime governing substances coming from the Moon and from other celestial bodies, including the principles governing activities in the use of the natural resources of the Moon and other celestial bodies"; cf. Report, 10th session, Legal Sub-Committee, para. 28.

32. Cf. B. Cheng, "Le Traité de 1967 sur l'espace", 95 *Journal du droit international*, 1968, No. 3, p. 565; Draft Code of Rules on the Exploration and Uses of Outer Space, David Davies Memorial Institute of International Studies, 1962, p. 2.1; H. Valladão, *The Law of Interplanetary Space*, Rio de Janeiro 1959, p. 8. For a different approach cf. C. Chaumont, *Le Droit de l'espace*, Paris 1960, p. 52. On the meaning of *res*, cf. R. Taubenschlag, *Roman Private Law* (in Polish), Warsaw, 1955, p. 124; J. Declareuil, *Rome et l'organisation du droit*, Paris 1924, p. 173.

Chapter V

The Frontiers of Outer Space

Having established that outer space is a distinct dimension, possessing a special legal status, we must ask the question: where are its frontiers?

It would be singular, to say the least, for the specific régime of a given environment to be determined without agreement as to the boundaries within which it is to operate. In fact, the determination of the frontiers of outer space has been a subject of lively controversy for years.

It should not, however, be forgotten that two frontiers are involved: the outward and the inward. As to the first, we have to plead sheer ignorance; for all that humanity may know, outer space may be infinite; it has, apparently, no frontier. In fact, any attempt to define it would be of little practical value. One may safely postulate that the realm of the law of outer space extends to infinity.

The Inner Frontier

Quite different is the situation of what may be called the inner frontier, that shared with airspace, where the law of the air prevails. This question arose in 1959, at an early stage in discussions on the law of outer space, and it was found that the task of delimiting it was not one of urgency;[1] thus the matter was not pursued and the first documents of the law of outer space bypassed the problem.[2] Only the elaboration of the Space Treaty (1966) was to give rise to a renewed approach.[3] Yet, throughout the intervening time it retained the particular interest of representatives of both theory and practice.

A large number of proposals were submitted, many theories advanced and solutions offered. Various criteria were suggested: some made an attempt to establish the boundary line between the two environments on a physical or geophysical basis;[4] others relied on the structure and methods of propulsion of vehicles.[5] Others, again, accepted the test of effective control.[6] Yet others proposed a specifically defined frontier.[7]

Another approach was of a functional nature. It laid less emphasis on the location of the line to be drawn, much more on the character of activities of States in outer space and the objectives they pursue.[8] This approach has led also to suggestions for the establishment of different frontiers for different types of activity, rendering them conditional on the degree of tolerance accorded to them by the subjacent States.[9]

With so many possible proposals we seem to be facing a dilemma. But is it really one? To begin with, it may be worth while to survey briefly the validity of some of them.

As regards environmental criteria, difficulties arise in view of the different approaches adopted by the various branches of science concerned. Although environing space can be divided into several strata, these join and overlap so that the line of separation between them is hardly discernible. Moreover, they are subject to fluctuations.

Difficulties would thus arise for instance if the earth's atmosphere, the gravitational field or the radiation belt were adopted as criteria: none of them having visible or clearly discernible frontiers, they would require therefore additional qualifications.

The same could be said of those which rely on the structure of vehicles or their methods of propulsion. It is true that an upper limit to the actual reach of aeroplanes or balloons can be established, so can the lowest perigee of satellites. Yet both these limits are subject to change, since they reflect the present state of technology in the respective fields. In fact, the issue has already been affected by the appearance of new types of vehicle which do not rely solely on aerodynamics (e.g., rocket-planes, which combine elements of traditional aircraft and of space-ships) and thus fly above traditional air space.

All this goes to show that any frontier relying on such criteria cannot be endowed with certainty, precision or permanence. The same applies to multi-layer frontiers, or a combination of physical and technical considerations, as these would be beset by the difficulties characteristic of both types.

As for the test of effective control, it is fraught with serious dangers. For it is not only the degree and form of control that are involved. It is much more a question of principle.[10] States which do not command an adequate technological or military potential would be deprived of rights which should be theirs as equal subjects of international law. This test could ultimately confer a premium on the stronger Power. Here then is a catalogue, though not an exhaustive one, of the many, frequently conflicting solutions offered.[11]

With these reflections in mind, one may return to the question: Is there any real dilemma?

In order to offer an adequate reply one has to consider the scope of such a frontier, the value and true interest of its establishment. As to the first, from a purely practical point of view, the whole issue is reduced to a rather limited part of space–stretching over the land and seas of our globe. This is the belt between the uppermost limit attained by aircraft and the lowest perigee of a spaceship. It is a safe assumption that its width will gradually be reduced–with aeroplanes reaching greater heights and the orbit of spaceships descending ever lower. Ultimately the path of their journeys will meet. Within this perspective, indicated by the development of technology, lies the real issue.

The value and interest of the frontier are linked in their turn with the basic motivation by which States have been guided in their claims to sovereignty over the area bordering with outer space. There can be little doubt that this has been, and remains, national security. As long as the State had not been threatened from above, it limited itself to the affirmation of the principle itself, and there was no valid reason for it to make any further detailed arrangements to this effect. With the advent of aircraft, States became anxious to protect themselves against whatever threat to their security these new flying objects might entail. This is clearly reflected in the principles and rules of aerial navigation. A State's rights over the air above its territory, as indicated earlier, were reasserted. How jealously they have been guarded and applied is illustrated by the practice of the last half-century.

Now, new objects have made their appearance in space. Though much further away, circling in their orbits or shooting upwards and coming down, do they constitute a new factor affecting the security of the States below? The developments during the last few years offer an unequivocal reply. The issue of security has not only retained its decisive importance: it has acquired an even greater emphasis. This is so whatever the point or line chosen, since the danger looming in outer space cannot be measured by distance. Modern technology has created possibilities for penetrating a State's exclusive domain from much greater distance than ever before. Hence the interest of States that activities in the vast dimensions above their territories should not become a threat to their security. Hence also their desire to take into account the nature of any activity carried out in the new dimension, to consider it on its merits, to judge it by its objectives and the consequences it produces within the areas of the sovereign rights of States.

Bearing in mind both theoretical and practical considerations, I advanced some years ago the view that there were no cogent reasons for States to proceed with the delimitation of the frontiers between airspace and outer space, maintaining that while the dimensions of a State's sovereignty above its territory are limited, the boundaries thereof need not necessarily be defined.[12] In fact, the lack of an established frontier has not so far created any special difficulties, nor has it constituted an obstacle to the formation and development of principles and rules of outer space law.[13]

However, with the growth of activities in outer space such a delimitation would offer clear advantages.[14] It would prevent the misunderstanding or even friction to which uncertainty tends to give rise, facilitate international co-operation. Thus we have now come some way nearer to the need for proceeding to that delimitation. Are we also any nearer the possibility of effecting it?

The attempts hitherto made to fix the frontier have proved abortive, and it has been confirmed that "it is not possible at the present time to identify scientific and technical criteria permitting the elaboration of a precise and lasting definition of outer space".[15] But the difficulties encountered are inherent in the methods which have been employed. There is however the possibility of adopting a purely conventional boundary which would only subsidiarily rely on specific environmental or functional criteria. Agreement on it in the not-too-distant future would evidently be facilitated by and should be sought in the context of further progress on wider issues of substantive law.

In pursuing the search for a solution it is essential to bear in mind the purpose it is intended to serve, i.e., to secure greater effectiveness of the law.[16]

The Way into Outer Space

As indicated, the law has traced no frontier between airspace and outer space. Wherever that frontier may eventually be fixed, any object journeying from earth to outer space, or the reverse, must traverse airspace. This does not give rise to any international legal problems if the flight carries the object solely over the State from whose territory it was launched[17] or over the high seas.[18] Such problems do arise, however, once the space object enters the airspace of other States.[19] In this context it may perhaps be useful to see whether the events of past years offer any guidance. They indicate, that:

1. States engaged in space activities:
   (*a*) Confined themselves to giving public notice of the launching of space objects;
   (*b*) did not inform States whose airspace was likely to be traversed of their intentions to launch space objects;
   (*c*) nor did they seek prior consent from those States.
2. States over whose territories space objects were flying did not, so far as is known:
   (*a*) Protest against, or endeavour to hinder or terminate, such flights;
   (*b*) reserve for themselves the right to bar such flights;
   (*c*) claim that such flights might in the future require their consent.

As this practice had begun at a time when the régime of outer space had not been formally determined, it was argued that it expressed only the recognition by States of the freedom of outer space and had no bearing on what might be called "the right of passage" through airspace.[20]

However true this may be, the very same practice has continued even after the acceptance of the written law on the status of outer space.

This action and this silence on the part of the States concerned have continued while an ever-growing number of space objects of different types have been crossing the airspace of many States. Can one therefore speak of a right of overflight established in the course of these years?

Scores of rockets and satellites have crossed the airspace of many States, affording a like number of opportunities for the States concerned to make their protests or objections known. These have not been forthcoming. Thus there is every reason to assume that a consensus has come into existence whereby launching States do not hold that their activities infringe the sovereign rights of other States, while the States overflown seem to have silently agreed that their rights were not so affected. Though this practice has continued for barely a dozen years, which may be held insufficient in itself, it should be considered in proportion to the number of opportunities offered to States to assert their rights or protest against their violation.[21] Within this perspective the conclusion seems to be warranted that an unwritten rule of law has gradually come into being.[22]

This view seems entirely compatible with the conclusions imposed by a more teleological approach. Thus when it is declared that outer space is "free for exploration and use to all States", a principle generally accepted by the whole community of nations, the law relating to access to outer space must, if that principle is to be effective, facilitate and not frustrate the endeavours of any State to avail itself for lawful purposes of the rights flowing from it. This holds good quite irrespective of such changing factual aspects as the scientific, industrial or economic capabilities of the State in question or the geography of its territory. If, in other words, the status of outer space is to be regarded not as a pious figment or abstract desideratum, but as a reality in terms of law, the legal conditions must be created for States to avail themselves of the rights it bestows.[23] This means that something in the nature of "freedom of innocent passage" through airspace must be recognized for the purpose of lawfully exploring and using outer space, as a necessary corollary of the declaration of the freedom of outer space made in written law. To think otherwise would be to postulate a right on the one hand and frustrate its essential purposes on the other.

This right of innocent passage should on principle be attributed to all States without discrimination. It implies reciprocity, even though the value of this, vis-à-vis most States, may remain purely theoretical for the foreseeable future.

However, it should not be forgotten that the acceptance of "innocent passage" through airspace, even though (as in other domains of international law) it does not prejudice the rights of sovereignty over the routes or space through which it is effected, implies the renunciation of some important options on the part of the territorial sovereign. It should therefore not be lightly presumed, especially where it does not result from any express declaration of will.[24] Thus while acquiescence may create a presumption of acceptance, it precludes the assumption that States have renounced, once and for all, the right to object to *any* activity connected with outer space that may be carried on in their airspace. More particularly, the right of passage does not connote activities which may be contrary to the principles and rules of outer space law or international law in general, or which are directed against a subjacent State or jeopardize its rights.

Nevertheless, if the exploration and use of outer space develop in the direction envisaged, i.e., for peaceful purposes and in the interests of overall international co-operation, there will be little basis for objecting to them as potentially violating the rights of subjacent States. With the gradual growth of rules corresponding to these general principles and objectives of the law, greater precision will have to be conferred on the concept of "innocent passage", and so the right to such passage through airspace may be expected, in time, to be embodied in the written law.

Notes to Chapter V

1. "It was generally believed that the determination of precise limits for air space and outer space did not present a legal problem calling for priority consideration at this moment": Report of the *Ad Hoc* Committee on the Peaceful Uses of Outer Space, A/4141, 14 July 1959.
2. At the first session (1962) of the Legal Sub-Committee it was raised by representatives of only two States; it was mentioned in the Report as one of six items referred to in the discussion. The report noted suggestions that the Sub-Committee should at a later stage examine *inter alia* the "demarcation between outer space and atmospheric space" (Report, para. 14, p. 8). The question was not pursued at subsequent sessions up to 1966.
3. Cf. statement of French representative in the Political Committee of the General Assembly, Twenty-First Session, 19 December 1966, A/C.l/SR.1492, pp. 8 ff., also a statement by the representative of Mexico, who suggested that the treaty be in future supplemented by a provision on the subject. Resolution 2222 (XXI), 19 December 1966, recommended to the Committee on the Peaceful Uses of Outer Space, *inter alia*, "to begin ... the study of questions relative to the definition of outer space ..." (para. 4 (*b*)). Thus the item found its way into the agenda of the Sixth Session of the Legal Sub-Committee (1967). The discussion resulted in a request addressed (in the form of a questionnaire) to the Scientific and Technical Sub-Committee "to draw up a list of scientific criteria that could be helpful to the Legal Sub-Committee in its study relative to a definition of outer space" and "to give its views on the selection" of these criteria (Report of the Legal Sub-Committee, 6th Session, 1967, p. 8). The problem was placed before the Scientific and Technical Sub-Committee at its Fifth Session in New York (A/AC.105/C.1. SR.44, 45 and 46; A/AC.105/39 of 6 September 1967, p. 7, para. 36 (*a*)). Following its Report the representative of France, while admitting the difficulties involved, suggested in the Political Committee of the General Assembly a "new study of this question": G.A., twenty-second session, 17 October 1967, A/AC.1/PV.1498, p. 12. During further discussion at the seventh session of the Legal Sub-Committee views were again divided; cf. proposal by the representative of France (A/AC.105/C.2/SR.102-110, pp. 1 ff. and 32 ff.; statements by the representatives of Italy, p. 7, and Canada, pp. 28 f.), while some delegations felt the time unripe for establishing the definition and others stressed the complexity of the problem (*ibid.*, pp. 4-10 and 26-28). The recommendation of the Legal Sub-Committee was "to place consideration of the study of questions relative to the definition of outer space on the agenda of the next session" (Report, 7th session, 1968, para. 16, pp. 11-12; Report of the Committee on the Peaceful Uses of Outer Space to the twenty-third session of the General Assembly, A/7285, p. 136; cf. G.A. resolution 2453 (XXIII) of 20 December 1968, B 2 (*b*)). At its 8th session the Legal Sub-Committee requested the Committee on the Peaceful Uses of Outer Space to invite the Secretary-General to prepare "a background paper for the next session of the Legal Sub-Committee on the question of the definition and/or delimitation of outer space" and "on the results of the studies to be furnished by the specialized agencies and the International Atomic Energy Agency in accordance with General Assembly resolution 2453 (XXIII)" (cf. Report, 1969, resolution

B, pp. 4-5). The General Assembly having endorsed this request the paper (A/AC.105/C.2/7) was submitted to the ninth session of the Legal Sub-Committee (1970) which did not consider the issue (cf. Report, paras. 9, 28 and 29, pp. 3, 10-11). By resolution 2733C (XXV), 16 December 1970, the General Assembly "requested the Committee on the Peaceful Uses of Outer Space to continue its study of questions relative to the definition of Outer Space"; following a further exchange of views at the tenth session of the Legal Sub-Committee, the matter was adjourned (Report, 1971, para. 29, pp. 14 f.).

4. The *upper limit of "the atmosphere"*, as the immediate environment of the earth, has often been proposed: what has traditionally been regarded as "air-space" (cf. the early view of V. Mandl, *Das Weltraumrecht*, 1932, p. 31; E. Pepin, "Space Penetration", *Proceedings A.S.I.L.*, 52nd Annual Meeting, 1958, p. 229). However, the atmosphere is not a uniform entity but comprises several layers, the ceiling of some of which (troposphere, stratosphere, ionosphere, even exosphere) have been suggested as possible boundary lines (cf. B. Cheng, "From Air to Space Law", 13 *Current Legal Problems*, London 1960, pp. 228 f.; V. I. Lisovsky, *International Law* (in Russian), Moscow 1961, p. 196; Jenks, *Space Law*, p. 191). It has also been proposed that the assumed boundary of the "meteorological atmosphere" (80 to 85 km. up), beyond which physical phenomena seem to have no effect on earth's surface, be taken as the inner frontier of space (representative of France in the Legal Sub-Committee, 5 July 1967, A/AC.105/C.2/SR.80, pp. 3 ff.).

The *limit of earth's gravitational effects*, where terrestrial gravity gradually fades away and that of another celestial body predominates has also been proposed as the boundary. It is estimated that the Earth's attraction extends up to 327,000 km. in relation to the Moon; it is almost sixfold in regard to the Sun. Cf. J. Kroell, "Eléments créateurs d'un droit astronautique", 16 *Revue générale de l'air*, XVI, 1953, No. 3-4, pp. 222 ff.; H. Strughold and O. Ritter, "Planetary Gravispheres", *Astronautics*, January 1962, pp. 26 f.

5. Here the suggested boundary would coincide with the *demarcation-line between aeronautics and astronautics*. This itself, however, according to the criterion adopted, could be for example (i) the "Von Karman primary jurisdictional line", defined as the height at which aerodynamic lift ceases and centrifugal force takes over (about 83 km. up), a suggestion put forward by Von Karman at a speech delivered in 1957 at the University of California, later modified by Haley, who applied the diagrams of Masson and Gazley (see A. G. Haley, *Space Law and Government*, New York 1963, pp. 77 and 97-107); cf. H. J. Abraham, *Das Recht der Luftfahrt*, Cologne 1960, Vol.I, p. 27; (ii) O. Schachter suggested (as far back as 1952) that the term "airspace" referred to that part of the atmosphere which would support flight by aircraft ("Legal Aspects of Space Travel", *Journal of the British Interplanetary Society* 1952, p. 14). Cf. also Jessup and Taubenfeld, *Controls for Outer Space and the Antarctic Analogy*, New York 1959, pp. 207 f., and Smirnoff, "The Real Possibilities and the Main Principles of a Future International Convention on Outer Space", *Proceedings*, Second Colloquium on the Law of Outer Space, London 1959, p. 324; (iii) the lowest perigee of a satellite (see resolution adopted at the 53rd Conference of International Law Association, Buenos Aires, August 1968). "The term 'outer space' as used in the Treaty, includes all space and above the lowest perigee achieved by the 27 January 1967, when the Treaty was opened for signature, by

any satellite put into orbit, without prejudice to the question whether it may or may not later be determined to include any part of space below such perigee" (Report, p. XXII) and J. E. S. Fawcett, *International Law and the Uses of Outer Space*, 1968, p. 23; and cf. the earlier views of R. Jastrow, "Definitions of Air Space", *Proceedings*, First Colloquium on the Law of Outer Space, p. 82, and G. P. Zadorozhny, *Basic Principles of the science of the Law of Outer Space* (in Russian), Moscow 1962, p. 40; (iv) a multi-layer frontier–the proposed setting-up of several frontiers, e.g., one to demarcate the sphere of territorial sovereignty of subjacent States and cover the area of aerodynamic flights, another beyond which space, freely accessible to all vehicles, would lie, and a special "contiguous zone" in between, something in the nature of a neutral zone with a special régime (see J. C. Cooper, "The Legal Problems of Upper Space", 23 *Journal of Air Law and Commerce*, 1956, p. 308, and "Legal Problems of Upper Space", *Proceedings*, American Society of International Law, 1956, pp. 85-94, and cf. his letter "Who Owns the Upper Air?" in *The Times*, 2 September 1957, and "The Rule of Law in Outer Space", 47 *American Bar Association Journal*, 1961, pp. 23 f.; cf. also A. Wolczek, First Colloquium on the Law of Outer Space, 1958, *Proceedings*, p. 115).

6. The decisive factor would be a State's possibility of securing effective control over the expanse above its territory. Cf. A. Dean, Letter to the Editor, *New York Times*, 25 October 1960. In this context it may be interesting to note one legislative act which lays down that national sovereignty "shall extend to the altitude to which the defensive weapons of the country are able to rise" (Bolivia, Decree regulating Air Service, 24 October 1930, Art. 1). See also J. C. Cooper, "High Altitude Flights and National Sovereignty", 4 *International Comparative Law Quarterly* 1951, pp. 411-418, who while admitting the possibility of such a solution, suggests a uniform rule applicable to every State, thus depriving the test of its rationale.

7. A series of proposals, while relying on some of the criteria already mentioned, or on others, have suggested that the frontier be fixed at some specific height from 20 to 800 kilometres and more. See *inter alia* R. T. Murphy, "Air Sovereignty Considerations in Terms of Outer Space", 19 *Alabama Lawyer*, 11,1958; *Draft Code of Rules on the Exploration and Uses of Outer Space*, David Davies Memorial Institute of International Studies, London, p. 7; C. Reintanz, *International Affairs* (in Polish), XI, No. 12, December 1958; cf. J. Rivoire, "Design for a Law of Space", *Proceedings*, First Colloquium on the Law of Outer Space 1958, p. 100; E. Fasan, *Weltraumrecht*, Mainz 1965, p. 52; and the proposals listed in L.P. Bloomfield, "Outer Space: Prospects for Man and Society", *The American Assembly*, New York 1962, pp. 154-156, and Fasan, *op. cit.*, pp. 53 f. Cf. discussion in the Legal Sub-Committee, 6th session, statements of the United Kingdom and Poland (A/AC.105/C.2/SR.81); Romania, Australia, USSR, Canada, Austria (SR.82); Bulgaria, India, Belgium, USA and Japan (SR.83). See also the Report of the Legal Sub-Committee, 6th session, 1967, Annex III, pp. 1-3; Working-Papers on the Definition of Outer Space submitted by the Government of France and Canada, A/AC.105/C.1/WP.V.1 and 2.

8. Cf. Quadri, *op. cit.*, pp. 519-521. Chaumont, *op. cit.*, pp. 147 ff., and D. Wadegaonkar, "Legal Problems of Outer Space", *Indian Journal of International Law*, Vol. 9, No. 1, January 1969, p. 56; also N. M. Matte, *op. cit.*, pp. 44 ff.

9. Cf. F. Zwicky, "The Morphology of Justice in the Space Age", *Proceedings*, Fourth Colloquium on the Law of Outer Space, Washington 1961, and "The Morphology of Justice in the Space Age and the Boundaries of Outer Space", *Acta Astronautica*, 14, 1969, pp. 615 ff. Cf. also J. F. McMahon, "Legal Aspects of Outer Space", 38 *B.Y.I.L.*, 1962 (he suggested that the drawing of a border-line–at the height of 100 km.–be linked "with an agreement on what activities above that point are to be permitted or prohibited": pp. 356 f.).
10. Cf. O. Schachter, "Legal Aspects of Space Travel", *loc. cit.*, p. 14; R. Probst, "Rechtliche Probleme des Raumflugs unter besonderer Berücksichtigung ihrer Bedeutung für ausländisches öffentliches Recht und Völkerrecht", 19 *Zeitschrift für ausländisches öffentliches Recht und Völkerrecht*, 1958, pp. 654-657; cf. also Chaumont, *op. cit.*, p. 47.
11. W. Strauss, in his paper "Air Law and Space Law" delivered at the McGill University, Montreal, in March 1962, estimated that fourteen different proposals had up to then been made on the subject: "the multiplicity of proposals for fixed boundary lines between air space and outer space makes it quite apparent that there is little agreement on the scientific facts", p. 25. Significantly, several of the authors of these proposals changed them more than once within a very short period of time. It is also noteworthy that some of these suggestions originated prior to the launching of the first satellite, or immediately afterwards.
12. "The International Law of Outer Space", 113 *R.C.A.D.I.*, 1964, pp. 39 f.
13. The great majority of replies to a questionnaire circulated among specialists in space law, including members of the United Nations Committee on the Peaceful Uses of Outer Space, stated that the determination of the frontier of outer space was not an urgent issue for the further development of the law on the subject, see P. B. Larsen, "A Sample of Space Law Opinion", 27 *Ohio State Law Journal*, 1966, No. 3, p. 468.
14. Cf. earlier comments on the advantages and disadvantages of determining a frontier of outer space; Lipson and Katzenbach, *Report to the National Aeronautics and Space Administration on the Law of Outer Space*, Chicago 1961, pp. 16 ff., and Zhukov, *op. cit.*, pp. 271 ff. Cf. in particular I. Brownlie, "The Maintenance of International Peace and Security in Outer Space", XL, B.Y.I.L., 1964, pp. 3 ff.
15. Report of the Scientific and Technical Sub-Committee of the UN Committee on the Peaceful Uses of Outer Space, A/AC.105/39, 6 September 1967, para. 36 (*a*), p. 7. Stating its consensus on this conclusion the Sub-Committee added that "a definition of outer space, on whatever basis recommended, is likely to have important implications for the operational aspects of space research and exploration, and that it is therefore appropriate that the Scientific and Technical Sub-Committee continue consideration of this matter at future sessions", para. 36 (*c*). Cf. also E. A. Brun, Chairman of a round table on "The Determination of Scientific Factors for Defining Outer Space" held during the XIX International Astronautical Congress, New York, 15 October 1968 (pp. 4 f.), and the earlier resolution adopted at the 51st Conference of the International Law Association, Tokyo 1964, *Report*, pp. XXXI f.
16. It was suggested that this could be "based on mutual political accommodations rather than on the 'scientific' merits of the proposal": cf. H. J. Taubenfeld, "Outer Space: the 'Territorial' Limits of Nations", 38 *Fordham Law Review*, 1969-1970, p. 6.

17. Cf. Articles 1 and 2 of the 1944 Chicago Convention on Civil Aviation.
18. "Freedom of the high seas" comprises *inter alia* "freedom to fly over the high seas", Article 2, para. 4, the 1958 Geneva Convention on the High Seas. One may also include the right to fly over the Antarctic, within the terms of the Antarctic Treaty (Arts. I, II, IV and V), Washington 1959.
19. Cf. C. Q. Christol, "The International Law of Outer Space", *International Law Studies*, 1962, Naval War College, Washington 1966, p. 171; D. Goedhuis, "Reflections on the Evolution of Space Law", *Netherlands International Law Review*, 1966, Issue 2, pp. 136 ff.
20. Cf. G. J. Feldman, "An American View of Jurisdiction in Outer Space", *Proceedings*, First Colloquium on the Law of Outer Space, The Hague 1958, pp. 47-49; A. G. Haley, *Space Law and Government:* "Under the principles of existing international law, any sovereign State could have declared that no man-made earth satellite might pursue an orbit over its territorial domain and that if such a satellite were launched, having such an orbit, the consequent violations of its territory would constitute an act of war" (p. 67). Cf. also the Draft Code of Rules on the Exploration and Use of Outer Space, David Davies Memorial Institute of International Studies, para. 2.
21. "With regard to the time factor, the formation of law by State practice has in the past frequently been associated with the passage of a long period of time. There is no doubt that in some cases this may be justified. However, the great acceleration of social and economic change, combined with that of science and technology, have confronted law with a serious challenge: one it must meet, lest it lag even farther behind events than it has been wont to do". *(I.C.J. Reports 1969,* Dissenting Opinion, p. 230.)
22. Cf. M. Cohen (ed.), *Law and Politics in Space,* Montreal 1964, p. 13; W. Wengler, *Völkerrecht,* Berlin 1964, Vol. II, p. 1091. Cf. Report of the 51st Conference of the International Law Association, Tokyo 1964, pp. 658-660: the right of passage through airspace was described as a "natural and functional necessity of space navigation" (P. Chauveau, pp. 676 f.).
23. Cf. the régime of the high seas, which have been declared "open to all nations ... coastal and non-coastal States" (Art. 2 of the 1958 Geneva Convention on the High Seas). A right of "innocent passage" through the territorial sea has been established, and its beneficiaries are all States, "whether coastal or not" (Art. 14 of the Convention on the Territorial Sea and the Contiguous Zone, which lays down conditions for the exercise of this right). Cf. Higgins, *Law of the Sea,* 8th ed., para. 42, p. 198, A. S. Bustamante y Sirven, *La Mer Territoriale,* Paris 1930, p. 205. As for the law of the air, cf. Articles 5, 6 and 8 of the 1944 Chicago Convention on International Civil Aviation. Cf. further Article 2, paragraph 2, of the Convention and Statute on Freedom of Transit, Barcelona, 20 April 1921, 7 *League of Nations Treaty Series,* p. 11; the Barcelona Convention and Statute on the Régime of Navigable Waterways of International Concern, 20 April 1921, *loc. cit.*, p. 35; E. Lauterpacht, "Freedom of Transit in International Law", 44 *Transactions of the Grotius Society,* 1957, p. 113 and pp. 317 f.; also the Convention on Transit Trade of Land-Locked States, 8 July 1965, *UN Treaty Series,* Vol. 597, p. 3; A. H. Tabibi, *The Right of Transit of Land-Locked Countries,* Kabul 1968.
24. Some writers question the existence of this right: cf. Footnote 20 above, also: Taubenfeld, "Outer Space: The 'Territorial' Limits of Nations", *loc. cit.*, p. 20.

He admits, however, that "a concept of free innocent passage might help the development of space capabilities for some small nations", p. 21. Cf. the earlier view of Jenks, *Space Law*, pp. 232 f.

Chapter VI

The Legal Situation of Objects Launched into Outer Space and of Astronauts

Not only are more and more devices being launched into outer space, but the number of types of instrument is constantly increasing. Recently the catalogue has been enriched, for example, by long-range manned stations or laboratories orbiting the earth. This diversity raises a preliminary question of definition. Should all these objects be placed in a common category? Many qualifications have been resorted to and terms borrowed from other environments: land, sea and air.[1] With growing frequency an overall formula, "objects launched into outer space", covering all vehicles and instruments moving into the new environment, is being used.[2] But, whatever the term, it does not solve the substantive problem–that of definition. A common denominator is required, a feature characteristic of all man-made space objects and distinguishing them from all other objects suspended above our globe or in motion beyond it.

It is worth recalling that the basic international treaties which shaped the law of the air, from Paris (1919) to Chicago (1944), refrained from laying down binding definitions of the term "aircraft". These are contained in subsidiary documents, which could be more easily amended.[3] Nor have such definitions been included in later agreements.[4]

This obvious reluctance to establish a detailed and specific definition, confirmed by a practice stretching over half a century, is very significant. It seems that an even stronger case can be made for flexibility in the definition of an "object launched into outer space".[5] In particular, there is one important factor which disqualifies attempts to resort for the purpose to existing instruments. This is the unpredictable potential of technological development, which could render the definition inadequate or even obsolete.[6]

It would therefore be preferable to adopt a definition broad enough to include any object designed:

1. to be placed:
   (*a*) in orbit as a satellite of the earth, the moon, or any other celestial body;
   (*b*) on the moon or any other celestial body;
2. to traverse some other course to, in or through outer space.

This, imperfect though it may be, can serve as a useful guideline for the effective application of the existing rules, and leaves room for elaboration in accordance with the growth of the body of law on the subject.

Following these preliminary considerations, two key problems call for reflection: those of jurisdiction and property.

1. Jurisdiction in General

Jurisdiction is of course a basic attribute of a State, whereby it exercises fundamental powers as a subject of international law. No reminder is needed that these powers, in terms of both domestic and international law, are not unlimited.[7] The bounds placed upon them are determined by the rights of other States and the requirements of co-operation in international relations.[8]

On the subject under consideration we face questions of jurisdiction arising beyond State territory, and many illustrations of rights invoked hereunder can be found in all dimensions. There have been many occasions when such claims led to confrontations, reflecting in particular the "old conflict" between territorial and personal jurisdiction.[9]

In view of the legal régime of outer space, only questions of jurisdiction over men and objects are involved.

It has been laid down that the State "on whose registry an object launched into outer space is carried shall retain jurisdiction and control over such object and over any personnel thereof while in outer space or on a celestial body.[10]

As this rule indicates, the law adds to the notion of "jurisdiction" another one: that of "control", criterion from which certain rights and obligations may result.[11] The term implies that the "State of registry" (see below) has a right to require other States to refrain from interfering with the direction and supervision of the object or with any of the technical arrangements necessary for the fulfilment of its mission of exploration and use of outer space. It should also be interpreted as implying certain obligations for the State concerned, in particular those of ensuring (*a*) that the object or the personnel thereof do not infringe the legitimate rights of other States and (*b*) that the mission they are intended to perform does not conflict with the rules of law of outer space.[12]

2. Legal Status of Space Objects

Thus the principle adopted with regard to space objects does not follow the old maritime rule of the "law of the flag" or the law of the air, which relies on the notion of "nationality".[13] Instead, reliance is placed on the institution of jurisdiction and it is within that framework that the issues are viewed and solutions solved. Its exercise is linked with two essential elements:

(*a*) the registry;
(*b*) the location of the space object within a defined environment.

The registry in question is not the same as that which the Secretary-General of the United Nations has been requested to maintain and for which States are called upon to furnish information.[14] It is one to be established and kept by States. No further provisions have been laid down on the subject. However, in view of the international consequences involved, a series of additional requirements should already be presumed; further, more detailed rules are sure to crystallize, and States will obviously have to enact special legislation or adopt regulations in this respect.

Of particular importance is the determination of criteria for entries in the registry.[15] No difficulties arise whenever a State launches its own object from its own territory; the same applies to objects owned or launched by non-governmental agencies registered in that State. However, in cases of joint launching, agreement between the parties is required as to which of them is to be deemed the "State of registry".[16] A similar agreement is also necessary when a launching is carried out by an international organization.[17]

Jurisdiction as defined extends over both the "objects" themselves and the "personnel" thereof. The legal status of the object and that of the men aboard are therefore inter-related.

As to the first, the problem raises no doubts: the jurisdiction extends over the whole, or over such parts thereof as may be detached and continue the journey in outer space as separate entities or land on celestial bodies. It also covers those parts of the space object which are severed from the main body owing to unforeseen circumstances. Finally, objects which after having landed on a celestial body are put together and become a new entity as "stations, installations, equipment" are also covered.

3. Legal Status of Space Personnel

The term used in this context is "personnel" (referring to those aboard a space vehicle); in another context it is "astronauts".[18]

These terms call for some reflection. Whom do they include? All members of the crew ought to be covered, including those who are in control of the vehicle as well as those who perform other functions, such as scientific tasks. Thus all persons aboard a space vehicle should share a common legal status. One may even venture one step further. Although for the time being no distinction can be made between crew and passengers, as the latter category is not yet in existence, one cannot ignore the certainty that one day passengers will be carried; to accord them the same status would be logical in the circumstances. However, greater clarification of the law on the subject will be necessary.

Now man has ventured outside his space vehicle, he has landed on the moon and moved upon it. Men may land upon other celestial bodies. In all these movements, whatever their nationality, men remain under the jurisdiction of the State "on whose registry" the space object in which they travelled is carried.[19] It may well be envisaged that they shall remain under that jurisdiction even if they enter an installation or station established on a celestial body by another State.[20]

Nevertheless the above considerations do not exhaust the issues, since on the way to and from outer space the object and the personnel are bound to find themselves in other environments. Problems may present themselves in the context of passage over or landing upon the territory of a State other than that of registry. Given the probable rarity of incidents in this regard, the questions involved may seem rather theoretical. Nonetheless they merit some brief attention.

The law having established the jurisdiction of the State of registry only with respect to outer space and celestial bodies, matters concerning jurisdiction elsewhere have to be dealt with in accordance with general international law and the specific rules concerning the environments in question. The only exception may arise from the obligation to ensure the safe and prompt return of the personnel of a space-ship to "the State of registry" or "the launching authority" in the event of accident, distress, emergency or unintended landing.[21]

Moreover, the inferred "right of passage" over foreign territory may be construed, as already suggested, in the sense of a right of "innocent passage", and, within that ambit, the subjacent State would therefore have no claim to jurisdiction.[22]

Both these situations may, of course, like others in this field, be given specific solutions by the elaboration of further rules.

Generally speaking, in interpreting the law it should be borne in mind that astronauts are to be regarded as "envoys of mankind in outer space".[23] The mission they perform and the risks they incur justify the special standing and legal protection afforded them. Yet this should not imply that they are placed above the law and are therefore exempted from bearing the consequences of any unlawful acts they may commit while, for instance, in the airspace of another State or after having landed on its territory.

4. Ownership

Outer space itself, including the moon and other celestial bodies, cannot (as we have shown) become the subject of proprietary rights. Any such rights existing in space objects, however, are protected as a consequence of the recognition extended by international law to what in principle is a category of municipal law. It has now been specified that ownership of space objects, "including objects landed or constructed on a celestial body", and of their component parts "is not affected by their presence in outer space or on a celestial body, or by their return to earth".[24] Thus the ownership of space objects is at every stage of their journey and in all environments, protected by the law.

The practical consequence of the recognition of ownership is the owner's right to claim the return of such objects or component parts thereof (as the case may be) and a corresponding obligation to return them.[25]

Special problems may arise should the space object constitute the property of several States or parts of it be supplied by them, or again when the object or part thereof is the property of an international organization.[26]

In the light of these provisions of the law there can be no question of assimilating objects launched into space, to meteorites, abandoned ships, *res derelicta* or *res nullius* in the wider sense, as was once in fact suggested.[27] However, the possibility of such an object's being abandoned and thus becoming *res nullius* cannot be excluded. But by renouncing rights of ownership the State concerned is not released from those obligations which rest upon it as the result of launching the object or from the further consequences thereof.[28] Finally, there is also the possibility of changes in ownership during the journey of the space object or its stay on a celestial body. While the first is probably very theoretical, the latter possibility may not be excluded, in particular with regard to objects permanently established on a celestial body. This would obviously require corresponding changes in the registry, with all that this implies.

Notes to Chapter VI

1. These are some of the terms which have been used: space-vehicle (employed in particular in Article 19 of the ELDO Convention), space-ship, spacecraft; kosmichesky korabl (Russian); engin spatial, véhicule spatial (French); vehiculo espacial (Spanish).
2. Cf. the French terms: *objet spatial, objet lancé sur l'espace, objet lancé sur orbite ou au-delà*. The Declaration of Legal Principles, 13 December 1963, uses the term "object" in paras. 7 and 8, and "space vehicle" in para. 9. The Space Treaty of 1967 employs the term "object" in Arts. IV, VII, VIII, X and "space vehicle" in Art. V. For the preamble to the earlier-agreed provisions of the Agreement on Assistance to and Return of Astronauts and Space Vehicles the expression "space craft and other space objects" was employed on my proposal (Legal Sub-Committee, Report, 2nd Part, 3rd session, 1964, Ann. III, p. 2). The final Agreement on Rescue of Astronauts, Return of Astronauts and Return of Objects Launched into Outer Space (1968) uses "spacecraft" in all cases where manned objects are concerned, and in other cases (as well as in the title) "object". The instrument on international liability (1971) is entitled "Convention on International Liability for Damage caused by Space Objects" and defines the latter term as also covering component parts of space objects as well as launch-vehicles and their parts (Article 1 (*d*)). The Agreement establishing Intelsat (20 August 1964) employs the term "space segment" (*secteur spatial*), comprising "communications satellites and the tracking, control, command and related facilities and equipment required to support the operation" of them (Article 1 (*b*) (*i*)).
3. Cf. Annexes 6 and 8 to the 1944 Chicago Convention: "*Aircraft*: any machine that can derive support in the atmosphere from the reactions of the air"; also R. H. Mankiewicz, "De l'ordre juridique dans l'espace extra-aéronautique", V *Annuaire français de droit international*, 1959, pp. 129 ff.
4. Such as the Convention for the Unification of Certain Rules Relating to International Transportation by Air, Warsaw, 12 October 1929, and the Convention on Damage Caused by Foreign Aircraft to Third Parties on the Surface (1) Rome, 1929, (2) Rome, 7 October 1952. On the other hand, the 1933 Hague International Sanitary Convention concerning Air Navigation does contain a definition.
5. Here are some of the definitions suggested: "*Space vehicle*. A vehicle designed to be placed in orbit as a satellite of the earth or of another heavenly body, or to be caused to traverse some other path in space" (Convention of the European Organisation for the Development and Construction of Space Vehicle Launchers (ELDO), Art. 19, Annex). "*Spacecraft*: A man-made vehicle, which is intended to go beyond the major portion of the Earth's atmosphere" (International Radio Regulations, Final Acts, Geneva 1971, Annex 1, Article 1, Add. 84BAA, p. 45). Cf. also the proposals made by (*a*) the David Davies Memorial Institute of International Studies: "'Spacecraft' means any craft capable of orbital movement or manoeuvre in outer space and includes any craft which is being operated as a space station" (para. 1 and Commentary); (*b*) Australia and Canada: "'Space object' means an object or any of its component parts which a launching State has launched or attempted to launch into outer space" (Legal

Sub-Committee, Third Session 1964, Second Part, Report, Annex I, p. 9); (*c*) Argentina: "For the purpose of this Agreement the term 'space vehicle' means any device launched by man exclusively for peaceful purposes, for the exploration or use of outer space, including the Moon and other celestial bodies, as well as the equipment used for launching and propulsion and any parts detached therefrom" (Legal Sub-Committee, Sixth Session 1967, Report, Annex II, p. 18).

6. The first attempts in this direction employed a somewhat negative approach: "By 'space device' shall be understood any device which is intended to move in space, remaining there by means other than the reaction of the air" (Working Paper submitted by Belgium on the Unification of Certain Rules Governing Liability for Damage caused by Space Vehicles, Art. 1, para. (*b*); Legal Sub-Committee, Second Session 1963, Report, Annex I, p. 11); or "'Space object' means space ships, satellites, orbital laboratories, containers and any other devices designed for movement in outer space and sustained there otherwise than by the reaction of air, as well as the means of delivery of such objects and any parts thereof" (Art. 1, para. 3, of the Draft Agreement concerning Liability for Damage Caused by the Launching of Objects into Outer Space, presented by Hungary, Legal Sub-Committee, Third Session 1964, First Part, Report, Annex II, p. 8). Cf. the critical comments of the Representative of Argentina on these proposals, at the Sixth Session of the Sub-Committee, 23 June 1967, and his own proposal in the preceding footnote. Cf. also a definition proposed by India (Legal Sub-Committee, Report, seventh session, 1968, Annex I, p. 67). Different criteria were suggested by Italy: "any man-made object designed to reach outer space and to move there (either) naturally or by means of radio-electric signals or the control exercised by pilots on board" (*ibid.*, p. 82. Cf. also criteria listed by Verplaetse, "On the Definition and the Legal Status of Spacecraft", *Journal of Air Law and Commerce*, Spring 1964, pp. 131 ff.
7. Cf. *inter alia* Judgment of the Central American Court of Justice, *Salvador* v. *Nicaragua*, 9 March 1917, *A.J.I.L.*, 1917, pp. 718 f; *Nationality Decrees in Tunis and Morocco, P.C.I.J. 1921, Ser. B., No. 4*, pp. 23 f.
8. "Can the island of Tobago pass a law to bind the rights of the whole world? Would the world submit to such an assumed jurisdiction?" Cf. Lord Ellenborough in *Buchanan* v. *Rucker* (1808), 9, East, 192; Lord Blackburn in *Schibsby* v. *Westenholz* (1870), L.R. 6, Q.B. 155, p. 160. From a rich literature on the subject"cf. M. Bourquin, "Règles générales du droit de la paix", *R.C.A.D.I.* Vol. 35, 1931-I, pp. 102 ff.; F. A. Mann, "The Doctrine of Jurisdiction in International Law", 111 *R.C.A.D.I.* 1964, pp. 9 ff.; R. Y. Jennings, "The Limits of State Jurisdiction", 32 *Nordisk Tidskrift for International Ret*, 1962, pp. 209 ff.
9. Cf. *Rights of United States Nationals in Morocco, I.C.J. Reports, Judgment, 1952*, p. 191.
10. Article VIII of Space Treaty, 1967; cf. also Declaration of Legal Principles, 1963, para. 7 (the latter referred to "outer space" only).
11. This term is to be found in other legal instruments both municipal and international. Cf. Proclamation of the President of the United States, 28 September 1945, referring to the natural resources of the subsoil and sea-bed of the Continental Shelf beneath the high seas, and declaring them "as appertaining to the United States, subject to its jurisdiction and control", 40 *A.J.I.L.*, 1946, Suppl., pp. 45 ff.; Article 5, para. 1, of the Convention on the High Seas (1958) states

inter alia: "the State must effectively exercise its jurisdiction and control in administrative, technical, and social matters over ships flying its flag".

12. Cf. *Costa Rica Packet*, 1897, Moore, *International Arbitrations*, Vol. V, p. 4592; as Brownlie rightly points out "The right to enjoy the protection of the law balances the responsibility of the flag State for the behaviour of its ships", *Principles of Public International Law*, Oxford 1966, p. 212.
13. Cf. *Lotus, P.C.I.J. Ser. A, No. 10*, 1927, p. 25; Report by J. P. A. François, International Law Commission, Doc. I.L.C.ACN/4/17, p. 7; Article 6 of the Convention on the High Seas (1958) and Article 17 of the Convention on International Civil Aviation, Chicago, 1944. In regard to outer space, cf. a resolution of the International Law Association: "Resolves to draw the attention of the United Nations Committee on the Peaceful Uses of Outer Space to the desirability of avoiding nationality as a necessary element in the rules to be drafted concerning legal status, liability and jurisdiction in respect of space vehicles" (Report, 51st Conference, Tokyo, p. 741).
14. Cf. UN General Assembly resolution 1721 (XVI) of 20 December 1961, part B: "1. *Calls upon* States launching objects into orbit to furnish information promptly to the Committee on the Peaceful Uses of Outer Space, through the Secretary-General, for the registration of launchings; 2. *Requests* the Secretary-General to maintain a public registry of the information furnished in accordance with paragraph 1 above."
15. It is highly desirable that the entry should reflect a link between the State which keeps the registry and the space object; cf. Article 5, para. 1, of the Convention on the High Seas: "There must exist a genuine link between the State and the ship ...".
16. The principle of registration by one State only reflects the law of the sea: "Ships shall sail under the flag of one State only" (Article 6, para. 1, of the Convention on the High Seas); in regard to aircraft, cf. Articles 17 and 18 of the 1944 Convention on International Civil Aviation; cf. also Art. 18, paras. 1 and 3, of the Convention on Road Traffic, Geneva, 19 September 1949. The text of Article VIII of the Space Treaty leaves no doubt that the same principle should apply to "objects launched into outer space". Article XIII of the Treaty takes account of joint activities of several States or of international organizations. Where two or more States are involved, the proper implementation of the provisions in question, i.e., the exercise of "jurisdiction and control over such objects and over any personnel thereof", requires that they agree on the subject.
17. In regard to ships, the specific question was raised as to what the effect would be of their being owned by the United Nations, registered by it and flying its flag. It was stated that this would not assimilate the latter to the flag of a State. Cf. J. P. A. François, "Report on the Rights of International Organisations to Sail Vessels under their Flags", *Yearbook of the International Law Commission* 1956, II, pp. 102 ff.; a similar question was discussed in ICAO: cf. *ICAO Bulletin*, Vol. XV, No. 10, 1960. As to the law of outer space, an international organization may of course lay down rules and regulations, and make other arrangements concerning operations conducted by it, and the personnel thus employed; this, however, does not resolve the issue of jurisdiction (cf. also footnote 16 above). All this indicates that further elaboration of the law is highly desirable. Cf. Draft Convention Concerning the Registration of Objects Launched into Space for the Exploration or Use of Outer Space, submitted by

France (Legal Sub-Committee, Seventh Session 1968, Report, Annex II, pp. 1-3) and statement by the Representative of France, 19 June 1968 (A/AC.105/C.2/SR.102-110, p. 3). The objective of the Convention is "the establishment of common rules governing the registration of objects launched ..." (Preamble, para. 2). It provides that "Any object launched ... shall be registered by entry in a register kept by a service under the supervision of one or more Governments Parties to this Convention" (Article 1, para. 1). "There shall be only one registration of each object" (Article 1, para. 2). Among the data to be recorded are envisaged: "the law applicable to the object and to the persons carried in it when an inter-governmental agency or a group of natural or juridical persons ... procures the launching" (Article 2, paras. (*c*) and (*e*) respectively). Cf. also statement on the Registration with the United Nations of Objects Launched into Outer Space, delivered by the Chief of the Outer Space Affairs Division of the United Nations (Legal Sub-Committee, 13 June 1969, Eighth Session 1969, Report, Annex IV, pp. 1 ff. At the same session the Legal Sub-Committee requested that the Scientific and Technical Sub-Committee undertake a study of the technical aspects of registration, and that appropriate information on registration of ships, aircraft, etc., be obtained from specialized agencies, as well as from Cospar: Resolution A, Report, para. 13). Cf. also the exchange of views on the subject at the 112th meeting of the Legal Sub-Committee. At its Tenth Session the Legal Sub-Committee recommended that the question be included among important subjects for its further consideration.

18. Articles IV, para. 2, and VIII of the Space Treaty, 1967, use the term "personnel", while Article V speaks of "astronauts"; the Agreement on Rescue of Astronauts, Return of Astronauts and Return of Space Vehicles uses in the text the term "personnel". In another context, that of stations, installations, equipment and space vehicles on the Moon and other celestial bodies being open to visit the Space Treaty uses the term "representatives" (Art. XII); the Convention on International Liability uses the term "persons ... on board ... a space object" (Articles III and IV).
19. An earlier provision laid down that the State of Registry "shall retain jurisdiction and control over 'objects launched into outer space' and 'any personnel thereon'" (Declaration of Legal Principles, 1963, para. 7). The Space Treaty replaced the word "thereon" by "thereof", thus extending this jurisdiction to wherever astronauts may move in space or on a celestial body. Cf. statements by the representatives of Canada and USSR in the Legal Sub-Committee, Fifth Session, 25 July 1966, A/AC.105/C.2/SR.66, pp. 11 and 55-56.
20. Cf. Article XII of the Space Treaty, 1967.
21. This is, of course, limited. Cf. Article 39 of the Vienna Convention on Diplomatic Relations (1961): Chapter VII hereunder.
22. Cf. footnote 23 to Chapter V, above.
23. Article V, para. 1, of the Space Treaty 1967; para. 9 of the Declaration of Legal Principles, 1963; cf. also para. 9 of the Draft Declaration proposed by the USSR, Legal Sub-Committee, First Session, 1962, Report, para. 11, p. 4.
24. Article VIII of the Space Treaty, 1967; Declaration of Legal Principles, 1963, para. 7.
25. "Such objects or component parts found beyond the limits of the State Party to the Treaty on whose registry they are carried shall be returned to that State

Party, which shall, upon request, furnish identifying data prior to their return." Article VIII as above *in fine*. We return to the subject in Chapter VII.

26. Here again the parties concerned should make proper arrangements so as to avoid any difficulties. Cf. provisions concerning ownership in Intelsat: "The space segment shall be owned by individual shares by the signatories to the Special Agreement in proportion to their respective contributions to the costs of the design, development, construction and establishment of the space segment" (Article III, Agreement Establishing Interim Arrangements for a Global Commercial Communication Satellite System, Washington, 20 August 1964). The Draft Agreement on the Establishment of an International Communications System Using Artificial Earth Satellites (Intersputnik) provides: "The outer-space complex shall be the property of 'Intersputnik' or shall be leased from its member States" (Article 3, para. 2). Cf. also para. 3, Doc. A/AC.105/46 of 9 August 1968; cf. also V. S. Vereshchetin, *Legal Aspects of Orbiting International Laboratories*, USSR Academy of Sciences, Moscow 1970, pp. 3 ff.
27. Proposals to this effect were made in the earlier stages of the exploration of outer space when it was still uncertain whether man could retain control over space objects. Thus it was suggested that "once a satellite is launched it is beyond the control of human beings; locked by gravitation to the earth, it resembles a meteorite revolving around the sun": M. T. Levit, "Space Age Question: Who owns a Fallen Satellite?" *Army-Navy-Air Force Register: The U.S. Military Review*, 1959, No. 4102-4103. Cf. also A. A. Cocca, "Reflecciones sobre el Derecho Interplanetario", 28 *Revista Nacional de Aeronautica*, Buenos Aires 1958, p. 195; E. Danier and M. Saporta, "Les Satellites artificiels", *Revue Générale de l'Air*, No. 3, 1955, pp. 29 ff. It may be of interest to recall that Blanchard's balloon was seized by the owner of the field where it landed, who not only refused to return it but destroyed it, claiming that he was entitled to do so since it was an object fallen from heaven. Blanchard got little consolation from the law: the court refused his claim for compensation and even ordered him to pay damages.
28. There remains its liability. Cf. Chapter XI.

Chapter VII

Assistance to Astronauts, Return of Astronauts and Space Objects

Evident dangers are involved in journeys into outer space. Hence the need for international co-operation in rendering assistance to those who undertake them, in the event of accident or distress, in the rescue and return of both men and space objects. To this problem special attention has been paid ever since the early days of law-making in the field.[1] It has been possible to draw lessons from arrangements concluded to similar ends in other environments, such as the sea and the air.[2]

I. Rescue and Return of Astronauts

The basic principles laid down in this respect provide for:

1. Assistance to astronauts in the event of accident, distress, or emergency landing;
2. their safe and prompt return;
3. mutual assistance between astronauts of different States in outer space and on celestial bodies.[3]

The beneficiaries of these provisions were originally designated "astronauts"; subsequently the term "personnel" was introduced. The humanitarian character of the action concerned imposes an extensive interpretation, whereby all persons aboard a space vehicle should be comprised herein.[4]

In the language of the detailed provisions of the law, action is called for when "the personnel of a space craft have suffered accident", "are experiencing conditions of distress" or "have made an emergency or unintended landing":[5]

(*a*) in territory under the jurisdiction of a State,[6]
(*b*) on the high seas, or
(*c*) in any other place not under the jurisdiction of any State.[7]

1. Notification

The State which receives information, or itself discovers, that one of these events has occurred shall immediately:

(*a*) "notify the launching authority", or

(*b*) "make a public announcement" instead, in case it "cannot identify and immediately communicate with the launching authority", and
(*c*) notify the Secretary-General of the United Nations.

Both the State concerned and the Secretary-General, the first for its announcement and the latter for the dissemination of the information, should use "all appropriate means of communication" at their disposal.[8]

Thus States are under no obligation to watch the objects launched into outer space during their flights or emergency landing. Information about the accident may be received in any way: in the course of the normal operation of State organs or services, directly or indirectly, or through private individuals. It is only at the moment that the event in question comes to a State's knowledge that the obligation to act arises. The notification of the launching authority should create no difficulty once it is identified. However, a fallen space object may be spotted in a relatively inaccessible area, or for other reasons there may be no means of establishing the identity of the launching authority or of communicating with it. It is in these circumstances that a public announcement should be made, so that the interested State may without delay receive information about its space object.

The requirement that the Secretary-General of the United Nations be notified is a corollary of the provisions stipulating that the United Nations be informed of all undertakings in the exploration and use of outer space, and is intended as a supplementary means of contacting the launching authority.[9]

2. *Assistance and Rescue of Astronauts*

A. The State exercising jurisdiction over the territory in which personnel of a space-craft land "owing to accident or distress", make an "emergency or unintended landing" shall "immediately take all possible steps to rescue them and render to them all necessary assistance". It shall also inform the launching authority and the Secretary-General of the United Nations of the steps "it is taking and of their progress".[10]

The qualifications concerning these operations have both objective and subjective connotations. Objectively, rescue action may require the most modern equipment and special technical devices, which are not everywhere readily available. If they are not, the test is whether all means at the disposal of the State concerned are deployed.[11] Their possible insufficiency explains the insertion of a reference to the assistance of the launching authority, which is called upon to co-operate in the operations whenever such collaboration:
(*a*) would help "to effect a prompt rescue",
(*b*) would "contribute substantially to the effectiveness of search and rescue operations".[12]

This assistance is not optional, it is an obligation which the launching authority should discharge. The State exercising jurisdiction is entitled to call for this aid, but is it under an obligation to seek it or to accept it if offered? It is really a question as to who shall decide whether such assistance would "help" or "contribute substantially" to the success of the operations. Here again, in view of their humanitarian character, it is to be presumed that the State concerned will not refuse such assistance, and thus take upon itself the responsibility for the possible failure of the action, without compelling reasons. In any case, the State which exercises jurisdiction over the territory:

(*a*) is vested with the right of "direction and control" of the search and rescue operations,

(*b*) has the obligation to "act in close and continuous consultation" with the launching authority.[13]

The above right derives from the exercise of jurisdiction, while the obligation arises from the need to afford the launching authority the possibility of discharging its special responsibility for the safety of the personnel.[14] However, as indicated earlier, all the obligations of the State exercising jurisdiction are limited to cases of accident, distress, emergency or unintended landing. It will not always be possible to ascertain beforehand whether any of these conditions did occur and were the principal cause of the landing. In any case, here, once again, the humanitarian character of the provision calls for latitude in its interpretation.

B. If the personnel of a space-craft "have alighted on the high seas or in any other place not under the jurisdiction of any State", a State which receives information to this effect is under the obligation to extend its assistance in the search and rescue action. This obligation covers only cases in which (*a*) it is in a position to offer assistance, and (*b*) such assistance is necessary.[15]

Here again, subjective and objective criteria are involved. Several States may be involved, their ships or aircraft being in the vicinity. The need for their taking action will arise only if the launching authority is unable to carry out the rescue operations alone.[16] Should they take action, they shall inform the launching authority and the Secretary-General of the United Nations.[17]

The obligation of mutual assistance also extends to astronauts in outer space and on a celestial body. This is stated in very general terms and the need for more detailed stipulations will no doubt arise.[18]

3. *The Return of Astronauts*

The last stage of every successful rescue operation will be the return of the astronauts to the launching authority. Wherever they may have been found, the State which has rescued them is to extend them all the protection necessary for their safe and prompt return. The obligation in this respect is unequivocal; they have to be returned to "representatives of the launching authority". If the latter is a State, they may be handed over to its diplomatic representatives or other persons delegated for this purpose in the very place where they landed, aboard ship or at any other suitable location.[19] Appropriate arrangements will be necessary if the launching authority is an international organization.

II. Recovery and Return of Objects Launched into Outer Space

Similar, though not identical problems arise in cases where an object launched into outer space has returned to earth and is found in territory under the jurisdiction of another State, on the high seas, or in any other place not under the jurisdiction of any State.

1. *The Obligation of Notification*

Any State acquiring knowledge of such an occurrence or discovering such an object shall notify (*a*) the launching authority, and (*b*) the Secretary-General of the United Nations.[20]

This obligation is much more limited than that in cases concerning astronauts: no stress is laid on "immediate" communication with the launching authority; in case it cannot be identified, there is no need to make an immediate public announcement. The obligations of the Secretary-General are similarly limited, though he will have to take measures to identify and notify the launching authority if the State concerned is unable to do so.

2. *The Obligation to Recover the Object*

(i) The State which exercises jurisdiction "over the territory on which a space object or its component parts has been discovered" shall take action leading to its recovery, but (*a*) this obligation arises only where the launching authority makes a request to that effect; (*b*) it involves only "such steps" as the State concerned "finds practicable"; and (*c*) it may request assistance from the launching authority.[21]
The initiative has thus been left to the launching authority. However, the State exercising jurisdiction over the territory on which the object is discovered remains in charge of the operations, and has the free choice of the means to be employed.

(ii) Any assistance in the recovery of space objects found outside the territorial jurisdiction of any State (e.g., on the high seas) is deemed to be voluntary and depends on the goodwill of States.[22]

3. *The Obligation to Remove Objects of a Hazardous or Deleterious Nature*[23]

Objects launched into outer space or their component parts may, by their return to the earth, have become hazardous or deleterious to life and health, or harmful to the environment. The launching authority is therefore under an obligation to take (*a*) immediate and (*b*) effective steps "to eliminate possible danger of harm".

When the object has been discovered in territory under the jurisdiction of another State, or recovered by it elsewhere, the action is to be carried out "under the direction and control" of that State.

For this obligation to arise it suffices for the State concerned to notify the launching authority that it "has reason to believe" that the object is of "a hazardous or deleterious nature". The provision in question has the character of a *lex specialis.*[24]

4. *The Return of Space Objects*

This is the ultimate purpose of all search and recovery operations.

(a) The Claim

The first step leading to return of the object is a request made by the launching authority whenever its space object (or parts thereof) is found beyond its territorial limits.[25] No specific provisions are made as to the form of such request, except that the claim has to be substantiated by the provision of identifying data.[26] (In order to facilitate the process it would be advisable to introduce some generally binding rules providing for identification marks on all space objects.) As to the timing of the request no difficulties should arise in practice. It is rather unlikely that any launching authority would delay claiming the return of any object of whose landing it is advised, especially when the recovery operation is to be conducted at its request. However, it is conceivable that on some occasions the claim may be renounced.

(b) The Obligation

The claim gives rise to a corresponding obligation on the part of the State against which it is made.

This obligation can be discharged by (i) the return of the object, or (ii) holding it at the disposal of persons duly authorized to collect it.

This alternative meets the difficulties the physical return may present to the finding State, which has therefore the right of choice.[27]

III. Expenses incurred in the Rescue, Recovery and Return of Astronauts and Space Objects

There can be little doubt that in view of the high costs which may be involved in these operations, the reimbursement of the expenses incurred by other States is fully justified, the more that such provisions are well known in other fields, such as sea and air navigation. In general, remuneration is provided for salvage of property. On the other hand, there is a clear trend towards excluding any financial remuneration wherever assistance in saving human life is involved.[28] As to outer-space activities, no provision has been adopted as to remuneration or the refund of expenses incurred in rendering assistance to and the return of astronauts. This silence of the law warrants the conclusion that no compensation can be demanded.[29] Different is the situation with regard to the recovery and return of space objects or their competent parts. The expenses are to be borne by the launching authority.[30] Thus any State incurring such expenses, wherever the action which led to them took place, on its territory or beyond its frontiers, may present a claim for their refund. It may even request an advance payment.

The launching authority remains under the obligation to cover these expenses even when, having requested the recovery of the object, its return, or its being held at its disposal, it later fails to claim it or expressly renounces the right to its return. It may similarly be held that reimbursement is due even if the action undertaken by another State is unsuccessful, unless, in carrying it out, it failed to comply with the specific provisions of the law.

IV. "The State of Registry" and "The Launching Authority"

Both terms are used in the context of rescue operations and the return of astronauts and spaceships. The provisions of one of the instruments (the basic one) stipulate that astronauts shall be returned "to the State of Registry of their space vehicle"; that objects launched into outer space or their competent parts shall be returned to the State "on whose registry they are carried".[31] The provisions of the other instrument–(the Agreement on Rescue and Return–constituting a *lex specialis* on the subject) confer corresponding rights upon "the launching authority".[32]

This raises the important question: do these appellations identify the same subjects of the rights involved? Consequently, is the difference one of terminology or one of substance? The right to keep a registry has been reserved exclusively to States. In this context it should be recalled that the institution of "registration" of space objects has further implications, as it constitutes a title for the exercise of jurisdiction and control over them.[33] On the other hand "the launching authority", following the definition given by the very instrument which uses the term, may be:

(1) A "State responsible for the launching" or

(2) "an international or intergovernmental organization" responsible for launching; the latter under the following conditions:
  (*a*) that it "declares its acceptance of the rights and obligations" laid down by the international instrument dealing with rescue, assistance and return (the agreement), and
  (*b*) that "the majority of the States Members of that organization are Contracting Parties" of two instruments (the Space Treaty and the Agreement).[34]

The history of the provisions in question, the process that led to their adoption, indicate that a similar if not identical meaning has been ascribed to both terms.[35] The essential issue which remained, in this and other contexts for some time concerned the status of international organizations.[36] Once it was resolved, and given the solution agreed upon, the term "State" had to be replaced by another, more comprehensive term, hence the word "authority",[37] the criterion of "registry" having become inadequate.[38] It is clearly in the interest of States engaged in outer space activities, more particularly for the sake of the effective assistance and rescue of astronauts, that a uniform interpretation of this terminology should be accepted.[39] It would be as well for States to take account of these questions in the process of drafting specific international rules. Apart from the further elaboration already suggested it will in due course also be necessary to lay down special provisions covering objects constructed in outer space or on celestial bodies.

Before we leave the subject of assistance in cases of accident or emergency, the problem of distress signals should be mentioned, though this is connected rather with the succeeding chapter, concerning telecommunication in outer space. Special arrangements have been made in their regard. Bearing in mind the possibility of manned space vehicles or satellites being forced down in emergency anywhere on the earth's surface, the application of the existing Radio Regulations has been extended so as to cover astronauts and space-vehicles.

Accordingly, distress signals from stations outside the atmosphere have been given absolute priority. Moreover a special frequency has been selected for purposes of search and rescue in outer space–to augment those already designated in the Radio Regulations for distress, emergency and survival-craft. Thus specific technical means have been made available in the interest of effective rescue operations.[40]

So much *de lege lata.* However, the ever-increasing complexity of technological links in all dimensions will require, apart from the development of specific rules, a more general approach: a closer co-ordination of assistance and rescue operations on land, at sea, in the air and in outer space.

Notes to Chapter VII

1. The question was raised for the first time in 1959 in the Report of the Legal Sub-Committee of the *Ad Hoc* Committee on the Peaceful Uses of Outer Space, p. 7. In 1962 two proposals were submitted to the Legal Sub-Committee: one by the USSR, a Draft International Agreement on the Rescue of Astronauts and Spaceships Making Emergency Landings, A/AC.105/C.2/L.2; and the other by the USA, a Draft Resolution of the General Assembly, commending to States a series of principles, A/AC.105/L3; cf. Report, 1962, pp. 4-6. The same year the General Assembly of the United Nations requested the Committee on the Peaceful Uses of Outer Space "to continue urgently its work" *inter alia* "on assistance to and return of astronauts and space vehicles" (resolution 1802 (XVII) of 14 December 1962). The 1963 Declaration of Legal Principles contained general provisions on the subject but this could be considered only as a first step. By General Assembly resolution 1963 (XVIII) the Committee was requested "to arrange for the prompt preparation of a draft international agreement ... on assistance to and return of astronauts and space vehicles" (Part. I, para. 2 *in fine*). Following this request, the Legal Sub-Committee dealt with the issue in detail during the first (9-26 March 1964) and second parts (5-23 October 1964) of its Third Session. Two Draft Agreements were submitted respectively by the USSR and the USA, while a proposal by Australia and Canada was presented as a working paper: see Legal Sub-Committee, Reports, first part, pp. 3 f. and Annex I, pp. 1-24, and second part, pp. 2 f. and Annex I, pp. 1-14, Annex III, pp. 1-4, and Annex IV, pp. 1-6. An informal working party of the Sub -Committee succeeded in reaching preliminary agreement on the Preamble and some provisions, cf. Annex III, *ut supra*. Discussion continued. Cf. Legal Sub-Committee, Fourth Session 1965, Report, pp. 1 f., and Annex I, pp. 1-5. The Space Treaty of 1967 reaffirmed and amplified the principles contained in the Declaration of 1963. The General Assembly again requested the Committee on the Peaceful Uses of Outer Space "to continue its work on the elaboration of ... an agreement on assistance to and return of astronauts and space vehicles" in resolution 2222 (XXI) of 19 December 1966. At the Sixth Session of the Legal Sub-Committee new drafts were submitted by the USSR and, jointly, by Australia and Canada; the USA maintained its proposal of 1964 as amended by it in 1965. Further proposals and amendments were presented, but no agreement was reached. Cf. Report, pp. 2-4 and Annex I, pp. 1-14. The issue then returned to the General Assembly, which adopted resolution 2260 (XXII) of 3 November 1967, requesting that the work on the agreement be continued "with a sense of urgency". Meanwhile further negotiations were held outside the Committee and they resulted in the elaboration of an Agreement, the text of which was sponsored by the USSR and the USA and presented to the Legal Sub-Committee at a special meeting convened for the purpose on 14 December 1967, A/AC.105/C.2.L.28. The deliberations of the Sub-Committee (14-15 December 1967) resulted in some changes in the text (A/AC.105/C.2/SR.86-89); the Committee approved it with amendments. The Agreement was subsequently commended in General Assembly resolution 2345 (XXII) of 19 December 1967, Annex. It was opened for signature on 22 April 1968 and entered into force on 3 December 1968.

2. Among those one may cite: (*Sea-navigation*) Convention for the Unification of Certain Rules with respect to Assistance and Salvage at Sea, Brussels 1910, International Convention for the Safety of Life at Sea, London 1948; (*Air-Navigation*) Convention for the Unification of Certain Rules relating to Assistance and Salvage of Aircraft or by Aircraft at Sea, Brussels 1938; Convention on International Civil Aviation, Chicago 1944. Cf. also Agreements, USA/Mexico, 13 June 1935; USA/Canada, 24 and 31 January 1949, 21 February 1952; Sweden/USSR, 29 September 1954; USSR/Bulgaria/Romania, 11 September 1956.
3. See Article V, paragraphs 1 and 2, of the 1967 Space Treaty, and cf. Declaration on Legal Principles, 1963, para. 9.
4. The Agreement uses in its title and Preamble the term "astronauts" and in the operative part "personnel". Cf. Summary of Views expressed in Working Group I, Legal Sub-Committee, Third Session 1964, second part, Report, Annex IV, Addendum p. 6. Cf. also footnote 18 to Chapter VI above, and the proposal of Argentina: "An 'astronaut' is a civilian explorer, exclusively for peaceful purposes, who is carrying out his duties as a representative of mankind in outer space, including the moon and other celestial bodies". Report 6th Session 1967, Annex I. p. 11.
5. Article 1 of the Agreement on Assistance and Return.
6. The Space Treaty used the formula: "on the territory of another State Party ...". However, during the later discussion it was pointed out that space objects may land not only in territories over which a State exercises sovereign rights, but also in others over which it exercises only jurisdiction. Thus the term "territory under the jurisdiction or control of a Contracting Party" was suggested (cf. Arts. 3 and 4 of the Proposal by Australia and Canada, Legal Sub-Committee, Third Session 1964, first part, Report, Annex I, p. 11 and Report, second part, Third Session, Annex IV, Addendum 2, p. 10). The wider term, "in territory under its jurisdiction", was adopted: Articles 2, 3, 4 and 5.
7. The Space Treaty contains no such provision; cf. Agreement, Articles 1, 3 and 4. Antarctica was specifically mentioned in the draft presented by the USA, Article 2, para. 1. To this Japan submitted an amendment: "Any search or rescue operation conducted in Antarctica should not be construed as prejudicing the positions of States concerned with respect to Antarctica." Cf. Legal Sub-Committee, Third Session 1964, first part, Report, Annex I, pp. 7 and 13. It was suggested that the phrase related also to outer space, the moon and other celestial bodies, statement by USA, Legal Sub-Committee, 14 December 1967, A/AC.105/C.2/SR.86, p. 7; cf. however statement by France, *loc. cit.*, p. 13. Cf. also footnote 18.
8. Article 1 of the Agreement.
9. Cf. General Assembly resolution 1721 (XVI), 1961, part B, referred to above: the obligation to notify the Secretary-General of the UN concerns also States not members of the UN which become Parties to the Agreement, as they may (cf. Article 7, para. 1).
10. Article 2 of the Agreement.
11. It was suggested that in rendering assistance the State concerned should employ "every means at its disposal, including electronic and optical equipment, means of communication, and rescue facilities of different kind" (Draft Agreement by USSR, Article 1: Legal Sub-Committee, First Session 1962, Report, p. 4). During the discussions it was pointed out that in some situations States not

disposing of such equipment would not be able to carry out the obligation thus defined. An alternative suggestion was made by Lebanon: "within the limits of the means at its disposal" (Third Session 1964, first part, Report, Annex I, p. 13); cf. the 1967 interpretation of the text by Sweden: "action within the limits of the facilities at the Contracting Parties' disposal" (A/AC.105/C.2/SR.86, p. 20). The 1944 Chicago Convention on International Civil Aviation lays down the obligation for the State concerned "to provide such measures of assistance to aircraft in distress in its territory as it may find practicable ..." (Art. 25).

12. Article 2 of the Agreement. Cf. also Article 5, para. 2. Cf. Article 3 of the Soviet, Article 2, para. 2, of the American, and Article 3, para. 2, of the Australian and Canadian drafts. Legal Sub-Committee Report, 6th session, 1967, Annex I, pp. 2, 4 and 8. Cf. also earlier proposals by Lebanon, and Austria, Third Session 1964, first part, Report, Annex I, p. 13.
13. Agreement, Article 2, *in fine.*
14. Cf. the discussion on the subject in the Legal Sub-Committee, as above, Third Session, second part, 1964, Report, Annex IV, Addendum, p. 10, also the statement of the representative of the USA: "In the unlikely event that (the two States) did not agree, the territorial party would of course have the final say in this matter" (A/AC.105/C.2/SR.86, 14 December 1967, p. 8). Cf. also statements by the representatives of Iran, *ibidem*, pp. 9-10, India, p. 11, France, p. 13, and Sweden, pp. 19 f.
15. Article 3 of the Agreement. Cf. Article 4 of the USSR draft; Article 4 of the Australian and Canadian draft. Report, 6th session, Annex I, pp. 2 and 8. Cf. also discussion on the subject A/AC.105/C.2/SR.86, 14 December 1967, pp. 3, 20 and 21.
16. That this is so is clear from the language used, which is different from that applied to similar situations occurring in territory under the jurisdiction of another State. It is also different from that employed in the Space Treaty (Article V). Even so, here again the humanitarian character of the action calls for an extensive interpretation of the provisions of the Agreement. Cf. P. G. Dembling and D. M. Arons, "The treaty on Rescue and Return of Astronauts and Space Objects", *William and Mary Law Review*, Vol. 8, Spring 1968, No. 3, pp. 650 f. Cf. also the International Convention for the Safety of Life at Sea, London 1948: "The master of a ship at sea, on receiving a signal from any source that a ship or aircraft or survival craft thereof is in distress, is bound to proceed with all speed to the assistance of the persons in distress informing them if possible that he is doing so" (Chapter V, Regulation 10(*a*)). Also Article 12 of the 1958 Convention on the High Seas.
17. Agreement, Article 3, *in fine.*
18. It is only the Space Treaty which deals with it "In carrying on activities in outer space and on celestial bodies the astronauts of one Party shall render all possible assistance to the astronauts of other Parties" (Article V para. 2). The Agreement makes no specific mention of outer space or celestial bodies. As indicated (footnote 7 above) it was argued that the term "another place not under the jurisdiction of any State", used therein, may include outer space and celestial bodies. Yet, even so, the provision in question is limited to cases where the "personnel of a spacecraft have alighted" (Art. 3) which could only concern celestial bodies, cf. Dembling and Arons, *op. cit.*, p. 649. In view of inadequacy of the existing rules and the complexity of the issues involved it seems reason-

able to suggest that assistance and rescue in outer space and on celestial bodies will have to be dealt with in a special instrument. Cf. R. C. Hall, "Rescue and Return of Astronauts on Earth and in Outer Space", 63 *A.J.I.L.*, 1969, No. 2, pp. 197 ff. Cf. also Article 5 of the Agreement, and footnote 27 below.

19. Article 4 of the Agreement. There is a discrepancy between the terms of the Agreement and those of the Space Treaty. ("... they shall be safely and promptly returned to the State of registry of their space vehicle": Article V, para. 1. See, on this, footnotes 38 and 39 below.) Cf. also para. 9 of the Declaration of Legal Principles, 1963. In view of the jurisdictional problems involved–cf. Chapter VI, footnote 21–the drafting of this provision raised some problems. Article 3 of the USA draft, and Article 5 of the Australian and Canadian proposal (Third Session, Report, Annex I, pp. 7 and 11); cf. Article 5 of the revised draft submitted by the USSR (Legal Sub-Committee, Third Session 1964, second part, Report, Annex I, p. 4); amendment by France: "A Contracting Party shall not oppose the departure from its territory of persons on board a spacecraft which has made an emergency landing and shall do its utmost to assist them in making travel arrangements. The present article shall not be construed as preventing juridical or administrative proceedings, or the enforcement of measures resulting from such proceedings, instituted by reason of the deeds or words of such persons after the completion of operations relating to the emergency landing" (*idem*, p. 7). Cf. other views expressed (*loc. cit.*, Annex IV, Add. 2, pp. 17-20) and Sixth Session 1967, Report, Annex I, p. 13. Cf. further the comments made at the final stages, prior to the approval of the Agreement, by the representatives of France, maintaining that the return of astronauts was subject to the provisions of municipal law, Legal Sub-Committee, 14 December 1967, A/AC.105/C.2/SR/86, p. 14, and G.A. 1640 Plenary Meeting, 19 December 1967, para. 82, p. 8; of Austria, Legal Sub-Committee, 15 December, A/AC.105/C.2/SR.87, pp. 9-10; of the USA stressing the "Absolute and unconditional nature of the obligation to return", 16 December, A/AC.105/PV.52, p. 66, also Canada, *loc. cit.*, p. 51.
Cf. P. H. Houben, "A New Chapter of Space Law, the Agreement on the Rescue and Return of Astronauts and Space Objects", XV *Netherlands International Law Review*, 1968, pp. 127 ff., and G. P. Zhukov, "International Co-operation on the Rescue of Astronauts", Paper submitted to the UN Conference on the Exploration and Peaceful Uses of Outer Space, Vienna 1968, p. 25.

20. Article 5, paragraph 1, of the Agreement. (It refers specifically to "a space object or its component parts" which "has returned to Earth".) If the launching authority cannot be identified, then it is only the Secretary-General of the United Nations that can be notified. Here is an illustration: By a letter of 16 July 1968 the Deputy Prime Minister of Nepal informed the Secretary-General that "certain metallic pieces were discovered in Nepalese territory" and that they were believed to be parts of a space object, but that the Government of Nepal had been unable to identify the launching authority. Though the Agreement on the Rescue of Astronauts, the Return of Astronauts and the Return of Objects launched into Outer Space had, at the time, not yet come into force, the Government of Nepal, acting "in the spirit" of that Agreement had "decided to open them for examination by interested States and return them to the launching authority on receipt of identifying data" (UN press release, 17 July 1968).

21. Article 5, paragraph 2, of the Agreement. The determination as to what steps are "practicable" is thus left to the judgment of the State within whose jurisdiction the object is found. It may therefore be concluded that that State may also determine whether the recovery is "practicable" at all. Cf. S. Gorove, "The Recovery and Return of Objects Launched into Outer Space", 4 *International Lawyer*, 1970, No. 4, p. 686.
22. This conclusion seems justified in view of the question having been completely omitted by the Agreement. In such a situation the State which makes the discovery is only under the obligation to notify the launching authority and the Secretary-General of the United Nations (cf. Article 5, paragraph 1, as above).
23. Article 5, paragraph 4; this obligation is imposed "notwithstanding paragraphs 2 and 3", it is one to be discharged by the launching authority. Cf. the proposal of Argentina; Article 6, paragraph 4, of the Australian and Canadian draft; amendment by Japan: Legal Sub-Committee, Third Session 1964, second part, Report, Annex I, pp. 6, 11, 13 and 14. It is, of course, possible that the launching authority may not comply with the obligation "to eliminate possible danger or harm". This being a serious obligation linked with risks to life, health or property, it is reasonable to assume that any States affected are entitled to do so themselves and claim the refund of the costs involved, relying herein on general international law, as this is not specifically provided for by the Agreement. Cf. also, the Convention on International Liability (see Chapter XI below).
24. This is not a problem which strictly speaking comes within the framework of rescue operations or return of objects launched into outer space. It is much more linked with general obligations of States engaged in space activities, specifically their responsibility for them.
25. Article 5, paragraph 3. In the context of Article 5 as a whole the question has been raised as to whether the provisions also concern objects which though sent into outer space never reached it (cf. the words "has returned to Earth" in paragraph 1 of Article 5). Cf. Gorove, *op. cit.*, pp. 684 f., and some doubts expressed by Vallat, *op. cit.*, p. 756. However, the language, object and purpose of the Agreement leave no doubt that it covers all objects launched into outer space which left Earth, whether they reached or did not reach outer space. The 1967 Space Treaty, in Article VIII, makes no mention of "the request", which seems, however, essential. In view of the double notification provided for by Article 5, paragraph 1, it is highly unlikely that the information will not reach the launching authority. This could only be the case when the obligation to notify has not been complied with.
26. Agreement, Article 5, paragraph 3, *in fine*; cf. also proposal of Japan, Legal Sub-Committee, Third Session 1964, second part, Report, Annex I, p. 13.
27. Article 5, paragraph 3; this flexible wording was suggested by France, legal Sub-Committee, 14 December, A/AC.105/C.2/SR.86, p. 14; and accepted, *loc. cit.*, p. 21. Prior to the adoption of the Agreement different views were expressed on the scope of that obligation: cf. drafts of USSR, Article 9; USA, Article 3; Australia and Canada, Article 6; Legal Sub-Committee, Third Session 1964, Report, Annex I, pp. 4, 7, 11 and 12; revised draft of USSR, Article 6, paragraph 2, Legal Sub-Committee, Third Session 1964, second part, Report, Annex I, p. 4; drafts and proposals submitted at the 6th session, Report, Annex I, pp. 4, 5, 9, 13, cf. also statement by the representative of France that the Agreement applied only to experimental and scientific flights. "The rights of the signatory

States must be fully reserved with regard to the day when such flights may be utilitarian or commercial. When that happens it will doubtless be necessary to negotiate a new Convention", General Assembly, 1640 Plenary Meeting, 19 December 1967, para. 85; cf. earlier statement by France, 15 December 1967, A/AC.105/C.2/SR.89, p. 6, also statement of Japan, 14 December, SR.86, p. 11. Another issue worth mentioning is the "territorial" scope of the obligation. It applies only to "objects launched into outer space or their component parts" which have returned to Earth (Article 5, para. 1) (cf. footnote 18). It does not extend to those found on celestial bodies, and in this respect Article VIII of the Space Treaty may be viewed as wider (cf. Vallat, *op. cit.*, p. 756).

28. Cf., *inter alia*, 1910 Convention for the Unification of Certain Rules with respect to Assistance and Salvage at Sea: "No remuneration is due from the persons whose lives are saved, but nothing in this article shall affect the provisions of the national laws on this subject" (Article 9); "There shall be no payment for the saving of human lives" (Article 8 of Agreement between USSR, Bulgaria and Romania concerning Co-operation for Saving Human Lives and Assistance to Vessels and Aircraft in Distress in the Black Sea, 1956, 266 *UN Treaty Series*, p. 238).
29. Cf. earlier proposals on the Agreement: Article 8 of USSR draft and Article 3 of USA draft, Legal Sub-Committee, Second Session 1963, Report, Annex I, pp. 4 and 5; Article 5 of USSR revised draft, Report, Sixth Session, Annex I, p. 2.
30. Article 5, paragraph 5, of the Agreement. This applies to cases when requests have been made to this effect by the launching authority, paragraphs 2 and 3 of Article 5. Cf. Article 6, paragraph 7, of the proposal of Australia and Canada. Legal Sub-Committee, Sixth Session 1967, Report, Annex I, pp. 2 and 9.
31. Article V, first paragraph, and Article VIII *in fine*, Space Treaty 1967.
32. Articles 4 and 5, paragraph 3 of the Agreement.
33. Cf. Chapter VI, under 1. *Jurisdiction in General.*
34. Agreement, Article 6.
35. The term "State of registry" was used in the Declaration of Legal Principles, 1963, and later in the Space Treaty. Successive proposals made during the work on the Agreement embodied the terms "the launching State", "State or States or international organization responsible for launching", "the State which officially announced the launching", "the State of registry or international organization responsible for launching", or "the launching State or international organization responsible for launching" (cf. Legal Sub-Committee, First Session, Report, pp. 4-5 and 6; Second Session, Report, Annex I, pp. 3-4 and 5; Third Session, Report, Annex I, pp. 2-3, 6-7, 10-11; Third Session, second part, Report, Annex I, pp. 3-4, 9-11; Sixth Session, Report, Annex I, pp. 17-20.
36. In 1964 the wording agreed provisionally by the Working Group was: "the State which announced the launching" (Articles 2, 3 and 6) (Legal Sub-Committee, Third Session, second part, Report, Annex III, pp. 2-4). The issue had to be re-opened with reference to international organizations. The Legal Sub-Committee reported that at its Sixth Session the choice of term had been deferred and that no agreement had been reached on the inclusion of the words "or international organizations" (Legal Sub-Committee, Sixth Session 1967, Report, p. 4).
37. The text as it now appears in the Agreement was adopted at the final stage of the discussions (14 December 1967; cf. proposals by the United Kingdom,

France, Canada and Sweden, A/AC.105/C.2/SR.86, pp. 13, 18, 19-20). Cf. the International Convention on Liability, which uses the term "launching State" (Article 1).

38. From a practical point of view the following situations may arise:
    (*a*) If a State is responsible for the launching of a space object, it should enter it on its registry; thus the "state of registry" will be identical with the 'launching authority";
    (*b*) if the launching is carried out as a common enterprise of several States, it is for them to designate one from their midst as both "the state of registry" and "the launching authority";
    (*c*) if an international organization is responsible for the launching and it has not declared its acceptance of the Agreement and/or a majority of its members are not parties to the two instruments (i.e., the Space Treaty and the Agreement), it is again for States Members of that organization to designate one of their number as "the launching authority" and "state of registry";
    (*d*) if an international organization responsible for the launching has declared its acceptance of the rights and obligations provided by the Agreement and a majority of States Members of that organization are parties to the two mentioned instruments, the organization will be considered as the "launching authority". This indeed is the only case where "the launching authority" could not carry the space object on its registry. Cf. Article 8 of the Space Treaty, also the Draft Convention concerning the Registration of Objects Launched into Space, presented by France, Articles 1 and 2 (see Chapter VI above).

39. One could, of course, advance the view that the Agreement constitutes *lex specialis* in relation to the provisions of the Space Treaty of 1967. This would be the easiest approach. It is, however, doubtful whether it would be the wisest. Moreover situations may arise between States some of which are parties to both instruments, while others are parties only to one of them (*scil.* the Space Treaty). It may therefore be more advisable to agree upon an interpretation which would lead to an almost uniform approach (cf. preceding footnote). In the long run this should lead to the adoption of a general formula and uniformity in the agreements which will further develop the law on the subject.

40. Cf. Resolution No. 2A concerning space vehicles in distress and emergency, adopted by the Extraordinary Administrative Radio Conference, Geneva 1963. *Final Acts*, Resolution No. 2A. This resolution has been abrogated as the measures consequent upon it have been taken (*Final Acts*, World Administrative Radio Conference for Space Communications, Geneva 1971, Annex 3, Article 5, ADD.201A, p. 52).

Chapter VIII

Space Telecommunications

However impressive were the existing means of telecommunication, the venture into space opened up vast new possibilities. In fact telecommunications are inseparably linked with journeys into and through outer space: they are essential for maintaining contact with or between objects in space or on celestial bodies. Stations on earth follow objects launched into outer space through the successive stages of their journeys, transmit signals and instructions to them, and if necessary correct their trajectories. At the other end, instruments placed aboard space vehicles transmit the results of their observations and other signals. The crew is able to maintain continuous contact, both visual and vocal, with Earth.

However, the impact of space telecommunications is much wider, for they have also *inter alia* revolutionized several branches of science:

The "science of the stars" has been liberated from its dependence on the penetration of the atmosphere by earthbound instruments. Astronomers today have at their disposal highly sophisticated equipment for the collection, recording and transmission from outer space of formerly inaccessible data.

Weather satellites, by providing data on cloud movements or the formation of storm-centres, greatly increase the meteorological information so essential for maritime and aerial navigation. A new chapter has been opened by communication satellites: those which reflect waves and return them to the earth,[1] and those which receive, store, amplify and retransmit messages.[2] By vocal and visual channels contact can be established through outer space between the most widely distant points on the earth's surface.

However tempting it may be to dwell on the more fascinating aspects of these developments, the purpose of the present considerations is to examine their legal implications. On the day communications media first crossed State frontiers, there arose a need for their legal regulation on the international plane. One hundred and seven years ago, on 17 May 1865, representatives of 20 countries signed the first international instrument in this field at Paris, and the International Union of Telegraphy was born. Twenty years later the first international rules concerning communication by telephone were established. In 1906, the representatives of 27 States drafted the first international regulations on radio-communications. These, however, proved inadequate, as was strikingly illustrated when, in 1912, the radio-operator of the sinking *Titanic* was unable to summon the assistance of another ship in the vicinity because he could not establish contact with it. This event became an important stimulus to more effective co-operation: an international allocation of radio frequency-bands had become a necessity. The years which followed saw the growth of international rules and regulations, and the modern law of telecommunications came into being.[3]

It was soon to be confronted by new problems arising out of the development of space technology.[4] It has become essential to proceed to a new allocation of frequency-bands and to provide special protection for space radio-communications in view of the particularly difficult conditions under which they operate. For there had proved to be a growing necessity to prevent harmful radio-interference and protect space-research services and distress signals in space, since, despite the widening of the usable waveband-spectrum, overcrowding had become an imminent threat.[5]

Consequently, radio-electric systems, services and stations were identified and defined.[6] The spectrum of frequencies has been increased.[7] For the purpose of their allocation, the world is divided into three regions.[8] Special provisions have been made for meteorological satellites, radio-astronomy, for the use of new techniques, navigation services and amateur transmissions.

A special frequency has been allocated for search and rescue operations, enlarging those already designated for distress, emergency and survival of craft.[9] In order to decrease the possibilities of harmful interference, it has been provided that space-stations should cease emitting upon completion of the programme of their mission.[10]

There is no need here to dwell on the further details involved. Suffice it to state, in the light of what has been done so far, that the foundation-stones have been laid and a series of rules enacted for this important part of the law of outer space.[11]

The question of the co-ordination of national activities and of international co-operation also called for some basic decisions. As in other sections of the new law, it had become essential that the advantages of the new discoveries should be opened to all, on the basis of equality and that safeguards be provided against abuse. These requirements entail rights and obligations on both the transmitting and the receiving side. On the one hand the objective was to guarantee free access to the means of space-telecommunications, on a "non-discriminatory basis".[12] This found its expression in the recognition that "all Members and Associate Members of the Union" had "an interest in and right to an equitable and rational use of frequency-bands allocated for space-communications".[13] This was followed up by a decision recognizing "that the registration with the ITU of frequency assignments for space radio-communication services and their use should not provide any permanent priority for any individual country or groups of countries, and should not create an obstacle to the establishment of space systems by other countries".[14] That was how the basic principles of the freedom of outer space have been translated into space-telecommunication terms.[15-16]

On the wider plane, on both the transmitting and the receiving side, problems arose in connection with the setting-up of international communication-satellite systems,[17] and here, unfortunately, differences of view still subsist. Agreement on a global scale, though highly important, is not in sight. Yet time presses, for we may shortly face the prospect, among others, of a most promising experience made possible by space-technology: direct sound and image transmission through outer space to whole continents, to millions of listeners and viewers. This will bring important legal issues into play, some of which are already known in terrestrial dimensions: radio or television stations acting without the necessary authorization, and using frequencies not allocated to them. (Placed usually aboard ships or otherwise installed outside territorial waters, such emitters have become known as "pirate stations".)[18]

There is therefore some foundation for the view that the same *ratio legis* which lay at the basis of the corresponding rules of law concerning land, sea and air, ought *a fortiori* to apply to outer space, in view of the far-reaching implications and potentialities of the latter. Hence, to avoid chaos, the need to conclude adequate legal arrangements on a universal basis.[19] Here again, it is important that law should not lag too far behind technical developments.[20]

Finally, there is one more problem worthy of specific mention. Sound and image transmitted through and in outer space–as indeed through any dimension–may serve various purposes: good and evil. Efforts to secure that means of communication should serve constructive purposes only, the peaceful co-operation of nations, date back to the early days of radio phony. One of their tangible results was the conclusion of an international instrument–Convention on the Use of Radio in the Interest of International Peace.[21]

Attention was drawn to this problem at an early stage of lawmaking for outer space. A special provision was inserted in the preamble of the basic instrument, the Space Treaty: "taking account" of a General Assembly resolution "which condemned propaganda designed or likely to provoke or encourage any threat to the peace, breach of the peace or act of aggression" and considering it "applicable to outer space".[22] As formulated, this paragraph extends the application of the resolution to a new dimension. It may be added that it also extends it to States parties to the treaty which are not Members of the United Nations. It does not, however, alter the character of the original instrument, for the resolution is incorporated *qua* resolution.[23] In regard to its substance, it should be read in the context of Article 1, paragraph 1, and Article 2, paragraph 4, of the United Nations Charter. It is within this wider framework that one should view the condemnatory character of the resolution itself and the paragraph in question.[24]

To summarize the state of the law on space-telecommunications, important progress can be recorded. A whole series of rules is now in force. The waves that transmit sound and image, harnessed through man's genius, invention and labour, have been given their lawful place in the new dimension. Here as elsewhere, however, further agreements are required to secure that every State, without discrimination should not only benefit from the new achievements but also be protected from whatever harm they may bring in their wake.

Notes to Chapter VIII

1. This is the passive satellite: the first of this type was Echo I, launched 12 August 1960.
2. This is the active satellite. Two types of it ought to be mentioned: (*a*) the low-orbit satellite, such as Telstar (the first launched on 10 July 1962), Molnia (first launched on 23 April 1965); (*b*) the stationary satellite, so described because it rotates above the Equator at a speed which corresponds to that of the Earth round its axis; this category includes Syncom I (launched on 14 February 1963), and Early Bird (launched on 6 April 1965).
3. The 1932 Madrid Convention provided for the merger of the International Union of Telegraphy and the International Radio Telegraph Union into the International Telecommunication Union, which came into being in 1934. It was within its framework that the international law of telecommunications was thenceforth to take shape.
4. Since 1958 the Union has been engaged in serious work on the subject through the International Radio Consultative Committee (CCIR). In April 1959 a special Study Group (IV) was set up: "to study systems of telecommunications with and between locations in space". The ITU Plenipotentiary Conference of 1959 stressed "the importance of the role that telecommunications and, in consequence, the ITU will necessarily play in this field" (Resolution 34). The Administrative Radio Conference held the same year made the first attempt to cover telecommunications for and in outer space in the revised Radio Regulations. These were arrangements of a preliminary character only and it was recommended that an Extraordinary Administrative Radio Conference to allocate frequency bands for space radio-communications purposes and to settle related matters be convened in 1963. (Recommendation No. 36).
5. The Conference of 1963 carried out a partial revision of the Radio Regulations of 1959, and adopted a series of resolutions and recommendations: cf. *Final Acts* of the Conference. The Regulations entered into force on 1 January 1965. By Recommendation No. 3A the CCIR was invited to continue or undertake new studies on a wide range of problems concerning space communications. In the light of new needs (and in compliance with Recommendation 9A para. 4) a World Administrative Radio Conference for Space Telecommunications was convened in Geneva in 1971. The Radio Regulations were again revised, new measures introduced and clarifications made, and 8 resolutions and 15 recommendations were adopted. Cf. Final Acts of the Conference.
6. Cf. Article of the Radio Regulations of 1963, *Final Acts,* Annex I, pp. 1-01 to 1-06, amended in 1971, *Final Acts*, pp. 37-48.
7. Cf. the successive extension of the whole spectrum: from 1938 (in Cairo), 1946 (in Atlantic City), 1959 (in Geneva), 1963 to 1971. In 1959 only slightly above 1% of the spectrum was made available for space communications, but the proportion has since been very considerably increased. Revision of Article 5 of the Radio Regulations, *Final Acts,* Conference 1963, Annex 3, pp. 03-01; *Final Acts,* Conference 1971, Annex 3, pp. 51-113.
8. *Final Acts,* 1971, Annex 3, p. 51, Appendix 24, cf. Atlantic City Regulations (1947) 63 stat. 1581. T.I.A.S. No. 1901.

9. Cf. footnote 40 to Chapter VII, above. *Final Acts*, 1971, Annex 3, Article 5, ADD 201A, p. 52 and ADD 287A, p. 69. Cf. also a special Recommendation Relating to the Use of Space Radiocommunication Systems in the Event of Natural Disasters, Epidemics, Famines, and similar Emergencies, No.Spa 2-13, *Final Acts*, pp. 347-348.
10. "Harmful interference"–as defined by the Geneva Telecommunication Convention of 1959–denotes "any emission, radiation, or induction which endangers the functioning of a radionavigation service or of other safety services, or seriously degrades, obstructs or repeatedly interrupts a radio communication service operating in accordance with the Radio Regulations". Annex 3. Cf. also Article 47 of that Convention, Cessation of Emissions: "Space stations shall be fitted with devices to ensure immediate cessation of their radio emissions by telecommand, whenever such cessation is required under the provisions of these Regulations" (Annex 5, Article 7, 470 V, § 24, *Final Acts*, 1971, p. 133). Cf. also Recommendations Relating to the Coordination of Earth Stations No. Sp 2-9, and to the Criteria to be Applied for Frequency-Sharing between the Broadcasting-Satellite Service and the Terrestrial Broadcasting Service, No. Spa 2-10, *loc. cit.*, pp. 340-344.
11. Cf. H. K. Jacobson, "International Institutions for Telecommunications: the ITU's Role", in *International Law of Communications*, ed. E. McWhinney, Leyden 1971, pp. 51 ff.
12. The General Assembly expressed its belief "that communication by means of satellites should be available to the nations of the world as soon as practicable on a global and non-discriminatory basis": resolution 1721 (XIII), 1961, Part D, Preamble. Cf. also G.A. resolution 1802 (XVII), 1962, part IV, para. 3.
13. Cf. Recommendation No. 10A adopted at the ITU Conference in 1963, *Final Acts*, Rec. 10 A-01: it made consequential recommendations to all ITU Members and Associate Members, with specific reference to the above-mentioned resolutions of the UN General Assembly.
14. Resolution adopted at the Conference of 1971, Resolution No. Spa 2-1, *Final Acts*, pp. 311-312.
15-16. Cf. the question of geostationary satellites raised in the Scientific and Technical Sub-Committee of UNCOPUOS and its Working Group; working-paper by France, A/AC.105/62, 30 June 1969, pp. 3 ff. Cf. also Report: A/8020, 1970, paras. 37 and 53.
17. In this context mention should be made of: (A) Intelsat, created by the Agreement Establishing Interim Arrangements for a Global Commercial Communications Satellite System (accompanied by a Special and Supplementary Agreement) Washington, 20 August 1964. These were preceded by the establishment of the Communication Satellite Corporation (Comsat) on 31 August 1962 (Public Law No. 87-624, 76 Stat. 419). This Corporation has become the manager of Intelsat (Art. VIII of the Agreement). The membership of Intelsat comprises 77 countries, and it was within its framework that a series of communication satellites was launched transmitting television programmes and telegraph and telephone messages through five satellites and 63 earth-station antennae. The interim Agreement was renegotiated at conferences held in 1969 and 1970, the main issues concerning decision-making powers in launching, utilisation and control. (B) The establishment of a West-European Communication Satellite System has been set as a goal by the European Conference of Postal and Tel-

ecommunications Administrations and the European Broadcasting Union, within the framework of the European Space Conference established in 1966. Public telecommunication services (telephone, telegraphy and telex) as well as television are envisaged. It is planned that the system will be operational in the 1980's. (C) The Socialist States took the first steps in the same field at a conference held in Moscow in November 1965; two years later they suggested "the establishment of an international satellites communications system which would be open to all States wishing to participate in it" (cf. UN doc.A/6668, 10 May 1967). In 1968 Bulgaria, Cuba, Czechoslovakia, Hungary, Mongolia, Poland, Romania and USSR submitted a draft Agreement on the Establishment of an International Communication System Using Artificial Earth Satellites (Inter-sputnik): UN doc. A/AC.105/46, 9 August 1968. It emphasized "the need to promote the strengthening and development of comprehensive economic, cultural and other relations through the maintenance of communications, including radio and television broadcasting using artificial earth satellites" (Preamble, para. 1). An Agreement establishing the organization was signed by Bulgaria, Czechoslovakia, Cuba, the German Democratic Republic, Hungary, Mongolia, Poland, Romania and USSR (Moscow, 15 November 1971). It will be administered by a Council on which all member States will be represented, and remains open to all States. Cf. also the proposal of France for the creation of a special UN Space Agency, submitted to the UN Conference on the Exploration and Use of Outer Space, Vienna 1968 (A/Conf. 34.VIII, 13, p. 12). From the copious literature on the subject cf. Mateesco Matte, *op. cit.*, pp. 181 ff., *The International Law of Communications*, ed. E. McWhinney, 1971. *Communications Satellites*, Stockholm Papers, SIPRI, No. 1, 1969, pp. 18 ff.; V. S. Vereshchetin, "International Space Telecommunications Systems", paper submitted to the 13th Colloquium on Space Law, 1970.

18. "The establishment and use of broadcasting stations (sound broadcasting and television broadcasting stations) on board ships, aircraft or any other floating or airborne object outside national territories is prohibited": International Radio Regulations (Geneva 1959), Article 7 (§ 1) 1; cf. also European Agreement for the Prevention of Broadcasts transmitted from Stations outside National Territories, Strasburg, 22 January 1965. About 15 such stations have been active in or off Europe, mainly at sea, in recent years. Cf. N. M. Green, "Pirate Radio Stations", 35 *Annuaire A.A.A.*, 1965, p. 133; H. F. van Panhuys and M. J. van Emde-Boos, "Legal Aspects of Pirate Broadcasting", *60 A.J.I.L.*, pp. 303 ff.

19. J. Persin, "Will Space be open to Piracy", 30 *Telecommunication Journal*, No. 4, 1963, pp. 113 ff.; J. H. Glaser, "Infelix ITU, The Need for Space-Age Revisions to the international Telecommunications Convention", 23 *Federal Bar Journal*, No. 1, 1963, p. 26; cf. also draft article submitted by the United Arab Republic for inclusion into the Space Treaty then under discussion: Legal Sub-Commitee, Fifth Session, Report, Annex III, p. 9.

20. Cf. resolution 2260 (XXII) by which the General Assembly requested UNCOPUOS *inter alia* "to study the technical feasibility of communication by direct broadcast from satellites and the current and foreseeable development in this field and the implications of such development" (para. 13); by resolution 2453 (XXIII), 1968, a Working-Group on Direct Broadcast Satellites was established, which submitted two reports in 1969 and a third report in 1970 (cf. Annexes to UNCPUOS reports A/7621/Add.1 and A/8020); cf. General Assembly

resolution 2733 A (XXV), 1970; cf. an earlier decision of Unesco, resolution 4131 adopted by the General Conference of 1966, also *L'information à l'ère spatiale: le rôle des satellites de communication* (Unesco, Paris 1968). A Committee of Governmental Experts sat in cooperation with the World Intellectual Property Organisation (WIPO) to study problems arising in the field of copyright protection of performers, producers, etc. (April 1971). The question has been of particular interest to ITU, which dealt with it in 1963; *Final Acts*, Recommendation 5A-01. The 1971 Conference revised Article 6 of the Radio Regulations: Regulation No. 417 (§ 3), *Final Acts*, p. 115. Cf. Legal Sub-Committee, Reports, 7th session, para. 15, p. 11; 8th session, para. 15, p. 5 and Annex III, and 10th session, para. 29, p. 14. Cf. further the work of ILA on the subject, Report of 53rd Conference, 1968, and Report of the Chairman, Space Law Committee, Hague Conference, 1970, pp. 13 ff.

21. Geneva, 23 September 1936, *League of Nations, Treaty Series*, Vol. 186, pp. 302 f.; cf. also *Final Acts* of the Conference, *League of Nations, Official Journal*, Vol. XVII, 1936, pp. 1444 f. and Rules for the Application of the International Convention concerning the Use of Broadcasting in the Cause of Peace, *Official Journal*, Vol. XVIII, 1937, pp. 1068 ff.
22. General Assembly resolution 110 (II) of 3 November 1947, Space Treaty, 1967, eighth paragraph. Reference to that resolution was made earlier in the Declaration of Legal Principles, 1963, preamble, sixth paragraph; proposals by Brazil, A/5549/Add.l, 27 November 1963, p. 27; and later by the United Arab Republic *ad* Space Treaty: Legal Sub-Committee, 5th Session 1966, Report, Annex III, p. 9 (cf. footnote 19).
23. Cf. Chapter XII on the law-making process for outer space.
24. It should be noted that the resolution also contains the following positive provision: "*requests* the Government of each Member to take appropriate steps within its constitutional limits: (*a*) to promote, by all means of publicity and propaganda available to them, friendly relations among nations based upon the Purposes and Principles of the Charter; (*b*) to encourage the dissemination of all information designed to give expression to the undoubted desire of all peoples for peace;" (para. 2). In fact, this is echoed in the fifth paragraph of the preamble to the Space Treaty, which refers to "the development of mutual understanding and to the strengthening of friendly relations between States and peoples". The provision in question is placed within the general exposition of the object of the Treaty (paras. 1-5 and para. 9) and some references to other specific documents (paras. 6 and 7).

Chapter IX

Peaceful Use–Arms and Armament

Over the beneficial effects of the opening-up of outer space, the extension to it of the armaments race hangs like an ominous shadow. Inevitably attention has been paid to the possible use of outer space for the purpose of "perfecting" the modern armoury and seeking more effective safeguards for national security. It has even been advanced that military operations could concentrate on outer space and save the earth from destruction.[1] But it would indeed be strange to seek comfort in the prospect that the destiny of the human race might be decided in some faraway Armaggedon.

Many novel strategic and technical considerations have arisen. For the present, suffice it to note that ever since man-made instruments moved into outer space, the claim has been asserted that, in view of the dangers involved, outer space should be used solely for peaceful purposes, and endeavours have been pursued to ensure that this be so.

This preoccupation was reflected in the first General Assembly Resolutions on the subject, in which "the common interest of mankind as a whole in furthering the peaceful use of outer space" was stressed.[2] So was "the common interest of mankind in furthering the peaceful uses of outer space and the urgent need to strengthen international co-operation in this important field".[3] Furthermore, in the Space Treaty the desire was expressed "to contribute to broad international co-operation in the scientific as well as the legal aspects of the exploration and use of outer space for peaceful purposes".[4]

The same outlook has been clearly reflected in documents emanating from non-governmental organizations and in the writings of legal scholars.[5] However, even in the early stages of the development of the law on the subject the issue gave rise to certain difficulties. No sooner had the objective of the use of outer space for peaceful purposes been laid down than it became the subject of two conflicting interpretations: one claiming that the term excludes only "aggressive" but not "military" use, the other that both are forbidden.[6] Yet there seems to be little doubt as to the real meaning of these words.

If it was intended to forbid aggressive use only, mere reference to international law and the Charter of the United Nations would have sufficed. Is it not evident that such actions are prohibited in terrestrial environments?

Since (as indicated earlier) it has been laid down that "the activities of States and the exploration and use of outer space shall be carried out in accordance with international law, including the Charter of the United Nations", this dimension can be no exception to the rule. For the Charter, reflecting as it does contemporary international law, imposes upon States the obligation to "refrain in their international relations from the threat or use of force". A restrictive interpretation of this obligation (or of the sense of the "use of force") has no legal foundation. The threat or use of force is barred not only when directed "against the territorial integrity or political independence of any State", but also when used or brandished "in any other manner inconsistent with the Purposes of the United Nations".[7] Thus an attack or any other constraint against a ship, aircraft or any other vehicle moving in other dimensions, such as outer space, constitutes a violation of the law.

Had only this prohibition been contemplated, the additional words "for peaceful purposes" would have been redundant. And yet they were expressly written into the basic international instruments governing the question. They can therefore hardly be considered as meaningless, the expression of a pious desire devoid of legal effects.[8] Moreover, the same term "peaceful purposes" has been employed in other contemporary instruments and at the same time given an authentic interpretation which is unequivocal. Suffice it to mention the provision concerning "the contribution of atomic energy to peace, health and prosperity throughout the world", which is linked with the goal that it be "not used in such a way as to further any military purposes".[9] Or another provision, where the term "peaceful purposes" is linked with the prohibition of "any measures of a military nature".[10]

However, taking precedence over this analogy with other international documents, it is the immediate context of the words which underlines their importance and makes their meaning unequivocal. This meaning is further confirmed by the whole trend of the development of the law of outer space from its general principles to specific and detailed rules. Thus it has been provided that: "The Moon and other celestial bodies shall be used ... exclusively for peaceful purposes. The establishment of military bases, installations and fortifications, the testing of any type of weapons and the conduct of military manoeuvres on celestial bodies shall be forbidden".[11] Here is a stipulation which leaves little room for doubt. This is particularly valuable in a domain which all too often has been the object of far-reaching misinterpretation.

The sense of "peaceful" is thus clearly defined.[12] It may be argued that problems could hereby be created for the exercise of the inherent right of self-defence. However, self-defence should be viewed as a special exception to the rule.[13]

Following this clarification of the *verba legis* and of the intention of the lawmakers, the question arises of the extent to which the principle of peaceful use has been implemented in practice.

This brings us to the issue of arms and disarmament. While the development of this new branch of international law is taking place in the shadow of a huge armaments race, the goal of outer space being reserved for "peaceful purposes only" may appear unrealistic. There is of course no magic word whereby–to change the metaphor–the momentum of the wheel can be instantly checked, or an instant halt be called, but the sober realization of mutual and, indeed, universal interest in the limitation of armaments should lead to at least a gradual deceleration. Outer space will have to be considered in the context of developments on the subject relating to other environments.[14]

It is evident that all progress in the peaceful use of outer space would have beneficent effects upon international relations in regard to regions nearer earth, and that every step towards disarmament on earth–or, more generally speaking, every improvement in international co-operation–should conversely have a beneficent effect as regards outer space. Here the formal outlawing of military activities, and self-commitment to use certain environments, or parts thereof, solely for peaceful purposes is both realistic and attainable. The process in this direction has already begun.

One disarmament measure covering several environments is the ban on nuclear-weapon tests in the air, under water and in outer space. Here outer space, be it noted, is specifically mentioned.[15]

Another measure places on "non-nuclear-weapon" States the obligation

> "... not to receive the transfer from any transferor whatsoever of nuclear weapons or other nuclear explosive devices, or of control over such weapons or explosive devices directly or indirectly; not to manufacture or otherwise acquire nuclear weapons or other nuclear explosive devices; and not to seek or receive any assistance in the manufacture of nuclear weapons or other nuclear explosive devices".[16]

This obligation has a counterpart in the undertaking of "nuclear-weapon" States

> "... not to transfer to any recipient whatsoever nuclear weapons or other nuclear explosive devices, or control over such weapons or explosive devices directly or indirectly; and not in any way to assist, encourage or induce any non-nuclear-weapon State to manufacture or otherwise acquire nuclear weapons or other nuclear explosive devices, or control over such weapons or explosive devices".[17]

Though these last-mentioned provisions do not mention outer space specifically, it is obvious that the obligations at issue limit the freedom of States in all dimensions.

Measures have also been taken towards the complete demilitarization of certain parts of our globe, which parts should henceforth be used only for peaceful purposes. This is the case with Antarctica. The instrument in question prohibits

> "... *inter alia*, any measures of a military nature such as the establishment of military bases and fortifications, the carrying-out of military manoeuvres as well as the testing of any type of weapons".[18]

Here, by substantive provisions–i.e., by the elimination of certain types of military activity from all or some environments, and the outlawing of all types in certain environments–, the freedom of States to engage in such activities is being limited step by step and the goal of confining them to peaceable actions is being approached.

It is within this perspective that the rule of the peaceful use of outer space should be viewed. Its practical implications have been concretized in the instruments referred to, as well as in others concerning outer space alone:

(i) The USSR and the United States solemnly recorded their intention not to station in outer space any objects carrying nuclear or any other weapons of mass destruction.[19]

(ii) All States were called upon:
   (*a*) to refrain from placing in orbit round the Earth any objects carrying nuclear weapons or any other kind of weapons of mass destruction, installing such weapons on celestial bodies or stationing such weapons in outer space in any other manner;
   (*b*) to refrain from causing, encouraging or in any way participating in the conduct of the foregoing activities.[20]

(iii) The call of the General Assembly [(ii) (*a*)] was transformed into a solemn treaty obligation.[21]

(iv) As stated, the Moon and other celestial bodies shall be used "exclusively for peaceful purposes. The establishment of military bases, installations and fortifications, the testing of any type of weapons and the conduct of military manoeuvres on celestial bodies" was prohibited.[22]

This demilitarization of celestial bodies is in no way affected by the provision permitting "the use of military personnel", as their employment is allowed only "for scientific research or for any other peaceful purposes". The same applies to the freedom of use "of any equipment or facility", for they too can be used only if "necessary for peaceful exploration of the Moon and other celestial bodies".[23] Thus the mere presence of military personnel or equipment in no way alters the status of celestial bodies: nor does it affect the basic provisions of the law.

Thus far has man progressed towards the implementation of the principle enunciated in the first instruments on the subject: the use of outer space for exclusively peaceful purposes.[24] We cannot as yet confidently assert that we are near the goal. Hence it remains imperative that law-makers on the subject should keep in view the ultimate objective and continue their efforts to achieve it. The age of space has, no doubt, intensified the urgency of adopting meaningful and successive disarmament measures in all dimensions. Within the framework of man's endeavours to attain that goal, the law of outer space has no small role to play.

Notes to Chapter IX

1. M. N. Golovine, *Conflict in Space*, London 1962, p. 47; D. G. Brennan "Arms and Arms Control in Outer Space", in Bloomfield: *Outer Space: Prospects for Man and Society*, Englewood Cliffs N.J. 1962, p. 125; J. T. McNaughton in M. Cohen: *Law and Politics in Space*, Montreal 1964, p. 70.
2. General Assembly resolution 1472 (XIV) of 12 December 1959, Part A, first para. of preamble; cf. second para. of preamble to the 1963 Declaration of Legal Principles and the same language in second para. of preamble to the 1967 Space Treaty; cf. also the very cautious commentary by K. Zemanek, "The United Nations and the Law of Outer Space", *Yearbook of World Affairs*, London 1965, pp. 215 f.
3. General Assembly resolution 1721 (XVI) of 20 December 1961, Part A, first para. of preamble; this was recalled by resolution 1802 (XVII) of 14 December 1962, preamble first para.
4. Space Treaty, 1967, fourth para. of preamble, also earlier Declaration of Legal Principles, 1963, fourth para. of preamble.
5. Cf. resolutions adopted by: ILA, 49th Conference, Hamburg 1960, Report, p. IX, para. 3a; Institut de Droit International, Brussels 1963, *Annuaire* II, p. 362 (para. 1); Draft Treaty on Outer Space, the Moon and Other Celestial Bodies, prepared by the David Davies Memorial Institute, Cambridge 1966, Preamble, fifth para.
6. R. D. Crane, "Law and Strategy in Space", 6 *Orbis* (University of Pennsylvania), 1962, pp. 282 ff. R. Gardner, "Co-operation in Outer Space", 41 *Foreign Affairs*, 1963, No. 3, p. 18, also his "Outer Space. A Breakthrough for International Law", 50 *American Bar Association Journal* 1964, No. 30, pp. 32 f. On the other hand, cf. D. Goedhuis: "Report on General Questions of the Legal Régime of Space", 50th ILA Conference, Brussels 1962, Report, pp. 70 ff., at p. 83 and the discussion on the subject, pp. 31 f.; C. W. Jenks, "Le droit international des espaces célestes, Rapport Préliminaire", Institut de Droit International," Geneva 1963, pp. 43 f. and his *Space Law*, pp. 45 f.; B. Cheng, "Le Traité de 1967 sur l'espace", *loc. cit.*, p. 606.
7. Article 2, paragraph 4, of the Charter; cf. Lachs, "La nouvelle fonction des armistices contemporains", *Hommage au Président Basdevant*, Paris 1960, pp. 315 ff., at pp. 320-326; Brownlie suggests that a similar argument may be valid whenever "a new forum for international relations opens up": "The Maintenance of International Peace and Security in Outer Space", *loc. cit.*, at p. 14.
8. Cf. *North Atlantic Coast Fisheries*, P.C.A., *U.N.R.I.A.A.*, XI, p. 198.
9. Cf. the Statute of the International Atomic Energy Agency, 1956, Article II.
10. Cf. Antarctic Treaty, Washington 1959: Article I, paragraph 1.
11. Article IV, paragraph 2, of the Space Treaty, 1967; cf. also the statement made in connection with this provision by the representatives of the USA and the USSR, in the Legal Sub-Committee, Fifth Session, on 22 July 1966; cf., further, sometimes conflicting interpretations of the provision in question: J. F. McMahon, "Legal Aspects of Outer Space, Recent Developments", XLI *B.Y.B.I.L.*, 1965-1966, pp. 419 and 422; N. Pulantzas, "The Outer Space Treaty", 20 *Revue Hellénique de Droit International*, No. 1-4, 1967, pp. 66 ff.; G. Gal, *Space Law*, Budapest 1969, pp. 164-175.

12. It has however been pointed out that: "In outer space the most peaceful uses may be suffused with military potentials", Jessup-Taubenfeld: *Controls of Outer Space and the Antarctic Analogy*, New York 1959, at p. 223.
13. Cf. Quadri, *op. cit.*, p. 570; also J. G. Verplaetse, "The Law of War and Neutrality in Outer Space", 59 *Nordisk Tidsskrift for International Ret*, 1959, pp. 55 ff.
14. Cf. the successive proposals and the discussion in the ten-member, later the 18-member Disarmament Committee and in the Conference of the Committee on Disarma'ent (CCD). Cf. also M. Ghelmegeau et A. Bolintineanu, "Contribution au problèm" des principes juridiques réglementant l'activité des Etats dans l'utilisation de l'espace cosmique", 8 *Revue Roumaine des Sciences Sociales, Série des Sciences Juridiques*, 1964, No. 2, pp. 223 f.; A. E. Gottlieb, "Nuclear Weapons in Outer Space", *The Canadian Yearbook of International Law*, 1965, pp. 3 ff.; cf. the statement of U. Thant in the General Assembly of the UN on the adoption of the resolution on the Space Treaty (19 December 1966): "The crux of the difficulty is that space activity is already part of the arms race ... Space disarmament is but a segment of the broad overshadowing problem of world peace and disarmament with which the world has wrestled for so long with a growing awareness of the need, but without sustained success. Eventually nations must surely realize that their genuine interests lie in peaceful rather than in military activities and that their activities in space should thus be peace-orientated."
15. Treaty Banning Nuclear Weapon Tests in the Atmosphere, in Outer Space and Under Water, Moscow, 5 August 1963, Article I, paragraph 1(a).
16. Article II: Treaty on the Non-Proliferation of Nuclear Weapons, 1 July 1968.
17. Article I of the Treaty as above.
18. The 1959 Antarctic Treaty (quoted above); Article I, paragraph I.
19. General Assembly resolution 1884 (XVIII), 17 October 1963, which recalling resolution 1721 A (XVI) of 20 December 1961 "welcomes the expressions by the Union of Soviet Socialist Republics and the United States of America of their intention not to station in outer space any objects carrying nuclear weapons or other kinds of weapons of mass destruction" (para. 1).
20. Paragraph 2 of the resolution just cited.
21. 1967 Space Treaty, Article IV, paragraph 1.
22. Space Treaty, Article IV, paragraph 2. Cf. draft treaties of the USA (Article 9) and the USSR (Article IV) and the US working-paper No. 6/Rev. 1: Legal Sub-Committee, Fifth Session 1966, Report, Annex I, pp. 7 and 13, and Annex III, p. 4. Mention should be made of what was viewed as a divergence between the first and second sentences of the second paragraph of Article IV of the Treaty. While the first contains the words "the Moon and other celestial bodies", the second speaks only of "celestial bodies". Thus it was suggested that the prohibition laid down in the latter did not include the Moon (D. Wadegaonkar, "Legal Problems of Outer Space", 9 *Indian Journal of International Law* 1969, No. 1, p. 53; cf. McMahon, *op. cit.*, at p. 423). However this conclusion seems unwarranted, as both sentences must be considered as a whole. It is also to be noted that though the draft presented by the USA uses throughout the term "celestial bodies" without specifically mentioning the Moon, the title given to it is "Treaty Governing the Exploration of the Moon and other Celestial Bodies". Thus the "Moon" was obviously intended to be covered. Cf. also the records of

the meeting of the Legal Sub-Committee on 24 October 1966, A/AC.105/C2/SR.65, p. 10.

23. Cf. Article IV, second paragraph *in fine*. Cf. also second paragraph of Article I of the Antarctic Treaty.

24. One special issue that has aroused serious controversy is that of intelligence operations carried on through outer space: cf. L. C. Meeker, "Observation in Space" in *Law and Politics in Space*, ed. Cohen, Montreal 1964, p. 82, and comments, pp. 85-89. Cf. also A. M. Beresford, "Surveillance Aircraft and Satellites, A Problem of International Law", 27 *Journal of Air Law and Commerce*, 1960, Spring, pp. 106 f. R. Fisher in Cohen, ed., *op. cit.*, p. 85. On the other hand cf. G. Gal, *op. cit.*, pp. 179 f., D. Goedhuis, ILA 1962, *op. cit.*, pp. 77-81; B. Cheng, "The United Nations and Outer Space", *Current Legal Problems*, London 1961, p. 271; A. Haley, *Space Law and Government*, New York 1963, p. 74; Jenks, *Space Law*, p. 304; cf. also comments on the freedom of the air in the early days of aerial navigation: F. Fauchille, *Le Domaine aérien et le régime juridique des aérostats*, Paris 1901, p. 23. Without going into the details of the issues involved, it is to be hoped that in the further development of the law of outer space due account will be taken of this very important issue and adequate solutions found.

Chapter X

Rights and Obligations of States

As we near the end of this analysis, a pattern of mutually complementary provisions in the new law is emerging. Threaded in this pattern is the strand which draws all the various parts into one whole: a set of reciprocal rights and obligations.

The main subjects of these rights and obligations are States acting, either through their governmental organs or, through nongovernmental entities, physical or juridical persons.[1] However, allowance has also been made for the possibility of conferring certain functions upon international organizations, through which States can channel their efforts.

The role of such organizations in international law is of course growing steadily more important, which is why there is an increasing tendency to vest them with some of the many rights of which the State has heretofore been the sole subject. As so far elaborated, the rules have conferred on them a status within the scope of which States were prepared to recognize and co-operate with them.[2]

Certain of the rights and obligations of States under outer-space law have already been discussed. But there are others, within the general framework, which must be mentioned here: some of direct concern solely to States engaged in outer-space activities, some of a general nature, effective *erga omnes.*

I.(*a*) The obligation of States to inform other States, or the Secretary-General of the United Nations, of any phenomena they may discover in the course of exploration and scientific investigation which "could constitute a danger to the life or health of astronauts".[3] This means that a mutual warning system has been established. To be effective, the information supplied must be sufficient to permit all other States to take precautionary measures, depending on the nature of the phenomenon, to protect their astronauts or suspend certain types of experiment. To this obligation there corresponds the right of all States concerned to obtain such information, which may indeed be of vital significance for their future activities;

I.(*b*) The obligation of States whose space vehicles have landed on the moon or other celestial bodies, or which have established stations, installations or equipment thereon, to allow representatives of other States access to them.[4] This provision extends the general freedom of access to celestial bodies to cover man-made objects placed upon them. The corresponding "right of visit" is based on reciprocity and can therefore become operative only when at least two States have proceeded with an experiment or venture involving such possibilities. It has also been qualified by certain additional provisions. Thus representatives of other States must give "reasonable" notice of a projected visit. The purpose of this proviso is in order that (i) "appropriate consultations may be held" and that (ii) "maximum precautions may be taken to assure safety and to avoid interference with normal operations in the facility to be visited". The consultations thus envisaged will undoubtedly aim at fixing the details of the visit. These will naturally include the observance of adequate safeguards so as not to expose to danger either the visitors or the visited. Similarly, to obviate risk and damage, the avoidance of interference with the operation "in the facility" is prescribed.

The foregoing are no more than general directives, rules which will in the course of time require elaboration.[5]

II. The obligation to consider requests by States "to be afforded an opportunity to observe the flight of space objects launched by those States". Such requests are to be considered "on a basis of equality", and it is agreement between the States concerned which will determine the nature of the facilities offered and the conditions of their use.[6]

Much more fundamental, and wider in scope, is the question of harmful experiments, some of which may produce consequences of a far-reaching nature. Not only may further research be prejudiced by the pollution of space or of celestial bodies, the bacterial or radio-active contamination of celestial bodies or the alteration of their surface, but more permanent damage may be done to outer space and to our own atmospheric environment, with a consequent jeopardizing of health and life on our planet. Citizens of many countries, even mankind as a whole, could fall victim to such dangers. Every State, therefore, should be viewed as entitled to claim the performance of the obligations assumed.

The matter is of paramount importance. No reminder should be needed of the temptation to which States armed with the great potentialities of modern science are exposed: that of limitless experimentation. Prompted by the most praiseworthy motives, men are sometimes involutarily blind to the possible consequences of their experiments. Yet the results they may produce can be irreversibly deleterious to life, or even catastrophic.[7]

Not surprisingly, governments and scientists have been engrossed with the urgent necessity of taking all possible precautions and the problem has produced some lively debate in international forums.[8] A parallel development is to be seen in the requests frequently voiced for adequate and effective legal safeguards to be provided.[9]

The result so far achieved is the acceptance, by States pursuing the study and exploration of outer space and celestial bodies, of an obligation to avoid "harmful contamination" of them and "adverse changes in the environment of the Earth resulting from the introduction of extraterrestrial matter". The States concerned have undertaken to put in train appropriate measures to this effect.[10]

Furthermore, any State which "has reason to believe that an activity or experiment planned by it or its nationals in outer space, including the Moon and other celestial bodies, would cause harmful interference with activities of other States" engaged in the peaceful exploration and use of outer space and celestial bodies is placed under an obligation "to undertake appropriate international consultations before proceeding with any such activity or experiment". A corresponding right to request consultation is bestowed on any State which "has reason to believe" that the plans of another State could be productive of such effects.[11]

Thus consultations are to be entered into only if they are judged necessary by an experimenting State or by other States requesting them. Nothing has been provided as to the procedure to be followed, or the consequences if the consultations should end in disagreement or in the event of non-compliance with such agreement as might result. In fact, a whole range of questions arises, and these provisions can be viewed only as the adumbration of a set of rules on the subject of safeguards.

To take a broader view, the rights and obligations of States should be considered in the context of general international law and that of the principles and rules embodied in the law of outer space. In particular, it is to be recalled that:

1. The exploration and use of outer space and celestial bodies are to be pursued:
   (*a*) "for the benefit and in the interest of all countries ... and shall be the province of all mankind",[12] and
   (*b*) "in the interest of maintaining international peace and security and promoting international co-operation and understanding".[13]
2. Outer space and celestial bodies:
   (*a*) are "not subject to national appropriation", and
   (*b*) "shall be free for exploration and use by all States" on a basis of non-discrimination and equality.[14]

One might of course argue that the scientific progress and technical achievements of any one country automatically enrich mankind as a whole. To bring this about, however, no provisions of the law would have been necessary, but in practice every State would have remained free to keep all the advantages of its discoveries for itself. That this interpretation is not compatible with the principle enunciated, and that more was intended, has received further confirmation in a specific rule whereby States conducting activities in outer space have agreed "to inform the Secretary-General of the United Nations as well as the public and the international scientific community, to the greatest extent feasible and practicable, of the nature, conduct, locations and results of such activities".[15]

Though qualified,[16] this is an obligation of no mean importance. Moreover, it is to be recalled again that in these activities States "shall be guided by the principle of co-operation and mutual assistance" and they have undertaken to conduct all their activities "with due regard to the corresponding interests of all other States".[17] The "interests" of all States are protected–both those engaged and those not engaged in outer space activities.

These principles may have been couched in very general and broad terms and supplemented with only a few specific rules, some of which themselves lack precision. Be this as it may, the provisions in question can hardly be regarded as nominal or devoid of substantive meaning. Nor could the rights arising out of them be viewed as imperfect, for they have become *vincula juris*, thus it can hardly be suggested that they were not intended to become effective.[18] It may have been premature to enter into any more detailed specification of them or of the corresponding obligations. But the need for this will grow in confrontation with practice, while adequate interpretation will be called for in concrete situations. It is, however possible even now to estimate the broad consequences of these principles and rules.

The law was obviously not expected to abolish the great disparity in the scientific and technological potential of States, which has been made manifest in outer space more than in any other dimension. Its agreed purpose was to ensure that no State should arrogate exclusive rights to itself or use them at the expense of others. There can be no doubt that the freedom of action of States in outer space or on celestial bodies is neither unlimited, absolute or unqualified, but is determined by the right and interest of other States. It can therefore be exercised only to the extent to which as indicated it does not conflict with those rights and interests. These in turn are not confined to matters of security or of potential activities in the new environment, but also embrace whatever results from the obligation of co-operation and the benefits which these activities should produce for all. There should therefore be no antinomy between the freedom of some and the interest of all, and herein lies the close relationship between the subjective and the objective criteria delimiting the sphere of action of States.[19]

Taking an even wider view, the mutual relationship of rights and obligations of States in all environments must be seen *in motu* and in due perspective. States continue to expand their spheres of activity, secure to themselves new rights and enter new domains. However, this being a phenomenon concerning every State (though not to the same degree), it carries with it a growth of mutual obligations, and so the network of the law becomes ever tighter: States acquire new rights while at the same time experiencing an ever-greater contraction of their freedom of action. These two processes, only apparently contradictory, in fact complement each other. In view of the far-reaching consequences implicit in outer-space activities, it is the more imperative that adequate legal safeguards should be developed in good time, in order to protect the rights and interests of all concerned–and above all those of the international community as a whole.

Notes to Chapter X

1. Article VI of the Space Treaty, 1967 (as above).
2. Cf. Article XIII of the Space Treaty, also the proposal of the United Kingdom submitted to the Legal Sub-Committee, Fifth Session 1966, Report, Annex III, p. 8, also proposal of Italy, *ibid.*, p. 15. Cf. H. G. Darwin, "The Outer Space Treaty", XLII *B.Y.I.L.*, 1967, pp. 286-288; cf. also Article 6 of the Agreement on Rescue and Return, and Article XII of the Convention on International Liability for Damage Caused by Space Objects (see Chapter XI below).
3. Article V, third paragraph, of the Space Treaty.
4. Article XII of the Space Treaty 1967; cf. Article VI of the draft treaty submitted by the USA (Legal Sub-Committee, Fifth Session 1966, Report, Annex I, p. 7); proposals by USSR, Italy and Japan (*ibid.*, Annex III, pp. 12, 14 and 16).
5. Cf. Article VII of the Antarctic Treaty: "3. All areas of Antarctica, including all stations, installations and equipment within those areas, and all ships and aircraft at points of discharging or embarking cargoes or personnel in Antarctica, shall be open at all times to inspection by any observers ...".
6. Article X of the Space Treaty; cf. Article I, paragraph 1, of the draft treaty submitted by the USSR (Fifth Session 1966, Report, Annex I, p. 12) and Working Paper No. 23, Corr. 1, para. II (*ibid.*, Annex III, p. 12).
7. Cf. B. Lovell, "Danger Signals in Outer Space", *The Sunday Times*, 15 March 1964; also his "The Pollution of Space", 24 *Bulletin of Atomic Scientists*, No. 10, pp. 42 f., also earlier warnings by scientists, *inter alia*, International Space Science Symposium, Proceedings, Amsterdam 1960. Pollution or other dangerous effects of space experiments on the Earth's environment may be produced by "terrestrial" or "extraterrestrial" sources. Cf. P. H. Sand, "Space Programmes and International Environment Protection", 21 *I.C.L.Q.* 1972, pp. 43 f.
8. As early as 1958 the International Council of Scientific Unions set up a special Committee on Contamination by Extraterrestrial Exploration (Cetex). In March 1959 it submitted a report. The functions of this Committee have been taken over by Cospar (resolution of ICSU, September 1961), in particular by its Consultative Group on Potentially Harmful Effects of Space Experiments. In one of its first reports it dealt with upper atmospheric pollution by rocket exhaust and chemical injection experiments, potentially harmful effects of space experiments concerning the contamination of planets, and standards for space probe sterilization (Florence, 20 May 1964). Cf. similar studies carried out by WMO, following General Assembly resolution 1721 (XVI), and by other organizations. Cf. also Report of ICSU, *Bulletin*, No. 19, November, 1969.
   The question was also taken up by the Scientific and Technical Sub-Committee of the United Nations Committee on the Peaceful Uses of Outer Space. One of its early resolutions states: "considering that mankind, being concerned about potentially harmful effects of such experiments, seeks to be scientifically assured that such experiments will not adversely change the space environment or adversely affect other experiments in space . . . Recognizes the importance of the problem of preventing potentially harmful interference with peaceful uses of outer space" (UNCOPUOS Report, A/5549, 24 September 1963, para. 18, p. 8). Also Report of the Sub-Committee 1964 A/AC.105/20, pp. 16-17 and A/5785, 13 November 1964. Cf. also resolution of the Institut de Droit Interna-

tional of 11 September 1963, para. 12; J. E. S. Fawcett, *Outer Space and International Order*, David Davies 1964 Memorial Lecture, p. 8; G. P. Zhukov, *The Law of Outer Space* (in Russian), Moscow 1966, pp. 156 ff.; and L. Aronovitz, in *Journal of Geophysical Research*, 15 May 1968; F. Zwicky, "Examples of Activities in Extraterrestrial Space", paper submitted to the Scientific-Legal Liaison Committee, International Academy of Astronautics, 1970. Cf. also earlier studies on weather modification: J. and A. Baskin, "International Legal Aspects of Artificial Interference with the Weather", *Pravovedenie* (in Russian) 1968, No. 1, pp. 103 f.; R. and F. Taubenfeld, "Some International Implications of Weather Modification Activities", XXIII *International Organization*, No. 4, 1969, pp. 808 ff.

9. Cf. discussion in the Legal Sub-Committee, particularly at its Second and Fifth Sessions, 1963 and 1966; cf. also, *inter alia*, the Draft Treaty on Outer Space, the Moon and Other Celestial Bodies, by the David Davies Memorial Institute, 1966, Articles VI and VII.
10. Article IX of the Space Treaty, 1967; cf. Article 10 of the USA draft; Article VIII of the USSR draft: Legal Sub-Committee, Fifth Session, 1966, Report, Annex I, pp. 8 and 14.
11. Article IX of the Space Treaty, 1967; cf. Article VIII (second and third sentences) USSR draft, *loc. cit.*; paragraph 6 of the Declaration of Legal Principles, 1963. Cf. Sand, *op. cit.*, pp. 50 and 59.
12. Article I, first paragraph of the Space Treaty, 1967.
13. Article III, *in fine*, of the Space Treaty, 1967.
14. Article I, second paragraph, of the Space Treaty, 1967.
15. Article XI of the Space Treaty, 1967; it continues: "On receiving the said information, the Secretary-General of the United Nations should be prepared to disseminate it immediately and effectively". Cf. Article IV of the USA draft, Legal Sub-Committee, Fifth Session, Report, Annex I, p. 7; see also discussion on the subject in the Sub-Committee meetings, 21 and 22 July 1966; cf. General Assembly resolution 1721 (XVI), part B, paragraph 3 (*b*); Article IX, paragraph 1 b and c, of the Antarctic Treaty, 1959.
16. The qualification, as contained in Article XI, is linked with considerations which may affect the extent to which the new discoveries and benefits arising out of them will be shared.
17. Article IX of the Space Treaty (first sentence). Cf. paragraph 6 of the Declaration of Legal Principles, 1963; Article VIII of the USSR draft, *loc. cit.*; cf. Article 2 *in fine*, Geneva Convention on the High Seas, 1958; Quadri, *op. cit.*, pp. 569 f.
18. Cf. H. Lauterpacht, *The Development of International Law by the International Court of Justice*, London 1958, pp. 227 f.; even very general formulae have their meaning.
19. It has been suggested that any "interprétation subjective" may reveal contradictions in the Treaty as a whole: J.L. Vencatassin, "Problèmes économiques, juridiques et sociaux résultant de l'exploration et l'utilisation de l'espace extra-atmosphérique", paper submitted to the UN Conference on the Exploration and Peaceful Use of Outer Space, Geneva 1968, A/Conf. 34/IX.5, p. 1.

Chapter XI

Responsibility

The extension to outer space of the existing international legal order governing the rights and obligations of States bears an obvious corollary; the corresponding extension of responsibility.[1]

There is no need to review here the basic principles of an institution so well established in general international law,[2] nor recall how, in different domains, they have been inflected in specific rules. At an early stage in law-making for outer space the question likewise arose as to whether the basic general principles of responsibility would prove adequate for the purpose. After all, the venture into outer space, more perhaps than any other enterprise, exposed many besides those directly engaged to risks of harm or loss. Dangerous experiments (as indicated in the context of States' rights and obligations) may even affect mankind as a whole–change the Earth's environment, pollute the atmosphere and produce incalculable effects on life.[3] There are more limited dangers that space vehicles or rocket-parts may crash on earth and cause serious damage to life and property.[4] They may collide with aircraft or with other flying instruments.[5]

It would however serve no useful purpose to catalogue the actions or situations through which a State may incur international responsibility. At the present pioneer stage the list could not hope to be exhaustive. It might even be misleading, as has been found in the framework of general international law. At best one can broadly describe some categories of act or omission for which a State may be held liable, ranging widely from crucial questions of security to the infliction of damage in a particular case.[6]

The first step in the regulation of responsibility in respect of the new dimension was to lay down the basic principle that States "shall bear international responsibility for national activities in outer space, including the Moon and other celestial bodies", irrespective of whether it was the State itself or non-governmental entities which carried them out.[7] Another general provision spelled out the principle of international liability for such damage as might be caused to "another State" or "to its natural or juridical persons" by objects launched into outer space or their component parts "on Earth, in airspace or in outer space including the Moon and other celestial bodies".[8]

States bear international responsibility for any activity in outer space, irrespective of whether it is carried out by governmental agencies or non-governmental entities. This is intended to ensure that any outer space activity, no matter by whom conducted, shall be carried on in accordance with the relevant rules of international law, and to bring the consequences of such activity within its ambit.

The acceptance of this principle removes all doubts concerning imputability. How important this is will be appreciated by all those familiar with the serious difficulties to which this issue has so frequently given rise in practice.[9]

The law thus identified each State with any activity carried on under its colours in outer space, so that it bears direct responsibility for any such activity. From the very inception an international obligation is created, a duty to respond as between States.

It follows herefrom that States are under obligation to take appropriate steps in order to ensure that natural or juridical persons engaged in outer space activity conduct it in accordance with international law. States have taken upon themselves the explicit obligation that such activity will require their "authorization and continuing supervision".[10] The term "international responsibility" served simply to establish the objective principle, which in its turn required more precise elaboration in order to determine the obligations resulting from damage caused.

Efforts in this direction have so far concentrated on the problem of liability for damage caused by space objects, and resulted in the adoption of a special instrument–a *lex specialis*–on the subject.[11]

The provisions of this instrument deal with the subjective and objective elements of liability, exemptions from it, the measure of compensation, the applicable law, apportionment of the compensation and the procedure for the presentation and settlement of claims. From the subjective aspect, the essential task was to identify the State which would incur liability.

The criteria for this purpose have been established: it is the State that "launches", "procures the launching" of the "space object" or "from whose territory or facility" it is launched.[12] Moreover, the term "launching" has been defined as including "attempted launching", as damage may often be caused when the launching does not succeed.[13]

Whenever two or more States "jointly launch a space object, they shall be jointly and severally liable for any damage caused".[14] This should safeguard the interests of the victim and facilitate the obtaining of compensation. Even if the States participating in the launching agree among themselves on the apportionment of such liabilities as they may incur, this has no effect vis-à-vis the injured State, which remains entitled "to seek the entire compensation" from any or all of the launching States "that are jointly and severally liable".[15]

Although States are the principal subject of rights and obligations, this does not exclude the possibility of their joining their efforts and acting within an international organization. For this reason these organizations have been endowed with a special status. The general rule provides that in such cases the responsibility shall rest with the organization and the States participating in it.[16] In further detail: some of them complying with specific provisions of the law, have been given a status assimilating their liability to that of States.[17] They are jointly and severally liable with their member States. However, the claim has to be presented to the organization first, and only in case the latter fails to discharge its obligation by paying the amount agreed upon or determined within the time-limit provided for, may the liability of States members of that organization which are contracting parties to the special instrument be invoked.[18] Yet the corresponding rights of these organizations are limited; quite apart from the question of whether they can become parties to the instrument, they cannot, unlike their members, present claims for damage caused to them. This may be done only by a State member of the organization which is a party to the special instrument.[19] (As to other organizations, their existence has no effect on the rights and obligations of the States concerned.)

States and (within the limits defined) international organizations are thus liable if by act or omission they cause "loss of life, personal injury or other impairment of health; or loss or damage to property", whoever may own it: a State, a natural or juridical person or an international organization.[20] To produce the legal effect, the "damage" thus defined must be caused by the space object or component parts of it, or by the launch vehicle or parts thereof. The causal link between these elements sets in motion the machinery of law.

Of particular interest is the character of the liability, as it is here that the rules have made a notable contribution to the development of the law.

It need scarcely be recalled that, traditionally in general international law, only an illicit act by a State gives rise to international responsibility.[21] One hundred and seventy-four years ago a court held that: "Where there is no fault, no omission of duty, there can be nothing whereupon to support a charge of responsibility or justify a complaint".[22] Only gradually and in exceptional cases has the sphere of operation of responsibility been extended. This has been the obvious consequence of new requirements maturing in inter-State relations.[23] It has become ever more evident that to deny responsibility even in some cases where damage was caused and there was no omission of duty, no fault, no violation of a specific rule of law, would not only be inequitable but would defeat the very purpose of the law. Thus the principle of absolute (objective) responsibility was born and found its way into a series of international instruments. In this, modern technology and the risks resulting from its application have been primary factors. May it suffice to mention the domains of sea and air transport, and more especially that of nuclear energy. Sixty-two years ago a Convention dealing with damages resulting from collisions at sea required proof of fault as a basis for liability,[24] no presumptions being admitted. A Convention concluded in 1929 accepted a presumption of fault, subject to rebuttal.[25] However, a Convention drafted in 1952, concerning damage caused by foreign aircraft to third parties, provided that "Any person who suffers damage on the surface shall, upon proof only that the damage was caused by an aircraft in flight or by any person or thing falling therefrom, be entitled to compensation...".[26]

In the particular domain of nuclear energy it has been accepted that the operator of a nuclear installation is liable upon mere proof that damage or loss of life, damage or loss of property was caused "by a nuclear incident involving either nuclear fuel or radioactive products or waste in, or nuclear substances coming from such installations...". The operator of a nuclear ship is held liable for damage caused in similar circumstances.[27]

This departure from the traditional rules imposes the question: is it only a series of exceptions from them or much more, the opening of a new chapter, intended to deal with new phenomena, which to an ever-growing extent will require new legal solutions, in view of the risks and dangers they carry with them? For new and indeed fundamental issues are involved: not only limited to the particular case, sometimes a minor accident, but some of great magnitude, the consequences of which can hardly be predicted. There can be little doubt that this requires an approach which is unfettered by the narrow rules of yesterday.

Such were the considerations which the lawmakers for outer space activities obviously had to bear in mind. Should States engaged in these activities enjoy entire freedom in the choice of means and experiments by which to proceed? The risks involved are too great for law to hold aloof, or only intervene within the traditional limits.[28] Refuge may now no longer be sought in the formulae of *force majeure* or act of God.[29] In view of the intrinsic scale of the risks of modern technology, the maxim *qui jure suo utitur neminem laedit*, or even the requirement of due care, have become inept, anachronistic. The question of who should be legally liable for the risks attendant on technical progress has therefore to be given an answer commensurate to the dangers involved. We have, in fact, arrived at a turning-point where a new solution has become necessary: the imposition of specific responsibility for the risks of technical developments on those who employ them.

Relying on recent precedents, the law of outer space has accepted this approach. Thus a long way has been traversed, from the initial suggestion that no responsibility whatever should be attached to such activities, to absolute liability.

The principle of absolute liability has been adopted in regard to damage caused by a space object "on the surface of the earth or to aircraft in flight".[30] When such damage is itself the result of damage "being caused elsewhere than on the surface of the earth to a space object of one launching State or to persons or property on board such a space object by a space object of another launching State" and is sustained by a third State or its natural or juridical persons, the absolute liability is borne "jointly and severally" by both launching States.[31] However, provided that the damage has not resulted from activities which are "not in conformity with international law...", a launching State may obtain exoneration from absolute liability to the extent that it can establish gross negligence, or an act or omission intended to cause damage on the part of the claimant State or the person it represents.[32]

As between launching States, however, the requirement of fault of the State or persons for whom it is responsible has been retained for the event that damage may be caused elsewhere than on the surface of the earth by the space object of one State to the space object of another or persons or property aboard.[33] Should such an incident result, elsewhere than on the surface of the earth, in damage to a space object of a third State or to persons or property aboard, the same requirement of fault "of either of the first two States" obtains, and determines their joint and several liability vis-à-vis the third.[34]

The underlying premise of this solution is obviously that once space objects (including any that may suffer damage) have left the ground all launching States may be presumed to have taken similar risks. Thus none is favoured by the law. This appears well founded.

No claim under the Convention is allowed in respect of damage caused by a space object to a national of the launching State, nor are nationals of other States covered while "they are participating in the operation of that space object" or find themselves "in the immediate vicinity of a planned launching or recovery area" at the launching State's invitation.[35]

The possible limitation of the amount of compensation opens another issue.[36] A ceiling of that kind is known to have been accepted in maritime and air law, and in regard to nuclear damage.[31] Proposals on similar lines were made during the preparatory work on liability for outer space activities.[38] Nevertheless the law as adopted keeps silence on this subject, and has therefore rejected the principle, thus leaving the solution of each case to its merits.

The measure for compensation and the law to be applied are other questions deserving special attention. In regard to the latter a choice could have been made as between the law of the claimant, the law of the respondent State, or the *lex loci.* A formula of more universal character, such as reference to international law, was also advocated. The advisability of exclusively following any of these courses was however challenged, whether on the ground of uncertainties in the choice of law or because of the imprecision of reliance on general principles. The solution adopted combines reference to international law with other considerations and a definition of the objective which the compensation is meant to achieve. It thus constitutes a substantive rule of law. The compensation is to be determined "in accordance with international law, and the principles of justice and equity, in order to provide such reparation in respect of the damage as will restore the person, natural or juridical, State or international organization to the condition which would have existed if the damage had not occurred".[39]

Among the remaining provisions deserving mention are those which constitute the logical consequence of the principle of direct international responsibility of States: since claims are qualified as international, the need for the exhaustion of local remedies is dispensed with.[40] It was accepted that the claimant, whether a State, physical or juridical persons, are not barred from seeking remedies open to them before courts, administrative tribunals, or agencies of the respondent State or under other international agreements. By doing so, however, they make a choice and the State concerned shall not be entitled to present the claim under the *lex specialis.*[41] Lastly, the titles for presenting claims are defined and the procedures for doing so laid down.[42]

These are the basic rules governing liability for damage caused by space objects. They do not, of course, exhaust the question of responsibility for space activities in the much wider sense referred to earlier. In this respect only one step has so far been taken: it has been laid down that–

> "If the damage caused by a space object presents a large-scale danger to human life or seriously interferes with the living conditions of the population or the functioning of vital centres, the States Parties, and in particular the launching State, shall examine the possibility of rendering appropriate and rapid assistance to the State which has suffered the damage, when it so requests."[43]

This is clearly a very modest beginning and, before long, it is to be expected that law will have to respond to the need for further elaboration.

Notes to Chapter XI

1. Cf. *Spanish Zone of Morocco Claims, Report III* (1924), *U.N.R.I.A.A.* II, at p. 641.
2. Cf. Reports by R. Ago, Special Rapporteur on State Responsibility, International Law Commission: 1st: Doc. A/CN.4/217 (1969); 2nd: Doc. A/CN.4/233 (1970); and 3rd: Doc. A/CN.4/246 and Add. (1971).
3. Cf. Chapter X, footnotes 7-9.
4. These have been reported several times: cf. *New York Times*, 8 October 1961 and 28 March 1964. Also Lay and Taubenfeld, *The Law Relating to Activities of Man in Space*, New York 1970, pp. 137-138.
5. It is suggested that the likelihood of "collision" in space is one in a million. Yet in 1965 two communications satellites came so close to each other that their long antenna-like booms crossed: no damage was done, and the satellites continued their journey (*New York Times*, 11 October 1966).
6. Cf. P. Guggenheim, *Traité de droit international public*, II, Geneva 1954, pp. 2 ff.; E. Jiménez de Aréchaga, "International Responsibility", in *Manual of International Law*, ed. M. Sørensen, London 1968, pp. 534 ff.; R. Ago, Second Report, Article 1, at pp. 25 ff., and Article 2 at pp. 46 ff., and Third Report, at pp. 60 ff.; G. I. Tunkin, *Problems of Theory of International Law* (in Russian), Moscow 1970, pp. 430 ff.
7. Article VI of the Space Treaty, 1967. Cf. also the almost identical paragraph 5 of the Declaration of Legal Principles, 1963.
8. Article VII of the Space Treaty. Cf. paragraph 8 of the Declaration of Legal Principles.
9. Cf. S. Schwarzenberger, *International Law as Applied by International Courts and Tribunals*, I, London 1957, pp. 613 ff.
10. Article VI of the Space Treaty. Cf. also paragraph 5, Declaration of Legal Principles, 1963.
11. Cf. first proposal submitted by the USA, Legal Sub-Committee, First Session 1962, Report, pp. 6-8; Working Paper by Belgium on the Unification of Certain Rules Governing Liability for Damage Caused by Space Vehicles, Legal Sub-Committee, Second Session 1963, Report, Annex I, pp. 10-12, and Draft Agreement by Hungary, Third Session 1964, Report, Annex II, pp. 7-10. The Sub-Committee continued the consideration of these and other proposals and amendments at the second part of the Third Session, and at the Fourth, Sixth, Seventh, Eighth, Ninth; cf. Reports and Tenth Sessions, when work on the Convention on International Liability for Damage Caused by Space Objects was completed. Cf. also G.A. Resolutions 1802 (XVII), 1962; 1963 (XVIII), 1963; 2222 (XXI), 1966; 2345 (XXII), 1967; 2453 (XXIII), 1968; 2601 B (XXIV), 1969 and 2733 B (XXV), 1970.
12. Article I (*c*) of the Convention: cf. also Article VII of the Space Treaty; in the elaboration of the Convention in the Sub-Committee seven criteria were listed as essential for liability: (*a*) providing territory for the launching of a space object; (*b*) providing facilities for the launching of a space object; (*c*) exercising control over the orbit or trajectory of a space object; (*d*) owning or possessing a space object; (*e*) procuring the launching of a space object; (*f*) participation in the launching of a space object; and (*g*) registration (international or na-

tional) of a space object: Legal Sub-Committee, Fourth Session 1965, Report, p. 4. Cf. further, Seventh Session 1968, Report, pp. 4 and 5. Cf. also Eighth Session 1969, Report, p. 9, footnote 3. It was resolved by the definition adopted by the Convention (Article I (*c*) as above) and Article V, paragraph 3, of the Convention.

13. Cf. Legal Sub-Committee, Fourth Session 1965, Report paragraph 15. Cf. also the drafts of Belgium, Article 2, second paragraph; of the USA, Article I (*b*);, the draft of Hungary used the terms: "Liability is also incurred even if, for any reason, the space vehicle or other object has not reached outer space" (Article I, para. 2). Legal Sub-Committee, Seventh Session 1968, Report, Annex I, pp. 51, 52. The Convention states in Article I (*b*): "the term 'launching' includes attempted launching".
14. Article V, paragraph 1, of the Convention.
15. Article V, paragraph 2, of the Convention. However the same paragraph provides that: "A launching State which has paid compensation for damage shall have the right to present a claim for indemnification to other participants in the joint launching". Cf. other instruments dealing with similar issues: Convention on Third Party Liability in the Field of Nuclear Energy, Paris 1960, Article 5 (*d*); Convention on the Liability of Operators of Nuclear Ships, Brussels 1962, Article VII/1; Vienna Convention on Civil Liability for Nuclear Damage, 1963, Article II/3 (*a*).
16. Article VI *in fine* of the Space Treaty; earlier paragraph 5 of the Declaration of Legal Principles.
17. The legal status of international organizations in the Convention was the object of long exchanges. Cf. Legal Sub-Committee, Fourth Session 1965, particularly meetings of 29-30 September 1965, A/AC.105/C.2/SR.52 and 54. "There was general agreement that international organizations engaged in space activities should be liable under the Convention for damage caused by such activities": Fourth Session 1965, Report, paragraph 17, p. 4; cf. drafts by Belgium, Article VI, USA, Article III, and Hungary, Articles VI and VII, *ibid.*, Annex IV, p. 4; cf. also Legal Sub-Committee, Seventh Session 1968, Report, Annex I: proposals by India, Articles I (*d*) and IV, paragraphs 2 and 3, pp. 17 and 21, by Italy, Articles 5 and 6, pp. 32 and 33, and joint proposal by Austria, Belgium, France, Sweden and United Kingdom, pp. 42-43. However, no agreement was reached at the time on the question of rights of international organizations under the Convention, *ibid.*, p. 6 *in fine*; cf. also Eighth Session 1969, Report, paras. 19 and 22, p. 6, and Ninth Session 1970, Report, p. 4 *in fine*. The question was finally resolved by the provisions of Article XXII, para. 1, of the Convention.

    "In this Convention ... references to States shall be deemed to apply to any international intergovernmental organization which conducts space activities if the organization declares its acceptance of the rights and obligations provided for in this Convention and if a majority of the States members of the organization are States Parties to this Convention and to the Treaty on Principles Governing the Activities of States in the Exploration and Use of Outer Space, including the Moon and other Celestial Bodies." Cf. also paragraph 2.

18. Article XXII, paragraph 3, of the Convention provides for the joint and several liability of the member States. Some difficulties arose on the issue whether the liability of States members of the international organization: (*a*) should be residual and arise only in the event of default by the international organiza-

tion, or (*b*) should arise at the same time as the liability of the international organisation, cf. Legal Sub-Committee, Sixth Session 1967, Report, pp. 6-7. Cf. also Eighth Session 1969, Report, para. 22, p. 6.

19. Under Article XXIV, paragraph 1, only States may become Parties to the Convention and Article XXII, paragraph 4, provides that claims under the Convention by international organizations having accepted its rights and obligations shall be presented by a State member of it and party to the Convention.

20. Article I (*a*). The question was discussed whether nuclear damage should be dealt with in the Convention: cf. Legal Sub-Committee, Fourth Session 1965, Report, paragraph 13 (*a*); draft of Hungary, Article I (*b*) (which specifically excluded nuclear damage), Seventh Session 1968, Report, Annex I, p. 52; also same session A/AC.105/C.2/SR.90 and 101, pp. 38-47 and 51-59; proposal of the United Kingdom submitted at the Eighth Session 1969, Report, Annex II, p. 36, also of Japan, *ibid.*, at p. 33. However, when the definition of "damage" was adopted, no specific mention of nuclear damage was made: the general term "damage" was used. Cf. discussion at the 8th Session of the Legal Sub-Committee, A/AC.105/C.2/SR.111-131.

21. "States, according to a thoroughly established rule of international law, are responsible only for those injuries which are inflicted through an act which violates some principle of international law", Mexico-USA, General Claims Commission, *U.N.R.I.A.A.* IV, p. 701; *Spanish Zone of Morocco Claims, U.N.R.I.A.A.* II, p. 641; *Treaty of Neuilly, Article 179, paragraph 4 (Interpretation), Judgment No. 3, 1924, P.C.I.J., Series A, No. 3*, p. 8. Second Report by R. Ago, Article I: "Every international illicit act by a State gives rise to international responsibility", *ut supra*, 1970, p. 24; also Article II, pp. 46. Oppenheim-Lauterpacht, *International Law*, 8th ed., London 1955, pp. 343 ff. Also G. Cohn, "La théorie de la responsabilité internationale", 68 *R.C.A.D.I.*, 1939-II, pp. 267 ff.

22. *Jamaica* case, British/United States Claims Commission 1798, Moore, *International Adjudications, Modern Series*, IV, p. 499.

23. Cf. *Trail Smelter* arbitration: *United States* v. *Canada*, 1941, *U.N.R.I.A.A.* III, p. 1965.

24. International Convention for the Unification of Certain Rules of Law in Regard to Collisions, Brussels 1910, Article VI. It may be of interest to note the development of maritime law which, in its early stages, held the carrier liable for loss and damage to cargo with the exception of Acts of God, acts of public enemies, inherent defects in the goods, fault of the shipper or if the goods made the subject of general average sacrifice. Cf. G. Gilmore and C. L. Black, *Law of Admiralty*, New York 1957, pp. 119 ff. It was only later that the effect of steam navigation gave rise to disclaimers of liability in respect of perils of navigation "of whatever nature and kind" and the introduction of "exoneration clauses" or "negligence clauses". Cf. Report, I.L.A., 9th Conference, Cologne 1881, pp. 109 ff.; also the International Convention for the Unification of Certain Rules Relating to Bills of Lading, Brussels 1924, Article IV; cf. Tanker Owners' Voluntary Agreement Concerning Liability for Oil Pollution, 1969, which provides for liability "if a discharge of Oil occurs from Participating Tanker through the negligence of that Tanker (and regardless of the degree of its fault), and if the Oil causes damage by Pollution to Coast Lines within the jurisdiction of a Government, or creates a grave and imminent danger of Damage by Pollu-

tion thereto then the Participating Owner of that Tanker shall remove the Oil so discharged, or pay the costs reasonably incurred by the Government concerned to remove the said Oil ..." (Article IV), 8 *International Legal Materials*, 1969, No. 3, p. 500.

25. Convention for the Unification of Certain Rules Relating to International Transportation by Air, Warsaw 1929, Articles 17, 18 and 20; however, even at the time the possibility of establishing objective responsibility was being discussed, cf. 1ère Conférence Internationale de Droit Privé Aérien, Paris 1926, pp. 55-56; 2e Conférence, Warsaw 1929, pp. 26-30 and 34. Cf. on the subject J. Rajski, *Civil Responsibility of the Air Carrier in International and Municipal Law*, Warsaw 1968, pp. 53 ff.; cf. also International Convention for the Unification of Certain Rules Relating to the Carriage of Passengers by Sea, Brussels, 29 April 1961, which accepts presumption in cases of death or personal injury resulting from collision, stranding, explosion, fire on the ship or shipwreck. The presumption is rebuttable (Article IV).
26. Convention on Damage Caused by Foreign Aircraft to Third Parties on the Surface, ICAO, Rome 1952, Article I, paragraph 1; cf. also Article VII.
27. OECD Convention on Third Party Liability in the Field of Nuclear Energy, Paris 1960, Article III (*a*); Convention on Liability of Operators of Nuclear Ships, Brussels 1962, Article II, paragraph 1. Cf. also Vienna Convention on Civil Liability for Nuclear Damage, 1963, Article II, and Convention Supplementary to the Paris Convention of 29 July 1960 on Third Party Liability in the Field of Nuclear Energy, Brussels 1963, Article II.
28. Cf. L. F. E. Goldie, "Liability for Damage and Progressive Development of International Law", 14 *I.C.L.Q.*, October 1965, pp. 1189 ff., particularly pp. 1241 ff.; McDougal, Lasswell and Vlasic, *op. cit.*, pp. 613 ff.; W. Warkallo, "Atomic Energy and Liability in Civil Law", *Mélanges* K. Przybylowski, Warsaw 1965, pp. 439 ff., Jenks, "Liability for Ultra-Hazardous Activities in International Law", 121 *R.C.A.D.I.* 1966-I, pp. 105 ff.
29. Liability is "not subject to the classic exonerations for tortious acts, force majeure, acts of God, or intervening acts of third persons": Explanatory Memorandum, Convention on Third Party Liability in the Field of Nuclear Energy, Paris 1960 (quoted above), 8 *European Yearbook*, 1960, p. 249. For some exceptions cf. Article IX of the Convention.
30. Article II of the Convention; cf. Legal Sub-Committee, Fourth Session 1965, Report, p. 3; cf. Article I (*b*) of the Belgian draft; Article II, paragraph 1, of the USA draft and Article III of the Hungarian draft, Legal Sub-Committee, Fourth Session 1965, Report, Annex IV, p. 5; also cf. agreement reached at Sixth Session 1967, Report, p. 6, B; Eighth Session 1969, Report, Field of application: paragraph 1, p. 8.
31. Article IV, paragraph 1 (*a*) of the Convention.
32. Article VI, paragraphs 1 and 2 of the Convention. Cf. Legal Sub-Committee, Third Session 1964, Report, Annex II: proposal of USA, Article III, paragraph 1, p. 3; of Hungary, Articles III-VI, p. 8; of Italy, of Canada; pp. 22-23; also of India and UAR: "There should be no exceptions to the principle of absolute liability for damage caused by space objects", *ibid.*, p. 23; cf. agreement reached at Seventh Session 1968, Report, p. 7. The Convention provides that where damage results from activities incompatible with international law, including the UN

Charter and the Space Treaty, there can be no exoneration even if the conditions for it otherwise exist (see Article VI, para. 2).

33. Article III of the Convention.
34. Article IV, paragraph 1 (*b*). For the provisions of the Convention providing for the apportionment of compensation in cases of joint and several liability, see Article IV, paragraph 2.
35. Article VII of the Convention; cf. joint proposal of Belgium, Hungary and USA, Legal Sub-Committee, Sixth Session 1967, Report, Annex II, p. 22; also Seventh Session 1968, Report, p. 5, A. In 1969 Austria and France proposed an addition to the text, Legal Sub-Committee, Eighth Session 1969, Report, Annex II, p. 36; the text was finally agreed as inserted as Article VII of the Convention (*ibid.*, p. 9).
36. Cf. suggestions to this effect: Goldie, *op. cit.*, p. 1248-9; David Davies Draft Code, Article 6, paragraph 2.
37. Cf. Article 11, paragraphs 1 and 2, of the Convention on Damage caused by Foreign Aircraft to Third Parties on the Surface, Rome 1952: in some cases the liability is unlimited (Article 12); Warsaw Convention for the Unification of Certain Rules Relating to International Transportation by Air, as amended (Hague Protocol, 1955), Article XI; the Vienna Convention on Civil Liability for Nuclear Damage (1963) provides that "The liability of the operator may be limited by the Installation State to not less than $ 5 million for any one nuclear incident", Article V, paragraph 1; Convention on Third Party Liability in the Field of Nuclear Energy (Paris 1960), Article 7; Convention on the Liability of Operators of Nuclear Ships (Brussels 1962), Article III.
38. Cf. drafts proposed by Hungary (Article II, paragraph 1), USA (Article IX) and the Belgian proposal that "The extent of the liability for compensation shall be determined in accordance with the provisions of the national law of the person injured ...." (Article V, first para.): Legal Sub-Committee, Third Session 1964, second part, Report, Annex II, pp. 3, 10 and 20, and comments in Annex IV, pp. 65 f. Cf. Article V of the Indian draft, "A launching State shall be liable to pay compensation without limit ...", but also Article VI, Legal Sub-Committee, Eighth Session 1969, Report, Annex II, p. 26.
39. Article XII of the Convention. This was one of the issues which gave rise to prolonged exchanges until agreement could be reached. Cf. proposal of Belgium, Article II, first paragraph; drafts of USA, Article II, paragraph 4; Hungary, Article II: Legal Sub-Committee, Fourth Session 1965, Report, Annex IV, pp. 2-3; at the Seventh Session: proposal by India, Article VI, by Italy, Article VIII, Australia, also amended proposal by Belgium (Article II), Legal Sub-Committee, Report, Annex I, pp. 24, 33, 45 and 56. At the same Session "the question of the law to be applied to the assessment of compensation for damage" was left open. "It was agreed however that if there was agreement on the applicable law between the claimant and the respondent, then that law should be applied" (Report, p. 7). At the following Session the principle was accepted that compensation "should be determined in accordance with international law", while the formula adopted a year earlier was retained (Eighth Session 1969, Report, para. 21, p. 6). The way to the final solution was opened by a joint proposal of Belgium, Brazil and Hungary (A/AC.105/C.2/L.79) (Article XXII), submitted to the Tenth Session of the Sub-Committee, Report, Annex I, p. 18;

cf. statements by Belgium and Hungary, 22 June, Italy, Austria and Bulgaria, 24 June 1971.

40. Article XI, paragraph 1, of the Convention. Cf. Article IV (*b*) of the Belgian proposal, Article IX, paragraph 1, of the USA draft, Legal Sub-Committee, Sixth Session 1967, Report, Annex II, p. 36. Agreement on the principle was reached at the Seventh Session, Report, p. 9.

41. See Article XI, paragraph 2, of the Convention, and cf. Seventh Session 1968, Report, p. 9.

42. On presentation of claims: a State may present a claim for compensation for damage sustained:
    1. by it, or by its natural or juridical persons;
    2. in its territory by any natural or juridical person, if the State of nationality has not presented a claim;
    3. by its permanent resident, if neither the State of nationality nor the State in whose territory the damage was sustained has presented a claim or notified its intention of doing so.

    (Article VIII of the Convention.) Cf. Article II of the Belgian proposal, Article VI of the USA, and Article VIII of the Hungarian drafts, Legal Sub-Committee, Sixth Session 1967, Report, Annex II, p. 35; draft of India, Article V, draft of Italy, Article IX, paragraph 1, Legal Sub-Committee, Seventh Session 1968, Report, Annex I, pp. 18-19, and p. 86; cf. also the text agreed upon at that Session, Report, p. 7. On the procedure for presentation, see Article IX of the Convention. Further clauses concern the time-limits for the presentation of claims (Article X), and the currency in which the compensation is to be paid (Article XIII).

    A series of other provisions deals with the settlement of claims by providing for the establishment of a Claims Commission, its composition and functions (Articles XIV-XX).

    The subject is no doubt important in itself and merits special attention. However, it goes beyond the scope of the present study. Cf. proposals on the subject in the proposal of Belgium (Article IV, C), USA (Articles X and XII), Hungary (Article XI), Legal Sub-Committee, Sixth Session 1967, Report, Annex II, pp. 37-38; draft of Italy (Article X), and of India, Compulsory Protocol on Settlement of Disputes, Legal Sub-Committee, Eighth Session 1969, Report, Annex II, pp. 15, 16 and 28-30; finally, proposal of Belgium, Brazil and Hungary, A/AC/C.2/L.79, presented at the Tenth Session 1971, Report, Annex I, pp. 16-17.

43. Article XXI of the Convention. It adds: "However, nothing in this Article shall affect the rights or obligations of the States Parties to this Convention". Cf. Proposal of Morocco of 25 June 1971, Tenth Session 1971, Report, Annex I, p. 19.

Chapter XII

The Law-Making Process

In the foregoing survey of the principles and rules embodied in the law of outer space, the details may have obscured the whole, and it may therefore be as well to reassemble the strands and briefly recapitulate the sequence of events in order to review the law-making process.[1] In so doing, we may also sum up the reply to the questions: from where does the law of outer space derive its force, and how did it grow?

The fundamental issue that arose on the day the first man-made instrument was launched into outer space concerned the law that should be applied to this domain and activities directed towards it: the identity, nature and framework of that law.

This issue could only be resolved by recognizing that the realm of international law, by which States had been bound in all dimensions, must extend to the latest of those dimensions to become accessible. Thus it was necessary to agree that outer space never had been a lawless area or legal vacuum, but had been subject to international law, though the matter could never have been put to the test before.

This recognition set the process in motion. And gradually, as the new chapter of international law began to unfold, a range of problems practical as well as theoretical–emerged.

The first was the problem concerning the right to launch objects into outer space. This could not be isolated from the legal régime of the new dimension. The second related to the right of passage into outer space. As recalled, the launching States sought no consent before proceeding with their operations. What is more, no objection was raised by the States whose territories were overflown. And so it has continued. Thus the question arose of whether the practice that has developed has grown into a custom, like "a path across the common".[2]

Here it had to be considered whether a sufficient period had elapsed to produce such a result, the time-factor being traditionally regarded as essential in the formation of custom. However, the rhythm of change is immeasurably more rapid today, time, as it were, travels more swiftly. Communications also are incomparably faster, in a world community that is far more closely knit for the purposes of international action. The stage of *consensus omnium* may thus be reached far sooner than in the past. The States overflown, having very frequent–even daily–opportunities of manifesting their will by protesting when objects were launched into space and circled the globe, refrained from doing so. It seemed therefore justified to interpret their acquiescence as consent.[3] Nor, given the continual space activity of the decade, could the relative shortness of that period affect the conclusion that such consent, far from being haphazard, had acquired the requisite features of legal certainty and stability.[4] Thus, long before any written instrument had been agreed, important principles were established, their source being general practice accepted as law.[5]

Yet it was obvious from the outset that the law-making process could not be left to be shaped solely by practice. Developments were occurring too swiftly, and a proliferation of activities was giving rise to many new issues. No more could the world afford the leisurely pace at which some chapters of international law–notably the law of the sea–had evolved. Hence the early initiative to embark on the elaboration of written law.

The United Nations having been entrusted with this task, it had to make a choice of procedures, a choice which naturally fell to be made from out the range of techniques which have been developed by the Organization over the last quarter-century.[6]

It had been realized that the task was not one which could feasibly be accomplished by the adoption of a single instrument, but one which rather lent itself to a continuous process of adopting and gradually elaborating principles and rules of law. It could have been entrusted to an existing organ of the United Nations. Yet the decision was rightly taken to follow another path, for which there was also precedent in the practices of the Organization. A special committee was set up and one of its two Sub-Committees was to concentrate exclusively on the drawing-up of legal principles and rules for outer space.

Furthermore, a special procedure was laid down, in view of the overriding importance of harmony in the decision of such vital issues. The deliberations of the Committee were to be conducted in such a way that it would "be able to reach agreement in its work without need for voting".[7] Thus no document could pass the committee stage without having secured the consensus of all.[8] Only then would it be submitted to one of the Main Committees of the General Assembly for approval and transmission to the plenary. (This procedure is peculiar to only some of the Assembly's subsidiary organs.[9])

The process of law-making moved towards the enactment of substantive provisions in two stages.[10] The first was marked by a series of General Assembly resolutions embodying guidelines on the ways and means of international co-operation, and outlining certain basic principles and rules intended to pave the way to more definitive arrangements.[11]

Among the resolutions which were not the work of the Committee, one merits special attention in view of the procedure adopted. It is that whereby the General Assembly welcomed the expression by the USSR and the USA "of their intention not to station in outer space any objects carrying nuclear weapons or other kind of weapons of mass destruction" and called upon all States to refrain from such activities.[12] In this way, the common intention of two States, an "agreement" reached outside the United Nations by two of its Members, was communicated to and put on record by the General Assembly, thus acquiring a special status vis-à-vis the other Members and being declared as an "example" to be followed by them all.[13]

The culmination of this first stage of law-making was the adoption in 1963 of the Declaration of Legal Principles Governing the Activities of States in the Exploration and Use of Outer Space.

A brief evaluation of this stage is called for before we proceed to the second.

As the activities of international organizations have grown in scope and variety, the taking of formal decisions by their organs has become an everyday phenomenon. However of the almost 3,000 resolutions adopted in 27 years by the General Assembly of the United Nations only a few have made history.

These instruments do not, however, form part of the traditional process of law-making, and what legal scope they may have is naturally determined by the powers of the organ from which they emanate. Thus most of them are not creative of legal rights and obligations. A general discussion of their standing would here be out of place, and I would simply refer the reader to the abundant literature on a subject which has attracted many writers.[14]

For the purpose of the present considerations it may suffice to indicate that some of these resolutions have confirmed legal principles recognized as binding on States "even without any conventional obligation".[15] On some occasions they have performed the important function of determining a situation or of interpreting provisions of the Charter.[16]

On others, a resolution has constituted a stepping-stone, a stage in the political and legal processes, initiating the law-making process by traversing the threshold into the realm of law.[17] Thus they have become a significant factor in the contemporary development and codification of international law.[18]

In the case of the 1963 Declaration of Legal Principles, even apart from the solemn form implied in the title[19] the interpretation attached to it by member States of the United Nations, particularly those engaged in the exploration and use of outer space, is of particular importance. The representatives of the latter declared in unequivocal terms that their governments would "respect" the principles laid down in it.[20] Similar statements were made on behalf of other States. The statements of almost all the representatives who spoke on that occasion attached to the Declaration an importance similar to that resulting from legally binding instruments.[21]

Thus, by expressing their will to be bound by the provisions of the document in question, they consented so to be bound, and there is no reason why they should not be held to it. For their intention seems to have been clear, the question of form, therefore, ceased to be of the essence.[22]

This, furthermore, should be viewed within the framework of a wider phenomenon reflecting a visible trend towards dispensing with traditional forms of decision-making in international relations. The rapid expansion of inter-State activity has been leading to an increasing abandonment of formal requirements when the will and consent of States is clearly discernible.[23]

In the light of all these considerations, it is difficult to regard the 1963 Declaration as a mere recommendation: it was an instrument which has been accepted as law.

Today, the status of the Declaration, though it was a highly important question at the time, is no longer crucial for the law of outer space.[24] Its intrinsic interest for present purposes is thus historic, as a stage in the development of the law.

In this connection, may I venture to recall what I said on the occasion when I presented the text to the United Nations Committee on the Peaceful Uses of Outer Space:

> "In this and in a wider ... it ought to be made clear that principles as enumerated do not constitute a closed chapter. We have to welcome what has been achieved and strive for further agreements. The law of outer space is in its formative stage only. We must proceed with prudence and care–take full benefit of agreements reached ... make them a living reality and continue with our efforts for further agreements ... The draft once adopted by the General Assembly could and should become a document of basic importance for our future efforts to facilitate international co-operation, to regulate and offer protection of law to the great achievement of man's genius in outer space for the benefit of our generation and those who will succeed us".[25]

A new stage of law-making was attained in 1967 by the conclusion of the Treaty on Principles Governing the Activities of States in the Exploration and Use of Outer Space, including the Moon and other celestial bodies. It was not only declaratory, confirming in treaty language the principles and rules already adopted and accepted as law; it went further, enriching the law by a number of important substantive provisions.[26]

Thus the conclusion of that treaty not only carried the law-making process very much further, but obviously helped to dispel doubts as to the state of the law on the subject. When presenting the Treaty to the Political Committee of the General Assembly for its approval, on 16 December 1966, I stressed that it was "a first basic treaty in the history of the law of outer space ... The work must continue. Some of the principles laid down will require further clarification. Some specific issues will call for further elaboration." I went on to recall what seemed to be obvious:

> "Treaties have been, still are and will remain the most effective instruments by which States acquire rights and enter into obligations in their mutual relations ... some of them constitute milestones in the development of international relations. It was, therefore, clear and logical that the next step to take was to conclude a treaty on the very same subject–a treaty universal in scope and character."[27]

Meanwhile the Legal Sub-Committee of the Committee on the Peaceful Uses of Outer Space had been engaged in the elaboration of two specific instruments.

The process was not an easy one. This is reflected in the draft agreements, conventions, proposals and amendments submitted, and in the debate at the annual meetings of the Sub-Committee. Consultations were necessary both inside and outside the committee-room before final agreement could be reached. The beginnings were obviously difficult. As the result of the first session in 1962 the Sub-Committee reported: "No agreement has been reached on any of the proposals submitted to the Sub-Committee. However, it is the consensus of all delegations who participated in this session that the meetings offered the possibility for a most useful exchange of views."[28]

A year later, in the Spring of 1963, after a debate on the particular principles proposed for inclusion in the Declaration of Principles, it became possible to identify: "(*a*) those as to which there were no differences of views; (*b*) those as to which there has been a certain rapprochement of points of view; (*c*) those as to which differences of view remain".[29] Yet before the end of the year it became possible to agree on the text of the Declaration.

At the same session "a certain rapprochement and clarification of ideas was recorded" on the two specific issues.[30] At its third session in 1964, the Sub-Committee, after 37 meetings found that "although substantial prog ress has been made there had been insufficient time to draft the international agreements", and decided to resume the session the same year.[31] However, no substantial progress was registered.[32] At the end of the fourth session, 1965, substantial differences still remained. The Sub-Committee concluded its report by stating that the "summary of its work is presented for information and that the agreements noted are of a preliminary and provisional character".[33] The elaboration of the Space Treaty, to which the Sub-Committee turned in 1966, having been presented with two drafts, also went through several stages. At the first, agreement was reached on nine articles, ironed out by a working group; after an interval of five weeks the Sub-Committee reconvened and recorded some progress, but no final text was agreed upon.[34] Further consultations were necessary before the text was approved and submitted to the General Assembly.

Returning to its consideration of the Agreement and Convention, the Sub-Committee recorded little progress at its sixth session.[35] However, it was only some months later, again as the result of consultations, that a joint draft Agreement on Rescue of Astronauts, Return of Astronauts and Return of Objects launched into Outer Space was produced and submitted to a specially convened session.

After some amendment, it was agreed upon.[36]

The work on the Convention on Liability had to continue for four more sessions. In 1968 it was noted "that while progress was made ... there remained important elements on which rapprochement of views was necessary".[37] Again informal consultations were resorted to and further attempts were made in 1969 to reach agreement.[38] A year later the Sub-Committee approved a text comprising the title of the draft Convention, the preamble and thirteen articles. However, on the two main issues of the settlement of claims and the question of applicable law "no agreement was reached ... and the solution to these two issues was left outstanding".[39] It was only at the tenth session in 1971 that the text of the Convention as a whole was agreed upon.

The records of the deliberations bear witness to the fact that among the members of the Sub-Committee the representatives of States not engaged in space activities played a very active part, and put forward many constructive proposals which found their way into the final instruments. As was rightly stated: "Outer space law was being shaped with the co-operation of the international community as a whole. That fact was all the more instructive since, in practice, outer space was being explored and utilized by only a very small number of States."[40]

The task, as all those familiar with law-making will appreciate, was arduous and exacting, the more so in that it concerned a new domain, where analogies could not too frequently be resorted to. Moreover, the rules to be elaborated had to serve objectives much wider than the immediate interests of those engaged in the discussions. It is here that negotiation came into its own, though, as elsewhere, it could not "be a nimble or hurried art", as "time pressure leads to improvisation, improvisation to error or more often to imprecision, and imprecision to future misunderstanding and mutual reproach".[41]

Looking at the body of law now existing, it could not be claimed that the rules adopted attained all the required objectives. As indicated in the foregoing analysis, some of them demand further elaboration, while others are not free of imprecision, or leave room for improvement. Some others constitute a bare scaffolding for the law of tomorrow, indications or merely inklings of the trend to be followed. This notwithstanding, the balance-sheet is impressive. Principles and rules, instruments of law, have come into being which are universal in scope and character.[42] They are clear and unequivocal on many issues. Furthermore, important decisions have been taken by international organizations, and many agreements between States on specific subjects of co-operation (both bi- and multi-lateral) have been concluded.[43]

Notes to Chapter XII

1. Cf. my comments in McWhinney-Bradley, *New Frontiers of Space Law*, Leyden 1969, pp. 13 ff.
2. P. Cobbett, *Leading Cases in International Law*, London 1922, Vol. I, p. 5.
3. Cf. Chapter V, above. Cf. also S. Latchford, "The Bearing of International Navigation Conventions on the Use of Outer Space", 53 *A.J.I.L.*, 1959, pp. 407 ff.
4. Cf. Ch. Chaumont, "L'orientation actuelle du droit de l'espace", *Revue Générale de l'Air*, No. 1, 1965, pp. 8 f., but contrast J. F. McMahon, *op. cit.*, at p. 417.
5. *Asylum Case, I.C.J. Reports 1950*, pp. 276-7, also K. Wolfke, *Custom in Present International Law*, Wroclaw 1964, pp. 114 ff.
6. Following its procedure in regard to the law of the sea, diplomatic and consular relations or the law of treaties, it could have entrusted the task to the International Law Commission, and then convened a diplomatic conference, or it could have assigned it to one of the main committees of the General Assembly, as in the case of the Convention on the Prevention and Punishment of the Crime of Genocide (1948); to one of the functional Commissions of the Economic and Social Council (as in the case of human rights, in particular of the International Covenant on Economic, Social and Cultural Rights and the International Covenant on Civil and Political Rights (1966), or it could have convened an *ad hoc* conference like that which prepared the Single Convention on Narcotic Drugs (1961)); for more on the subject, cf. Lachs, "La Contribución de las Naciones Unidas al Desarollo del Derecho Internacional", XI *Foro Internacional*, Mexico City, No. 2, pp. 339 ff.
7. Cf. Chapter III, footnotes 21 ff.
8. Cf. Statement by the Chairman of the Committee, 19 March 1962, A/AC.105/PV.2. Similar statements were made by the Chairman of the Legal Sub-Committee, cf. First Session 1962, Report, para. 8, p. 2. Cf. also the Scientific and Technical Sub-Committee.
9. Cf. the 18-nation Committee on Disarmament, ENDC/1 and Add. 1-4; Special Committee on the Situation with regard to the Implementation of the Declaration on the Granting of Independence to Colonial Countries and Peoples, A/AC.109/L.27, para. 9; Special Committee on Principles of International Law concerning Friendly Relations and Co-operation among States. Drafting Committee, G.A. (XX), a.i. 90 and 94, A/5746, para. 12; United Nations Commission on International Trade Law, Report on its First Session, A/7216, para. 35, pp. 10-11; *Ad hoc* Committee to study the Peaceful Uses of the Sea-bed and the Ocean Floor beyond the Limits of National Jurisdiction, A/AC.135/SR.2.
10. Cf. similarly: Resolution on the Prevention and Punishment of the Crime of Genocide: General Assembly resolution 96 (I), 11 December 1946; followed by a Convention, approved in General Assembly resolution 260 (III) of 9 December 1948; Universal Declaration of Human Rights, General Assembly resolution 217 (III), 10 December 1948, followed by two International Covenants, 16 December 1966; Declaration on the Elimination of All Forms of Racial Discrimination, General Assembly resolution 1904 (XVIII), 20 November 1963, followed by an International Convention on the subject, resolution 2106 (XX), 21 December 1965.
11. Cf. footnote 30 to Chapter III.

12. Resolution 1884 (XVIII), 17 October 1963, quoted above.
13. The Report of the Political Committee of the General Assembly referred to "the agreement arrived at between the United States and the Soviet Union" (A/5571).
14. Particular value is to be attached to the reasoning of Judge Lauterpacht in *I.C.J. Reports 1955*, pp. 115 ff. and Judge Jessup in *I.C.J. Reports 1966*, pp. 441 ff.
15. *Reservations to the Genocide Convention, I.C.J. Reports 1951*, p. 23.
16. *I.C.J. Reports 1971*, Advisory Opinion, paras. 95 and 105. J. Castañeda, *Legal Effects of United Nations Resolutions*, New York, 1969, pp. 117 ff.
17. This view is shared by S. Bastid, "Observations sur une étape dans le développement progressif et la codification du droit international", *Mélanges Guggenheim*, Geneva 1968, pp. 134 and 139.
18. Cf. R. Ago, "La codification du droit international et les problèmes de sa réalisation", *Mélanges Guggenheim, op. cit.*, pp. 93 ff., particularly at p. 124; Bastid, *op. cit.*, p. 132.
19. In a memorandum of the Office of Legal Affairs of the United Nations it was pointed out: "In United Nations practice, a 'declaration' is a formal and solemn instrument, suitable for rare occasions when principles of great and lasting importance are being enunciated, such as the Declaration on Human Rights ... Apart from the distinction just indicated, there is probably no difference between a 'recommendation' or a 'declaration' in United Nations practice as far as strict legal principle is concerned ... However, in view of the greater solemnity and significance of a 'declaration' it may be considered to impart, on behalf of the organ adopting it, a strong expectation that members of the international community will abide by it ..." (E/CN.4/L.610, 2 April 1962). This seems to have been stressed by the language used in the text: the Declaration on Legal Principles called upon all States to: "observe faithfully and strictly the provisions of the Charter of the United Nations, the Universal Declaration of Human Rights and the Present Declaration". Cf. the introductory words of its substantive provisions: "*The General Assembly* ... ."–it states "solemnly declares that in the exploration and use of outer space States should be guided by the following principles."
20. The representative of the USA said that his Government "considered that the legal principles contained in the operative part of the draft declaration reflected international law as accepted by the Members of the United Nations. The United States intended to respect them and hoped the conduct they recommended in the exploration of outer space would become the practice of all Nations"; the representative of the USSR stated that: "The United States representative had said that in his Government's view the legal principles contained in the draft declaration reflected international law as accepted by the Members of the United Nations and that the United States for its part intended to respect them. The Soviet Union, in its turn, undertook also to respect the principles enunciated in the draft declaration if it were unanimously adopted." (*General Assembly, Official Records, 18th Session, 1st Committee*, 1342nd Meeting, 2 December 1963, pp. 159 and 161.)
21. At a meeting of UNCOPUOS on 22 November 1963, the representative of Italy stated: "... the Declaration will constitute a generally accepted set of international legal principles which could not be disregarded. My country for one would be scrupulously guided by it in any undertaking in outer space" (*GA*,

OR, XVIII, Annexes, item 28, p. 20; cf. his similar statement in the First Committee on 2 December 1963, *loc. cit.*, p. 164); the representative of Australia stated: "While in our view a General Assembly declaration of legal principles cannot itself be creative of legal duties, it is equally not the Australian delegation's view that such a General Assembly declaration can have no part in the development or creation of international law. It is our view that a declaration of legal principles by the General Assembly, especially if universally adopted and adhered to in practice, may be valuable evidence of international custom, which in turn is a most important source of law." (*GA, OR*, XVIII, Annexes, item 28, p. 18.) At the First Committee meeting mentioned, the representative of the United Kingdom said that his Government "intended to respect those principles and believed that all States would apply them, thus ensuring that exploration and use of outer space would be confined to peaceful purposes" (*loc. cit.*, p. 164). Similar statements were made by the representatives of Iran, Japan, Argentina, Canada and other States at First Committee meetings on 2-5 December 1963 (*loc. cit.*, pp. 167-191). Cf. however the statement of the representative of France, who said that: "While supporting the principles set forth in the draft declaration, he wished to stress that the latter could not be looked on as more than a statement of intention; legal obligations *stricto sensu* could only flow from international agreements ..." (*loc. cit.*, p. 183).

22. This view is shared by Castañeda, *op. cit.*, pp. 162 f. and C. Q. Christol, Paper submitted to the 13th Colloquium on the Law of Outer Space, Constance 1970, pp. 11 f. Cf. also the Report of the 51st Conference of the International Law Association, Tokyo 1964, pp. 670 ff. It has also been suggested that the unanimous vote "implies that these member States recognize the principles contained therein. This would appear to make a strong case for suggesting that these principles should be treated as General Principles of Law Recognized by Civilized Nations" (K. Zemanek, *op. cit.*, pp. 208 and 210). Verdross, dealing with wider aspects of general principles of law, enlarges upon this point (*Mélanges Guggenheim*, Geneva 1968, pp. 525 f.). Cf. A.E. Gottlieb, *op. cit.*, p. 32.

23. Cf. Lachs, "Some Reflections on the Question of Substance and Form in International Law", *Transnational Law in a changing Society*, 1972.

24. General Assembly resolution 1963 (XVIII), adopted at the same time, recommended: "That consideration should be given to incorporating in international agreement form, in the future as appropriate, legal principles governing the activities of States in the exploration and use of outer space".

25. *GA, OR*, XVIII, Annexes, item 28, p. 15.

26. For the negotiations on the Treaty, see Chapter III, and cf. Legal Sub-Committee, Fifth Session 1966, Report, *loc. cit.* Cf. also the records of the General Assembly First Committee meetings on 16 and 17 December 1966, A/C.1/PV.1492 and 1493, and of the plenary meeting of 19 December 1966, A/PV.1499, pp. 54-55. Cf. general comments on the Treaty by M. Mateesco, "Interprétation juridique du Traité du 27 janvier 1967", XXVIII *Revue Générale de l'Air*, 1968, No. 1, pp. 9 ff.; D. Goedhuis, "An Evaluation of the Leading Principles of the Treaty on Outer Space of 27 January 1967", XV *Netherlands International Law Review*, 1968, pp. 17 ff.; J. Dutheil de la Rochère, "La Convention sur l'Internationalisation de l'Espace", XIII, *A.F.D.I.*, 1967, pp. 607 f.

27. First Committee of the General Assembly, 16 December 1966 A/C.1/PV.1491, pp. 11, 13-15.

28. First Session 1962, Report, p. 9, para 16.
29. Second Session 1963, Report, p. 4, para. 11,I,2.
30. *Ibid.*, para. 11,II.
31. Third Session 1964, Report, p. 5, para. 17.
32. Third Session 1964, Report, 2nd Part, p. 3, para. 10 and p. 5, para. 18.
33. Fourth Session 1965, Report, p. 6, para. 23.
34. Fifth Session 1966, Report, pp. 1-2, paras. 3 and 4 and Annex II.
35. Sixth Session 1967, Report, pp. 3-4, para. 11, pp. 5-8, para. 17.
36. Cf. Special Session held 14-15 December, A/AC.105/C.2/L.28, followed by a meeting of the Committee.
37. Seventh Session 1968, Report, p. 9, para. 11.
38. Eighth Session 1969, Report, p. 1, para. 2 *in fine*, pp. 6-10, para. 21 and paras. 22, 24 and 26.
39. Ninth Session 1970, Report, p. 4, para. 17 and pp. 6-11, para 27.
40. Dr. Krishna Rao, representative of India at the Seventh Session, 6 June 1968, A/AC.105/C.2/SR.92. This is borne out by the records of the ten Sessions of the Legal Sub-Committee, and by the great number of proposals and amendments, both written and oral, presented throughout the deliberations. Cf. also on the subject, however, statements made at the Special Session, 14 December 1967, as above; also Tenth Session 1971, Report, p. 13, paragraphs 23-25.
41. H. Nicolson, "The Old Diplomacy and the New", David Davies 1961 Memorial Lecture, p. 5.
42. All three instruments are "open to all States for signature", cf. Space Treaty, Article XIV, paragraph 1; Agreement on Rescue and Return, Article 7, paragraph 1; Convention on International Liability, Article XXIV, paragraph 1.
43. Cf., above, Chapter III, footnotes 7-16, also Chapters VIII and IX. Further draft Agreements remain on the agenda of the Legal Sub-Committee of the UN-CPUOS, in particular: the draft Convention concerning the Registration of Objects Launched into Space for the Exploration or Use of Outer Space, submitted by France; draft Agreement on the Principles Governing Activities in the Use of the Natural Resources of the Moon and other Celestial Bodies, and a draft Agreement on Activities Carried out through Remote-Sensing Satellite Surveys of Earth Resources–both by Argentina; a draft Treaty Concerning the Moon, by the USSR. There are also several other proposals and suggestions, such as those concerning implications of space communications, delimitation of outer space and definition of space activities.

Conclusions

The great venture, the probing of outer space and the reconnaissance of celestial bodies, will of course continue. The 35 missions already directed towards the moon in the years 1959-1971 will be succeeded by others. Now Mars has come under close scrutiny; orbital stations and laboratories, astronomical, geophysical and biological observatories in space are an immediate prospect; a grand tour of the planets by space-probes–from Jupiter, through Saturn and Uranus to Neptune–is planned for the years 1978-1979; so is a shuttle service, a new approach to space transportation and the launching of ever bigger loads, of giant objects of great weight. Thus man will not only make deeper forays into space but may soon begin to use this great storehouse of energy and resources. Though the effects of the exploration and use of outer space on man's terrestrial life have been slower to make themselves felt than many expected, man is in time bound to become space-oriented.[1]

As these ventures proceed it will be essential for the men of law to read each fresh page of scientific discovery, to wait upon the replies of science to many questions still unresolved, and to be constantly mindful of the changing needs in the field of law which may be attendant on new achievements.

Thus new pages of law will be added to those already written. The synthesis of law will grow. Even now, as the preceding account may have shown, the results are noteworthy. Imperfect as some of the new rules may be, they have the distinction of timeliness, evolving as they have in the immediate wake of scientific progress. And so they have succeeded in establishing the rule of law in the new dimension before any points of no return were reached. Indeed, some of the concepts and rules of the new chapter may be usefully applied to other environments.[2] Some represent an even wider contribution to international law as a whole.[3] The actual process of law-making for outer space may influence the writing of other chapters of international law.[4]

Within a wider perspective, the body of principles and rules here discussed is only one illustration of the response of law to the great strides of modern science. At the turn of the half-century, John Boyd Orr was able to declare: "In the last fifty years science has advanced more than in the two thousand previous years and given mankind greater power over the forces of nature than the ancients ascribed to their gods." In the twenty years that have elapsed since then the scientific explosion has continued with yet greater force. Its impact on society and on economic development is today profounder than ever before.[5] Indeed, it has produced far-reaching consequences in many areas of international relations. It holds out great prospects, but serious dangers have also begun to loom to the environment and to man himself. For science has not only laid bare many of nature's most jealously guarded secrets but has released enormous energies[6] which, if uncontrolled, could bring limitless disaster to our planet but, if tamed, could be turned to beneficent use on a scale hitherto unknown.

At the same time, we are inescapably faced with the menace that stems from uncontrolled industrial power and its insidious side-effects.[7] Because the environment is not adequately protected, rivers carry dead water; millions of tons of garbage, radioactive waste and oil pollute the seas; the air is increasingly poisoned; the world of nature becomes poorer, hundreds of species of birds and animals having been destroyed; marine life is in danger. All this causes men to ask "why, despite the marvels of science and its service to society, the heavens reek, the waters below are foul …".[8] The use of natural resources and man-made energies is inadequately controlled and there is, moreover, inadequate protection against the hazards of new experiments.

To prevent man from becoming a prisoner of the forces he himself has let loose, and eventually their victim, to arrest this process of decay and to canalize the uses of science in the interest and for the good of mankind: that is law's paramount task. But in many areas it has lagged behind.[9] The warnings of both jurists and scientists go unheeded.[10] Some chapters of international law remain unfinished, some require rewriting, the writing of others has not even begun. The gap is increasing.

Yet international law is not doomed to stay behind. For, while it is essential that it should build on the foundations already laid, it may not remain past-oriented, myopic or parochial. It can move in good time, if there is an organized effort on the part of States, commensurate–and integrated–with the progress they have achieved in another sphere: that of science and technology. A continuous dialogue between scientists and jurists would facilitate the reduction of the gap.[11]

Thus law would be able to respond by providing rules of conduct, restraint or prevention; and by measures to inhibit hazardous activities and to ensure, by means of co-operation, that the great riches of the universe are used with conscious moderation in the interest of all nations. In coming to grips with these problems it will be useful, as we have suggested, to draw upon the lessons of law-making for outer space–of its successes and even its imperfections–in both its substantive and its procedural aspects. The illustrative and cautionary value of that experience will prove considerable.

Notes to Conclusions

1. N. M. Sissakian, "On the Way to the Inhabited Space", 15 *Impact of Science on Society*, 1965, No. 3, p. 146. "I had hoped", said with disappointment N. Armstrong, the man who first set foot on the moon, "that the impact would be more far-reaching." *International Herald-Tribune*, 20 July 1970.
2. Cf. *inter alia* General Assembly resolution 2749 (XXV) of 17 December 1970, which solemnly declared: "1. The sea-bed and ocean floor, and the subsoil thereof, beyond the limits of national jurisdiction (hereinafter referred to as the area), as well as the resources of the area, are the common heritage of mankind; 2. The area shall not be subject to appropriation by any means by States or persons, natural or juridical, and no State shall claim or exercise sovereign rights over any part thereof". Cf. the earlier resolutions 2340 (XXII), 2467 (XXIII) and 2574 (XXIV), and also W. Friedman, *The Future of the Oceans*, New York 1971.
3. Cf. Quadri, *op. cit.*, pp. 515 f. "Le Traité de l'Espace," wrote J. L. Vencatassin, "ménageant un sage équilibre entre règles traditionelles et principes nouveaux, marque une étape importante dans l'évolution du Droit International positif et dans la philosophie des relations internationales contemporaines". *Op. cit.* p. 1.
4. "We as space lawyers can, I think, take some justifiable pride in contributing to the development of processes for the creation and formalization of principles and rules of international law": C. Q. Christol, "General Report on Activities and Action of the U.N. in the Space Legal Field", paper submitted to the 13th Colloquium on the Law of Outer Space, Constance 1970, pp. 11 f. For pertinent general comments on the subject cf. O. Schachter, "Scientific Advances and International Law", 55 *California Law Review*, No. 2, 1967, pp. 423 ff.
5. Cf. "The Role of Science and Technology in Economic Development", Report, Unesco, Paris 1968, in 8 *Science Policy Studies and Documents*, pp. 11-52; interesting comments by Lord Zuckerman, "Scientific Expectations", TLS Lectures, 1 *Times Literary Supplement*, No. 3, 635, 1971, p. 1; J. Szczepanski, "Problems of Enhancing the Influence of Science on the Development of Society", 8 *Problems of Science*, Vol. 2, Warsaw 1971, pp. 139 ff.; B. G. Kuznietsov, *Science in the Year 2000*, Moscow 1969.
6. How right was Frédéric Joliot-Curie in the prophecy he made on the occasion of receiving the Nobel prize in 1935, "Nous sommes en droit de penser que les chercheurs construisant ou brisant les éléments à volonté sauront réaliser des transmutations à caractère explosif, véritables réactions chimiques à la chaîne. Si de telles transmutations arrivent à se propager dans la matière, on peut concevoir l'énorme libération d'énergie utilisable qui aura lieu." Cf. B. Lovell and T. Margerison, "The Explosion of Science" in *The Physical Universe*, London 1967, p. 5; and a Study on the Main Trends of Inquiry in the Natural Sciences, Dissemination of Scientific Knowledge and Application of such Knowledge for Peaceful Ends prepared under the auspices of Unesco in cooperation with the United Nations and other international organizations on a recommendation of Ecosoc: UN doc. A/4461, 24 August 1960, and Unesco doc. NS/Es/19, 1 February 1960.
7. M. Nicolson, *The Environmental Revolution*, London 1970, also G. A. Taylor, *The Doomsday Book*, London 1970.

8. B. Commoner, in "Science Gone Mad", *The Sunday Times,* 17 July 1968.
9. One need only recall the 1912 *Titanic* disaster (referred to earlier) or the case of the *Torrey Canyon,* which went aground off the Isles of Scilly and spilled thousands of gallons of oil into the sea, thus seriously affecting the ecology of the region. Cf. also E. W. Patterson, *Law in a Scientific Age,* New York 1963, pp. 1 ff.
10. To mention only Maurice Bourquin: "Nous sommes en retard sur cette révolution. Partout elle nous a dépassés. Nos doctrines et nos méthodes, nos moeurs et nos institutions ont besoin d'être renouvelées pour nous permettre de résoudre les problèmes devant lesquels elle nous place" ("Le pouvoir scientifique et le droit international", 70 *R.C.A.D.I.,* 1947-I, p. 337). Eleven years later Linus Pauling claimed: "During the past hundred years there have been astounding developments in science and technology, developments that have completely changed the nature of the world in which we live. So far as I can see, the nature of diplomacy, of conduct of international affairs, has changed very little" (*No more Wars,* New York 1958, p. 194). Though this may contain some exaggeration, the point is well taken.
11. In the world of science, the gulf is disappearing at much greater speed. There is ever-deeper interpenetration between science as a whole and the social sciences, between "human" and natural sciences, including technology. As Louis Armand said, addressing the Académie des Sciences Morales: "Toutes les années, tous les mois qui passent rendent plus impérative la liaison entre ce qu'on est habitué à appeler sciences physiques, d'un côté, et sciences humaines, de l'autre" (*Le Monde,* 6 January 1965). After a long period of disintegration, all roads lead to unity.

Annexes

Annex I. Space Treaty

Treaty on Principles governing the Activities of States in the Exploration and Use of Outer Space, including the Moon and other Celestial Bodies

The States, Parties to this Treaty

Inspired by the great prospects opening up before mankind as a result of man's entry into outer space,

Recognizing the common interest of all mankind in the progress of the exploration and use of outer space for peaceful purposes,

Believing that the exploration and use of outer space should be carried on for the benefit of all peoples irrespective of the degree of their economic or scientific development,

Desiring to contribute to broad international co-operation in the scientific as well as the legal aspects of the exploration and use of outer space for peaceful purposes,

Believing that such co-operation will contribute to the development of mutual understanding and to the strengthening of friendly relations between States and peoples,

Recalling resolution 1962/XVIII, entitled "Declaration of Legal Principles Governing the Activities of States in the Exploration and Use of Outer Space", which was adopted unanimously by the United Nations General Assembly on 13th December, 1963,

Recalling resolution 1884/XVIII, calling upon States to refrain from placing in orbit around the Earth any objects carrying nuclear weapons or any other kinds of weapons of mass destruction or from installing such weapons on celestial bodies, which was adopted unanimously by the United Nations General Assembly on 17th October, 1963,

Taking account of United Nations General Assembly resolution 110/II of 3rd November, 1947, which condemned propaganda designed or likely to provoke or encourage any threat to the peace, breach of the peace or act of aggression, and considering that the aforementioned resolution is applicable to outer space,

Convinced that a Treaty on Principles Governing the Activities of States in the Exploration and Use of Outer Space, including the Moon and Other Celestial Bodies, will further the purposes and principles of the Charter of the United Nations–*Have agreed* on the following:

Article I

The exploration and use of outer space, including the Moon and other celestial bodies, shall be carried out for the benefit and in the interests of all countries, irrespective of their degree of economic or scientific development, and shall be the province of all mankind.

Outer space, including the Moon and other celestial bodies, shall be free for exploration and use by all States without discrimination of any kind, on a basis of equality and in accordance with international law, and there shall be free access to all areas of celestial bodies.

There shall be freedom of scientific investigation in outer space, including the Moon and other celestial bodies, and States shall facilitate and encourage international co-operation in such investigation.

Article II

Outer space, including the Moon and other celestial bodies, is not subject to national appropriation by claim of sovereignty, by means of use or occupation, or by any other means.

Article III

States, Parties to the Treaty, shall carry on activities in the exploration and use of outer space, including the Moon and other celestial bodies, in accordance with international law, including the Charter of the United Nations, in the interest of maintaining international peace and security and promoting international cooperation and understanding.

Article IV

States, Parties to the Treaty, undertake not to place in orbit around the Earth any objects carrying nuclear weapons or any other kinds of weapons of mass destruction, install such weapons on celestial bodies, or station such weapons in outer space in any other manner.

The Moon and other celestial bodies shall be used by all States, Parties to the Treaty, exclusively for peaceful purposes. The establishment of military bases, installations and fortifications, the testing of any type of weapons and the conduct of military manoeuvres on celestial bodies shall be forbidden. The use of military personnel for scientific research or for any other peaceful purposes shall not be prohibited. The use of any equipment or facility necessary for peaceful exploration of the Moon and other celestial bodies shall also not be prohibited.

Article V

States, Parties to the Treaty, shall regard astronauts as envoys of mankind in outer space and shall render to them all possible assistance in the event of accident, distress, or emergency landing on the territory of another State Party or on the high seas. When astronauts make such a landing, they shall be safely and promptly returned to the State of registry of their space vehicle.

In carrying on activities in outer space and on celestial bodies, the astronauts of one State Party shall render all possible assistance to the astronauts of other State Parties.

States, Parties to the Treaty, shall immediately inform the other States, Parties to the Treaty, or the Secretary-General of the United Nations of any phenomena they discover in outer space, including the Moon and other celestial bodies, which could constitute a danger to the life or health of astronauts.

Article VI

States, Parties to the Treaty, shall bear international responsibility for national activities in outer space, including the Moon and other celestial bodies, whether such activities are carried on by governmental agencies or by non-governmental entities, and for assuring that national activities are carried out in conformity with the provisions set forth in the present Treaty. The activities of non-governmental entities in outer space, including the Moon and other celestial bodies, shall require authorization and continuing supervision by the appropriate State, Party to the Treaty. When activities are carried on in outer space, including the Moon and other celestial bodies, by an international organization, responsibility for compliance with this Treaty shall be borne both by the international organization and by the States, Parties to the Treaty, participating in such organization.

Article VII

Each State, Party to the Treaty, that launches or procures the launching of an object into outer space, including the Moon and other celestial bodies, and each State Party from whose territory or facility an object is launched, is internationally liable for damage to another State, Party to the Treaty, or to its natural or juridical persons by such object or its component parts on the Earth, in air space or in outer space, including the Moon and other celestial bodies.

Article VIII

A State, Party to the Treaty, on whose registry an object launched into outer space is carried shall retain jurisdiction and control over such object, and over any personnel thereof, while in outer space or on a celestial body. Ownership of objects launched into outer space, including objects landed or constructed on a celestial body, and of their component parts, is not affected by their presence in outer space or on a celestial body or by their return to the Earth. Such objects or component parts found beyond the limits of the State, Party to the Treaty, on whose registry they are carried shall be returned to that State Party which shall, upon request, furnish identifying data prior to their return.

Article IX

In the exploration and use of outer space, including the Moon and other celestial bodies, States, Parties to the Treaty, shall be guided by the principle of co-operation and mutual assistance and shall conduct all their activities in outer space, including the Moon and other celestial bodies, with due regard to the corresponding interests of all other States, Parties to the Treaty. States, Parties to the Treaty, shall pursue studies of outer space, including the Moon and other celestial bodies, and conduct exploration of them so as to avoid their harmful contamination and also adverse changes in the environment of the Earth resulting from the introduction of extraterrestrial matter and, where necessary, shall adopt appropriate measures for this purpose. If a State, Party to the Treaty, has reason to believe that an activity or experiment planned by it or its nationals in outer space, including the Moon and other celestial bodies, would cause potentially harmful interference with activities of other State Parties in the peaceful exploration and use of outer space, including the Moon and other celestial bodies, it shall undertake appropriate international consultations before proceeding with any such activity or experiment. A State, Party to the Treaty, which has reason to believe that an activity or experiment planned by another State Party in outer space, including the Moon and other celestial bodies, would cause potentially harmful interference with activities in the peaceful exploration and use of outer space, including the Moon and other celestial bodies, may request consultation concerning the activity or experiment.

Article X

In order to promote international co-operation in the exploration and use of outer space, including the Moon and other celestial bodies, in conformity with the purposes of this Treaty, the States, Parties to the Treaty, shall consider on a basis of equality any requests by other States, Parties to the

Treaty, to be afforded an opportunity to observe the flight of space objects launched by those States.

The nature of such an opportunity for observation and the conditions under which it could be afforded shall be determined by agreement between the States concerned.

Article XI

In order to promote international co-operation in the peaceful exploration and use of outer space, States, Parties to the Treaty, conducting activities in outer space, including the Moon and other celestial bodies, agree to inform the Secretary-General of the United Nations as well as the public and the international scientific community to the greatest extent feasible and practicable, of the nature, conduct, locations and results of such activities. On receiving the said information, the Secretary-General of the United Nations should be prepared to disseminate it immediately and effectively.

Article XII

All stations, installations, equipment and space vehicles on the Moon and other celestial bodies shall be open to representatives of other States, Parties to the Treaty, on a basis of reciprocity. Such representatives shall give reasonable advance notice of a projected visit, in order that appropriate consultations may be held and that maximum precautions may be taken to assure safety and to avoid interference with normal operations in the facility to be visited.

Article XIII

The provisions of this Treaty shall apply to the activities of States, Parties to the Treaty, in the exploration and use of outer space, including the Moon and other celestial bodies, whether such activities are carried on by a single State, Party to the Treaty, or jointly with other States, including cases where they are carried on within the framework of international intergovernmental organizations.

Any practical questions arising in connexion with activities carried on by international intergovernmental organizations in the exploration and use of outer space, including the Moon and other celestial bodies, shall be resolved by the States, Parties to the Treaty, either with the appropriate international organization or with one or more States, members of that international organization, which are Parties to this Treaty.

Article XIV

1. This Treaty shall be open to all States for signature. Any State which does not sign this Treaty before its entry into force in accordance with paragraph 3 of this article may accede to it at any time.
2. This Treaty shall be subject to ratification by signatory States. Instruments of ratification and instruments of accession shall be deposited with the Governments of the Union of Soviet Socialist Republics, the United Kingdom of Great Britain and Northern Ireland, and the United States of America, which are hereby designated the Depositary Governments.
3. This Treaty shall enter into force upon the deposit of instruments of ratification by five Governments including the Governments designated as Depositary Governments under this Treaty.
4. For States whose instruments of ratification or accession are deposited subsequent to the entry into force of this Treaty, it shall enter into force on the date of the deposit of their instruments of ratification or accession.
5. The Depositary Governments shall promptly inform all signatory and acceding States of the date of each signature, the date of deposit of each instrument of ratification of and accession to this Treaty, the date of its entry into force and other notices.
6. This Treaty shall be registered by the Depositary Governments pursuant to Article 102 of the Charter of the United Nations.

Article XV

Any State, Party to the Treaty, may propose amendments to this Treaty. Amendments shall enter into force for each State, Party to the Treaty, accepting the amendments upon their acceptance by a majority of the States, Parties to the Treaty, and thereafter for each remaining State, Party to the Treaty, on the date of acceptance by it.

Article XVI

Any State, Party to the Treaty, may give notice of its withdrawal from the Treaty one year after its entry into force by written notification to the Depositary Governments. Such withdrawal shall take effect one year from the date of receipt of this notification.

Article XVII

This Treaty, of which the Chinese, English, French, Russian and Spanish texts are equally authentic, shall be deposited in the archives of the Depositary Governments. Duly certified copies of this Treaty shall be transmitted by the Depositary Governments to the Governments of the signatory and acceding States.

IN WITNESS WHEREOF the undersigned, duly authorized, have signed this Treaty.

Annex II. Rescue Agreement

Agreement on the Rescue of Astronauts, the Return of Astronauts and the Return of Objects Launched into Outer Space

The Contracting Parties,

Noting the great importance of the Treaty on Principles Governing the Activities of States in the Exploration and Use of Outer Space, including the Moon and Other Celestial Bodies, which calls for the rendering of all possible assistance to astronauts in the event of accident, distress or emergency landing, the prompt and safe return of astronauts, and the return of objects launched into outer space,

Desiring to develop and give further concrete expression to these duties,

Wishing to promote international co-operation in the peaceful exploration and use of outer space,

Prompted by sentiments of humanity,

Have agreed on the following:

Article 1

Each Contracting Party which receives information or discovers that the personnel of a spacecraft have suffered accident or are experiencing conditions of distress or have made an emergency or unintended landing in territory under its jurisdiction or on the high seas or in any other place not under the jurisdiction of any State shall immediately:

(*a*) notify the launching authority or, if it cannot identify and immediately communicate with the launching authority, immediately make a public announcement by all appropriate means of communication at its disposal;

(*b*) notify the Secretary-General of the United Nations, who should disseminate the information without delay by all appropriate means of communication at his disposal.

Article 2

If, owing to accident, distress, emergency or unintended landing, the personnel of a spacecraft land in territory under the jurisdiction of a Contracting Party, it shall immediately take all possible steps to rescue them and render them all necessary assistance. It shall inform the launching authority and also the Secretary-General of the United Nations of the steps it is taking and of their progress. If assistance by the launching authority would help to effect a prompt rescue or would contribute substantially to the effectiveness of search and rescue operations, the launching authority shall co-operate with the Contracting Party with a view to the effective conduct of search and rescue operations. Such operations shall be subject to the direction and control of the Contracting Party, which shall act in close and continuing consultation with the launching authority.

Article 3

If information is received or it is discovered that the personnel of a spacecraft have alighted on the high seas or in any other place not under the jurisdiction of any State, those Contracting Parties which are in a position to do so shall, if necessary, extend assistance in search and rescue operations for such personnel to assure their speedy rescue. They shall inform the launching authority and the Secretary-General of the United Nations of the steps they are taking and of their progress.

Article 4

If, owing to accident, distress, emergency or unintended landing, the personnel of a spacecraft land in territory under the jurisdiction of a Contracting Party or have been found on the high seas or in any other place not under the jurisdiction of any State, they shall be safely and promptly returned to representatives of the launching authority.

Article 5

1. Each Contracting Party which receives information or discovers that a space object or its component parts has returned to Earth in territory under its jurisdiction or on the high seas or in any other place not under the jurisdiction of any State, shall notify the launching authority and the Secretary-General of the United Nations.
2. Each Contracting Party having jurisdiction over the territory on which a space object or its component parts have been discovered shall, upon the request of the launching authority and with assistance from that authority if requested, take such steps as it finds practicable to recover the object or component parts.
3. Upon request of the launching authority, objects launched into outer space or their component parts found beyond the territorial limits of the launching authority shall be returned to or held at the disposal of representatives of the launching authority, which shall, upon request, furnish identifying data prior to their return.

4. Notwithstanding paragraphs 2 and 3 of this article, a Contracting Party which has reason to believe that a space object or its component parts discovered in territory under its jurisdiction, or recovered by it elsewhere, is of a hazardous or deleterious nature may so notify the launching authority, which shall immediately take effective steps, under the direction and control of the said Contracting Party, to eliminate possible danger of harm.
5. Expenses incurred in fulfilling obligations to recover and return a space object or its component parts under paragraphs 2 and 3 of this article shall be borne by the launching authority.

Article 6

For the purposes of this Agreement, the term "launching authority" shall refer to the State responsible for launching, or, where an international intergovernmental organization is responsible for launching, that organization, provided that that organization declares its acceptance of the rights and obligations provided for in this Agreement and a majority of the States, members of that organization, are Contracting Parties to this Agreement and to the Treaty on Principles Governing the Activities of States in the Exploration and Use of Outer Space, including the Moon and Other Celestial Bodies.

Article 7

1. This Agreement shall be open to all States for signature. Any State which does not sign this Agreement before its entry into force in accordance with paragraph 3 of this article may accede to it at any time.
2. This Agreement shall be subject to ratification by signatory States. Instruments of ratification and instruments of accession shall be deposited with the Governments of the Union of Soviet Socialist Republics, the United Kingdom of Great Britain and Northern Ireland, and the United States of America, which are hereby designated the Depositary Governments.
3. This Agreement shall enter into force upon the deposit of instruments of ratification by five Governments including the Governments designated as Depositary Governments under this Agreement.
4. For States whose instruments of ratification or accession are deposited subsequent to the entry into force of this Agreement, it shall enter into force on the date of the deposit of their instruments of ratification or accession.
5. The Depositary Governments shall promptly inform all signatory and acceding States of the date of each signature, the date of deposit of each

instrument of ratification of and accession to this Agreement, the date of its entry into force and other notices.

6. This Agreement shall be registered by the Depositary Governments pursuant to Article 102 of the Charter of the United Nations.

Article 8

Any State, Party to the Agreement, may propose amendments to this Agreement. Amendments shall enter into force for each State Party to the Agreement accepting the amendments upon their acceptance by a majority of the States, Parties to the Agreement, and thereafter for each remaining State, Party to the Agreement, on the date of acceptance by it.

Article 9

Any State, Party to the Agreement, may give notice of its withdrawal from the Agreement one year after its entry into force by written notification to the Depositary Governments. Such withdrawal shall take effect one year from the date of receipt of this notification.

Article 10

This Agreement, of which the Chinese, English, French, Russian and Spanish texts are equally authentic, shall be deposited in the archives of the Depositary Governments. Duly certified copies of this Agreement shall be transmitted by the Depositary Governments to the Governments of the signatory and acceding States.

IN WITNESS WHEREOF the undersigned, duly authorized, have signed this Agreement.

Annex III. Convention on International Liability for Damage Caused by Space Objects

The States Parties to this Convention

Recognizing the common interest of all mankind in furthering the exploration and use of outer space for peaceful purposes,

Recalling the Treaty on Principles Governing the Activities of States in the Exploration and Use of Outer Space, including the Moon and Other Celestial Bodies,

Taking into consideration that, notwithstanding the precautionary measures to be taken by States and international intergovernmental organizations involved in the launching of space objects, damage may on occasion be caused by such objects,

Recognizing the need to elaborate effective international rules and procedures concerning liability for damage caused by space objects and to ensure, in particular, the prompt payment under the terms of this Convention of a full and equitable measure of compensation to victims of such damage,

Believing that the establishment of such rules and procedures will contribute to the strengthening of international co-operation in the field of the exploration and use of outer space for peaceful purposes,

Have agreed on the following:

Article I

For the purposes of this Convention:

(*a*) the term "damage" means loss of life, personal injury or other impairment of health; or loss of or damage to property of States or of persons, natural or juridical, or property of international intergovernmental organizations;

(*b*) the term "launching" includes attempted launching;

(*c*) the term "launching State" means:

- (1) a State which launches or procures the launching of a space object;
- (2) a State from whose territory or facility a space object is launched;

(*d*) the term "space object" includes component parts of a space object as well as its launch vehicle and parts thereof.

Article II

A launching State shall be absolutely liable to pay compensation for damage caused by its space object on the surface of the earth or to aircraft in flight.

Article III

In the event of damage being caused elsewhere than on the surface of the earth to a space object of one launching State or to persons or property on board such a space object by a space object of another launching State, the latter shall be liable only if the damage is due to its fault or the fault of persons for whom it is responsible.

Article IV

1. In the event of damage being caused elsewhere than on the surface of the earth to a space object of one launching State or to persons or property on board such a space object by a space object of another launching State, and of damage thereby being caused to a third State or to its natural or juridical persons, the first two States shall be jointly and severally liable to the third State, to the extent indicated by the following:
   (*a*) if the damage has been caused to the third State on the surface of the earth or to aircraft in flight, their liability to the third State shall be absolute;
   (*b*) if the damage has been caused to a space object of the third State or to persons or property on board that space object elsewhere than on the surface of the earth, their liability to the third State shall be based on the fault of either of the first two States or on the fault of persons for whom either is responsible.
2. In all cases of joint and several liability referred to in paragraph 1, the burden of compensation for the damage shall be apportioned between the first two States in accordance with the extent to which they were at fault; if the extent of the fault of each of these States cannot be established, the burden of compensation shall be apportioned equally between them. Such apportionment shall be without prejudice to the right of the third State to seek the entire compensation due under this Convention from any or all of the launching States which are jointly and severally liable.

Article V

1. Whenever two or more States jointly launch a space object, they shall be jointly and severally liable for any damage caused.

2. A launching State which has paid compensation for damage shall have the right to present a claim for indemnification to other participants in the joint launching. The participants in a joint launching may conclude agreements regarding the apportioning among themselves of the financial obligation in respect of which they are jointly and severally liable. Such agreements shall be without prejudice to the right of a State sustaining damage to seek the entire compensation due under this Convention from any or all of the launching States which are jointly and severally liable.
3. A State from whose territory or facility a space object is launched shall be regarded as a participant in a joint launching.

Article VI

1. Subject to the provisions of paragraph 2, exoneration from absolute liability shall be granted to the extent that a launching State establishes that the damage has resulted either wholly or partially from gross negligence or from an act or omission done with intent to cause damage on the part of a claimant State or of natural or juridical persons it represents.
2. No exoneration whatever shall be granted in cases where the damage has resulted from activities conducted by a launching State which are not in conformity with international law including, in particular, the Charter of the United Nations and the Treaty on Principles Governing the Activities of States in the Exploration and Use of Outer Space, including the Moon and Other Celestial Bodies.

Article VII

The provisions of this Convention shall not apply to damage caused by a space object of a launching State to:
(*a*) nationals of that launching State;
(*b*) foreign nationals during such time as they are participating in the operation of that space object from the time of its launching or at any stage thereafter until its descent, or during such time as they are in the immediate vicinity of a planned launching or recovery area as the result of an invitation by that launching State.

Article VIII

1. A State which suffers damage, or whose natural or juridical persons suffer damage, may present to a launching State a claim for compensation for such damage.

2. If the State of nationality has not presented a claim, another State may, in respect of damage sustained in its territory by any natural or juridical person, present a claim to a launching State.
3. If neither the State of nationality nor the State in whose territory the damage was sustained has presented a claim or notified its intention of presenting a claim, another State may, in respect of damage sustained by its permanent residents, present a claim to a launching State.

Article IX

A claim for compensation for damage shall be presented to a launching State through diplomatic channels. If a State does not maintain diplomatic relations with the launching State concerned, it may request another State to present its claim to that launching State or otherwise represent its interests under this Convention. It may also present its claim through the Secretary-General of the United Nations, provided the claimant State and the launching State are both Members of the United Nations.

Article X

1. A claim for compensation for damage may be presented to a launching State not later than one year following the date of the occurrence of the damage or the identification of the launching State which is liable.
2. If, however, a State does not know of the occurrence of the damage or has not been able to identify the launching State which is liable, it may present a claim within one year following the date on which it learned of the aforementioned facts; however, this period shall in no event exceed one year following the date on which the State could reasonably be expected to have learned of the facts through the exercise of due diligence.
3. The time-limits specified in paragraphs 1 and 2 shall apply even if the full extent of the damage may not be known. In this event, however, the claimant State shall be entitled to revise the claim and submit additional documentation after the expiration of such time-limits until one year after the full extent of the damage is known.

Article XI

1. Presentation of a claim to a launching State for compensation for damage under this Convention shall not require the prior exhaustion of any local remedies which may be available to a claimant State or to natural or juridical persons it represents.
2. Nothing in this Convention shall prevent a State, or natural or juridical persons it might represent, from pursuing a claim in the courts or

administrative tribunals or agencies of a launching State. A State shall not, however, be entitled to present a claim under this Convention in respect of the same damage for which a claim is being pursued in the courts or administrative tribunals or agencies of a launching State or under another international agreement which is binding on the States concerned.

Article XII

The compensation which the launching State shall be liable to pay for damage under this Convention shall be determined in accordance with international law, and the principles of justice and equity, in order to provide such reparation in respect of the damage as will restore the person, natural or juridical, State or international organization on whose behalf the claim is presented to the condition which would have existed if the damage had not occurred.

Article XIII

Unless the claimant State and the State from which compensation is due under this Convention agree on another form of compensation, the compensation shall be paid in the currency of the claimant State or, if that State so requests, in the currency of the State from which compensation is due.

Article XIV

If no settlement of a claim is arrived at through diplomatic negotiations as provided for in Article IX, within one year from the date on which the claimant State notifies the launching State that it has submitted the documentation of its claim, the parties concerned shall establish a Claims Commission at the request of either party.

Article XV

1. The Claims Commission shall be composed of three members: one appointed by the claimant State, one appointed by the launching State and the third member, the Chairman, to be chosen by both parties jointly. Each party shall make its appointment within two months of the request for the establishment of the Claims Commission.
2. If no agreement is reached on the choice of the Chairman within four months of the request for the establishment of the Claims Commission, either party may request the Secretary-General of the United Nations to appoint the Chairman within a further period of two months.

Article XVI

1. If one of the parties does not make its appointment within the stipulated period, the Chairman shall, at the request of the other party, constitute a single-member Claims Commission.
2. Any vacancy which may arise in the Claims Commission for whatever reason shall be filled by the same procedure adopted for the original appointment.
3. The Claims Commission shall determine its own procedure.
4. The Claims Commission shall determine the place or places where it shall sit and all other administrative matters.
5. Except in the case of decisions and awards by a single-member Commission, all decisions and awards of the Claims Commission shall be by majority vote.

Article XVII

No increase in the membership of the Claims Commission shall take place by reason of two or more claimant States or launching States being joined in any one proceeding before the Commission. The claimant States so joined shall collectively appoint one member of the Commission in the same manner and subject to the same conditions as would be the case for a single claimant State. When two or more launching States are so joined, they shall collectively appoint one member of the Commission in the same way. If the claimant States or the launching States do not make the appointment within the stipulated period, the Chairman shall constitute a single-member Commission.

Article XVIII

The Claims Commission shall decide the merits of the claim for compensation and determine the amount of compensation payable, if any.

Article XIX

1. The Commission shall act in accordance with the provisions of Article XII.
2. The decision of the Commission shall be final and binding if the parties have so agreed; otherwise the Commission shall render a final and recommendatory award, which the parties shall consider in good faith. The Commission shall state the reasons for its decision or award.
3. The Commission shall give its decision or award as promptly as possible and no later than one year from the date of its establishment unless an extension of this period is found necessary by the Commission.

4. The Commission shall make its decision or award public. It shall deliver a certified copy of its decision or award to each of the parties and to the Secretary-General of the United Nations.

Article XX

The expenses in regard to the Claims Commission shall be borne equally by the parties, unless otherwise decided by the Commission.

Article XXI

If the damage caused by a space object presents a large-scale danger to human life or seriously interferes with the living conditions of the population or the functioning of vital centres, the States Parties, and in particular the launching State, shall examine the possibility of rendering appropriate and rapid assistance to the State which has suffered the damage, when it so requests. However, nothing in this Article shall affect the rights or obligations of the States Parties under this Convention.

Article XXII

1. In this Convention, with the exception of Articles 24 to 27, references to States shall be deemed to apply to any international intergovernmental organization which conducts space activities if the organization declares its acceptance of the rights and obligations provided for in this Convention and if a majority of the States members of the organization are States Parties to this Convention and to the Treaty on Principles Governing the Activities of States in the Exploration and Use of Outer Space, including the Moon and Other Celestial Bodies.
2. States members of any such organization which are States Parties to this Convention shall take all appropriate steps to ensure that the organization makes a declaration in accordance with the preceding paragraph.
3. If an international intergovernmental organization is liable for damage by virtue of the provisions of this Convention, that organization and those of its members which are States Parties to this Convention shall be jointly and severally liable; provided, however, that:
    (*a*) any claim for compensation in respect of such damage shall be first presented to the organization; and
    (*b*) only where the organization has not paid, within a period of six months, any sum agreed or determined to be due as compensation for such damage, may the claimant State invoke the liability of the members which are States Parties to this Convention for the payment of that sum.

4. Any claim, pursuant to the provisions of this Convention, for compensation in respect of damage caused to an organization which has made a declaration in accordance with paragraph 1 of this Article shall be presented by a State member of the organization which is a State Party to this Convention.

Article XXIII

1. The provisions of this Convention shall not affect other international agreements in force in so far as relations between the States parties to such agreements are concerned.
2. No provision of this Convention shall prevent States from concluding international agreements reaffirming, supplementing or extending its provisions.

Article XXIV

1. This Convention shall be open to all States for signature. Any State which does not sign this Convention before its entry into force in accordance with paragraph 3 of this Article may accede to it at any time.
2. This Convention shall be subject to ratification by signatory States. Instruments of ratification and instruments of accession shall be deposited with the Governments of the United Kingdom of Great Britain and Northern Ireland, the Union of Soviet Socialist Republics and the United States of America, which are hereby designated the Depositary Governments.
3. This Convention shall enter into force on the deposit of the fifth instrument of ratification.
4. For States whose instruments of ratification or accession are deposited subsequent to the entry into force of this Convention, it shall enter into force on the date of the deposit of their instruments of ratification or accession.
5. The Depositary Governments shall promptly inform all signatory and acceding States of the date of each signature, the date of deposit of each instrument of ratification of and accession to this Convention, the date of its entry into force and other notices.
6. This Convention shall be registered by the Depositary Governments pursuant to Article 102 of the Charter of the United Nations.

Article XXV

Any State Party to this Convention may propose amendments to this Convention. Amendments shall enter into force for each State Party to the Convention accepting the amendments upon their acceptance by a majority of the States Parties to the Convention and thereafter for each remaining State Party to the Convention on the date of acceptance by it.

Article XXVI

Ten years after the entry into force of this Convention, the question of the review of this Convention shall be included in the provisional agenda of the United Nations General Assembly in order to consider, in the light of past application of the Convention, whether it requires revision. However, at any time after the Convention has been in force for five years, and at the request of one-third of the States Parties to the Convention, and with the concurrence of the majority of the States Parties, a conference of the States Parties shall be convened to review this Convention.

Article XXVII

Any State Party to this Convention may give notice of its withdrawal from the Convention one year after its entry into force by written notification to the Depositary Governments. Such withdrawal shall take effect one year from the date of receipt of this notification.

Article XXVIII

This Convention, of which the English, Russian, French, Spanish and Chinese texts are equally authentic, shall be deposited in the archives of the Depositary Governments. Duly certified copies of this Convention shall be transmitted by the Depositary Governments to the Governments of the signatory and acceding States.

IN WITNESS WHEREOF the undersigned, duly authorized, have signed this Convention.

Selected Bibliography

Abraham (H.J.), Das Recht der Luftfahrt. Köln-Berlin, 1960. 2 vols.

Adams (T.R.), Outer Space Treaty: An Interpretation in Light of the No-Sovereignty Provision. 9 Harvard International Law Journal, 1968, pp. 140 ff.

Ago (R.), La codification du droit international et les problèmes de sa réalisation. Mélanges Guggenheim 1968, p. 93 ff.

– Reports on State Responsibility, International Law Commission Doc. A/CN.4/217 (1969), Doc. A/CN.4/233 (1970), Doc. A/CN.4/246 (1971).

Baker (A.S.), Military Implications of Space, I.C.L.Q. Special Publication, No. 9, 1966, pp. 73 ff.

Baskin (I. and A.), International Legal Aspects of Artificial Interference with the Weather (in Russian). 1968 Pravovedenie, No. 1, pp. 103 ff.

Bastid (S.), Observations sur une étape dans le développement progressif et la codification du droit international. Mélanges Guggenheim, Genève, 1968, p. 139 ff.

Beresford (A.M.), Surveillance Aircraft and Satellites: A Problem of International Law. 27 Journal of Air Law and Commerce, 1960, pp. 106 ff.

Berezowski (C.), Rules of Liability for Injury or Loss Caused by the Operation of Space Vehicles. Report of the 50th ILA Conference, Bruxelles, 1962.

– Miedzynarodwe Prawo Lotnicze (International Air Law), Warsaw, 1964.

Bhat (S.), Legal Controls of Explorations and Use of the Moon and Celestial Bodies. 8 Indian Journal of International Law, 1968, pp. 33 ff.

Bierzanek (R.), La nature juridique de la haute mer, 1961 R.G.D.I.P., p. 233 ff.

Bloomfield (L.P.) Ed., Outer Space: Prospects for Man and Society. The American Assembly. Columbia University, 1962.

– Outer Space and International Cooperation. 18 International Organization, 1965, pp. 603 ff.

Bodenschatz (M.), Vorschläge zu einem internationalen Haftungsabkommen betreffend Schäden, verursacht durch Raumfahrzeuge, insbesondere im Hinblick auf die Tätigkeit privater Halter, 14 Zeitschrift f. Luftrecht und Weltraumrechtsfragen, 1965, pp. 312 ff.

Bourély (M.G.), Les organisations de l'espace. Juris-Classeur de droit international, Fascicule 195.

– Fondements juridiques de la coopération internationale dans l'espace. 93 Journal du droit international, 1966, p. 601 ff.

– Europe à la recherche d'une politique spatiale. 24 Revue française de droit aérien. 1970, p. 13 ff.

Bourquin (M.), Règles générales du droit de la paix. 35 R.C.A.D.I., 1931: I, p. 102 ff.

– Pouvoir scientifique et droit international. 70 R.C.A.D.I., 1947: I, p. 331 ff.

Brennan (D.F.), Arms and Arms Control in Outer Space, in Bloomfield (Ed.), Outer Space: Prospects for Man and Society. The American Assembly. Columbia University, 1962.

Brierly (J.L.), The Law of Nations. 6th edition. Oxford, 1963.

Brooks (E.), National Control of Natural Planetary Bodies: Preliminary Considerations, 32 Journal of Air Law and Commerce, 1966, pp. 315 ff.

– Legal Aspects of the Lunar Landings. 4 International Lawyer, April 1970, pp. 415 ff.

Brownlie (I.), The Maintenance of International Peace and Security in Outer Space. B.Y.I.L., 1964, pp. 1 ff.

– Principles of Public International Law. Oxford, 1966.

Bueckling (A.), Weltraumrecht und internationale Gerichtsbarkeit. 18 Juristenzeitung, 1963, pp. 300 ff.

– Friedliche Benutzung des Weltraums. 15 Zeitschrift f. Luftrecht und Weltraumrechtsfragen, 1966, pp. 237 ff.

– Weltraumvertrag und nationale Folgegesetzgebung. 17 Zeitschrift f. Luftrecht und Weltraumrechtsfragen, 1968, pp. 225 ff.

Bustamante y Sirven (A.S.), La mer territoriale. Paris, 1930.

Carlson (J.), Liability in International Law for Damage Caused by Space Vehicles. 15 Indian Yearbook of International Affairs, 1966-1967, pp. 227 ff.

Castañeda (J.), Legal Effects of United Nations Resolutions. New York, 1969.

Chandrasekharan (M.), Gemini Space Program and the Manned Orbiting Laboratory in Space–An Appraisal. 5 Indian Journal of International Law, 1955, pp. 334 ff.

– Space Treaty. 7 Indian Journal of International Law, 1967, pp. 61 ff.

Chaumont (Ch.), Le droit de l'espace. Paris, 1960.

– La résolution de Bruxelles de l'Institut de droit international sur le droit de l'espace, 1 Revue belge de droit international, 1965, p. 15 ff.

– L'orientation actuelle du droit de l'espace. 28 Revue générale de l'Air, 1965, p. 7 ff.

– Observations sur le régime international des satellites de télécommunications. 29 Revue générale de l'Air et de l'Espace, 1966, p. 86 ff.

Cheng (B.), From the Air Law to Space Law. 13 Current Legal Problems, 1960, pp. 228 ff.

– The United Nations and Outer Space. 14 Current Legal Problems, 1961, pp. 247 ff.

– The Extra Terrestrial Application of International Law. 18 Current Legal Problems, 1965, pp. 132 ff.

– United Nations Resolutions on Outer Space: An "Instant" International Customary Law? 5 Indian Journal of International Law, 1965, pp. 23 ff.

– Le Traité de 1967 sur l'espace. 95 Journal du droit international, 1968, pp. 532 ff.

– Communications Satellites. 24 Current Legal Problems, 1971, pp. 211 ff.

Christol (C.Q.), The International Law of Outer Space. International Law Studies 1962, Naval War College. Washington, 1966.

– Space Stations: A Lawyer's Point of View. 4 Indian Journal of International Law, 1964, pp. 488 ff.

– General Report on Activities and Action of the United Nations in the Space Legal Field. Paper submitted to the 13th Colloquium on the Law of Outer Space, Konstanz, 1970.

Cocca (A.A.), Refecciones sobre el derecho interplanetario. 28 Revista Nacional de Aeronautica, Buenos Aires, 1958, pp. 195 ff.

– Basic Statute for the Moon and Heavenly Bodies. 2 Revista di Diritto Aereo, 1963, pp. 141 ff.
– Benefits of World Exchanges, in "Communication in Space Age" Published by UNESCO. Amsterdam, 1968.
– Preliminary Report of the Special Working Group on Telecommunications by Satellites, Submitted at XI Colloquium of the I.I.S.L., New York, 1968.
Cohn (G.), La Théorie de la responsabilité internationale. 68 R.C.A.D.I., 1939: II, pp. 208 ff.
Cooper (J.C.), High Altitude Flights and National Sovereignty. 4 I.L.Q., 1951, pp. 411 ff.
– Roman Law and the Maxim "cujus est solum" in international law. 1 McGill Law Journal, 1952, pp. 23 ff.
– Legal Problems of Upper Space. 1956 Proceedings of the A.S.I.L., pp. 85 ff.
– The Rule of Law in Outer Space. 47 Am. Bar Association Journal, 1961, pp. 23 ff.
– Aerospace Law, Subject Matter and Terminology. 29 Journal of Air Law and Commerce, 1963, pp. 89 ff.
– Laboratoire habité sur l'orbite. Décision juridique et politique de première importance. 20 Revue française de Droit aérien, 1966, p. 269 ff.
– A qui appartiendra la lune? Nécessité d'une réponse. 20 Revue française de Droit aérien, 1966, p. 169 ff.
– Explorations in Aerospace Law. Montreal, 1968.
Craig (D.), National Sovereignty at High Altitudes. 24 Journal of Air Law and Commerce, 1957, pp. 387 ff.
Crane (R.D.), Law and Strategy in Space. 6 Orbis (University of Pennsylvania), 1966, pp. 282 ff.
Creola (P.), Raumfahrt und Völkerrecht. Zürich, 1967.
Csabafi (J.), and S. Rani, Law of Celestial Bodies. 6 Indian Journal of International Law, 1966, pp. 195 ff.

Dahm (G.), Völkerrecht. Stuttgart, 1958.
Danier (E.), Les voyages interplanétaires et le droit. 15 Revue générale de l'Air, 1952, p. 423 ff.
Danier (E.), et M. Saporta, Les Satellites artificiels. 18 Revue générale de l'Air, 1955, p. 297 ff.
Darwin (H.G.), The Outer Space Treaty, 42 B.Y.I.L., 1967, pp. 278 ff.
Deleau (O.), Responsabilité pour dommages causés par les objets lancés dans l'espace extra-atmosphérique. 14 A.Fr.D.I., 1968, pp. 747 ff.
Dembling (P.G.), Liability Treaty for Outer Space Activities. 19 American Law Review, December 1969, pp. 33 ff.
Dembling (P.G.) and D.M. Arons, The Treaty on Rescue and Return of Astronauts and Space Objects. 9 William and Mary Law Review, Spring 1969, pp. 650 ff.
David Davies Memorial Institute of International Studies; Draft Code of Rules on the Exploration and Uses of Outer Space, London, 1963.
– Draft Treaty on Outer Space, the Moon and Other Celestial Bodies, London, 1966.
Dutheil de la Rochère (J.), La Convention sur l'internationalisation de l'espace. 13 A.Fr.D.L, 1967, p. 607 ff.

Fasan (E.L.), Law and Peace for celestial bodies. Proceedings of the 5th Colloquium of the IISL, Varna, 1962, pp. 8 ff.

– Weltraumrecht. Mainz, 1965.

Fauchille (F.), Le domaine aérien et le régime juridique des aérostats, Paris, 1901.

Fawcett (J.E.S.), Outer Space and International Order. David Davies 1964 Memorial Lecture.

– International Law and the Uses of Outer Space. London, 1968.

– The Politics of the Moon. 25 The World To-day, 1969, pp. 359 ff.

Feldman (G.J.), An American View of Jurisdiction in Outer Space. Proceedings of the 1st Colloquium of the IISL, The Hague, 1958, pp. 47 ff.

– International Arrangements for Satellites Communications, in Cohen (Ed.), Law and Politics in Space, Montreal, 1964, pp. 23 ff.

Fenwick (G.G.), How High is the Sky. 52 A.J.I.L., 1958, pp. 96 ff.

Ferreira (E.A.), Statut des corps célestes. Commentaire des résolutions et textes approuvés par l'Assemblée Générale des N.U. 23 Revue française de Droit aérien, 1968, p. 369 ff.

Fitzgerald (G.F.), Participation of International Organizations in the Proposed International Agreement on Liability for Damage Caused by Objects Launched into Outer Space. 3 Canadian Yearbook of International Law, 1965, pp. 265 ff.

François (J.P.A.), Réflexions sur l'occupation. En Hommage à Paul Guggenheim, Genève, 1968, p. 795 ff.

Franke (H.), Zur Anwendbarkeit des Völkerrechts auf die Raumfahrt. 19 Zeitschrift f. Luftrecht und Weltraumrechtsfragen, 1970, pp. 34 ff.

Gal (G.), Space Law, Budapest, 1969.

Galina (A.), K voprosu o mezhplanetnom prave (On the Question of Interplanetary Law), 1958 Sovetskoe Gosudarstvo i Pravo, No. 7, pp. 52 ff.

– Mezhdunarodnye pravovye voprosy osvoeniya kosmicheskogo prostranstva (International Legal Problems on the Exploration of Space) 2 Sovetskii Ezhogodnik Mezhdunarodnogo Prava, 1959, pp. 51 ff.

Gardner (R.), Co-operation in Outer Space. 41 Foreign Affairs, 1963, No. 3, pp. 18 ff.

– Outer Space: A Breakthrough for International Law. 50 American Bar Association Journal 1964, pp. 32 ff.

Ghelmegeanu (M.), et A. Bolintineanu, Contribution au problème des principes juridiques réglementant l'activité des Etats dans l'utilisation de l'espace cosmique. 8 Revue Roumaine des sciences sociales, Série des sciences juridiques, 1964, No. 2, p. 223 ff.

Gidel (G.), Explosions nucléaires expérimentales et liberté de la Haute Mer. Mélanges Spiropoulos, Bonn, 1957, p. 173 ff.

Giraud (E.), La notion d'espace dans les relations internationales. 19 Z.f.A.O.R.V.R., 1958, p. 109 ff.

Glaser (J.H.), Infelix ITU: The need for space age revision to the International Telecommunications Convention. 23 Federal Bar Journal, 1963, pp. 23 ff.

Goedhuis (D.), General questions of the Legal Regime of Space. Report of the 50th ILA Conference, 1962, pp. 70 ff.

– Delimitation of Air Space from Outer Space. Report of the 52nd ILA Conference, 1966, pp. 191 ff.

– Conflict of Laws and Divergencies in the Legal Regime of Air Space and Outer Space. 109 R.C.A.D.I., 1963: II, pp. 263 ff.

– Reflections on the Evolution of Space Law, 12 Netherlands International Law Review, 1968, pp. 109 ff.

– An Evaluation of the Leading Principles of the Treaty on Outer Space of 27 January 1967. 15 Netherlands International Law Review, 1968, pp. 17 ff.

Gold (M.E.), Direct Broadcast Satellites: implications for less developed countries and for world order. 12 Virginia Journal of International Law, December 1971, pp. 66 ff.

Goldie (L.F.E.), Liability for Damage and Progressive Development of International Law. 14 I.C.L.Q., 1965, pp. 1189 ff.

Golovin (M.N.), Conflict in Space. London, 1962.

Gorove (S.), Legal Problems of the Rescue and Return of Astronauts. 3 International Lawyer, July 1969, pp. 898 ff.

– Interpreting Art. II of Outer Space Treaty. 37 Fordham Law Review, March 1969, pp. 349 ff.

– The Recovery and Return of Objects Launched into Outer Space. 4 International Lawyer, July 1970, pp. 682 ff.

Gottlieb (A.E.), Nuclear Weapons in Outer Space. 3 Canadian Yearbook of International Law, 1965, pp. 3 ff.

Green (N.M.), Pirate Radio Stations. 35 Annuaire de 1'AAA, 1965, pp. 133 ff.

Haley (A.G.), Law of Outer Space–a problem for international agreements, 7 The American University Law Review, 1958, pp. 71 ff.

– Space Law and Government. New York, 1963.

Hall (R.C.), Rescue and Return of Astronauts on Earth and in Outer Space, 63 A.J.I.L. 1969, pp. 197 ff.

Hannover (Wolf Heinrich Prinz, von), Luftrecht und Weltraum, Hannover, 1953.

Hingorani (R.C.), La souveraineté sur l'espace extra-atmosphérique, 20 Revue générale de l'Air, 1957, p. 248 ff.

Hosni (O.), Treaty Governing the Exploration of Outer Space, the Moon and Other Celestial Bodies, 25 Revue égyptienne de droit international, 1969, p. 29 ff.

Houben (P.H.), A New Chapter of Space Law, The Agreement on the Rescue and Return of Astronauts and Space Objects. 15 Netherlands International Law Review, 1968, pp. 127 ff.

International Law of Communications. Ed. by E. McWhinney, Leiden, 1971.

Jacob (N.H.), Droit interplanétaire. 15 Revue générale de l'Air, 1952, pp. 287 ff.

Jacobson (H.K.), International Institutions for Telecommunications: the ITU's Role, in "International Law of Communications". Edited by E. McWhinney, Leiden, 1971, pp. 51 ff.

Janovskii (M.V.), Rol OON v Formirovanii Norm Kosmicheskogo Prava (The Role of the U.N. in the formulation of space law). 1969 Sovetskoe Gosudarstvo i Pravo, No. 1, pp. 65 ff.

Jasentuliyana (N.), Regulatory Functions of ITU in the Field of Space Telecommunications. 34 Journal of Air Law and Commerce, 1968, pp. 62 ff.

Jenks (C.W.), International Law and Activities in Space. 5 I.C.L.Q., 1956, pp. 99 ff.

– Le droit international des espaces célestes. 1963 Annuaire de l'Institut de droit international, v. 50: I, pp. 128 ff.; II, pp. 60 ff.

– Space Law. London, 1965.

– Liability for Ultra-Hazardous Activities in International Law, 121 R.C.A.D.I., 1966: I, pp. 105 ff.

– Evolution of Space Law Continues. Mélanges Andrassy, The Hague, 1968, pp. 135 ff.

Jessup (Ph. C.), and Taubenfeld (H.G.), Controls for Outer Space and the Antarctic Analogy. New York, 1959.

Jiménez de Aréchaga (E.), International Responsibility, in "Manual of International Law", Edited by M. Sørensen. London, 1968, pp. 531 ff.

Johnson (J.A.), Law and Space Telecommunications, 2 Lawyer of the Americas, Fall 1970, pp. 2 ff.

Kiss (A.C.), Accord sur le retour et le sauvetage des astronautes et la restitution des objets lancés dans l'espace extra-atmosphérique. 14 A.Fr.D.I., 1968, pp. 736 ff.

– Le régime juridique applicable aux matériaux provenant de la Lune et des autres corps célestes. 16 A.Fr.D.I., 1970, pp. 767 ff.

Kopal (V.), Treaty on Principles Governing the Activities of States in the Exploration and Use of Outer Space, including the Moon and Other Celestial Bodies. 1961 Yearbook of Air and Space Law, pp. 463 ff.

Korovine (E.), La conquête de la stratosphère et le droit international. 1934 R.G.D.I.P., pp. 675 ff.

– International Status of Cosmic Space. Proceedings of the 4th Colloquium of the IISL, New York, 1961, pp. 1063 ff.

Kosmos i Mezhdunarodnoe Pravo (Outer Space and International Law). Ed. by E.A. Korovine, Moscow, 1962, pp. 5 ff.

Kosmos i Mezhdunarodnoe Sotrudnichestvo. (Outer Space and International Cooperation). Moscow, 1963.

Kovalev (F.N.) and Cheproy (I.J.), Na puti k kosmicheskomu pravu. (On the road towards a Space Law), Moscow, 1962.

Kroell (J.), Eléments créateurs d'un droit astronautique. 16 Revue Générale de l'Air, 1953, p. 22 ff.

Kuznetsov (B.G.), Nauka w 2000 godu (Science in the Year 2000) Moscow, 1969.

Lachs (M.), Le problème de la révision de la Charte des Nations Unies, 1957 R.G.D.I.P., p. 55 ff.

– Les développements et fonctions des traités multilatéraux. 92 R.C.A.D.I., 1957: II, p. 229 ff.

– La nouvelle fonction des armistices contemporains. Hommage au Président Basdevant, Paris, 1960, p. 315 ff.

– The International Law of Outer Space. 113 R.C.A.D.I., 1964: III, pp. 1 ff.

– Outer Space Treaty and Its Impact on International Law. 37/38 Annuaire de l'A.A.A., 1967/1968, pp. 186 ff.

– Statut juridique de l'espace extra-atmosphérique et des corps célestes. Mélanges T. Ionasco, 12 Revue Roumaine des Sciences Sociales, 1968, No. 1-2, p. 241 ff.

– The Law-making Process for Outer Space, in "New Frontiers in Space Law", Ed. E. McWhinney and M.A. Bradley, Leiden, 1969, pp. 13 ff.

– La contribución de las Naciones Unidas al desarollo del derecho internacional. XI Foro Internacional, Mexico City, No. 2, pp. 339 ff.

– Some Reflections on the Question of substance and form in International Law, 11 Columbia Journal of Transnational Law, Spring 1972.

Larsen (P.B.), A sample of Space Law Opinion, 27 Ohio State Law Journal, 1966, No. 3, pp. 468 ff.

Latchford (S.), The Bearing of International Navigation Conventions on the Use of Outer Space. 53 A.J.I.L., 1959, pp. 405 ff.

Lauterpacht (E.), Freedom of Transit in International Law. 44 Transactions of the Grotius Society, 1957, pp. 313 ff.

Law and Politics in Space. Edited by M. Cohen. Montreal, 1964.

Lay (S.H.) and Poole (R.E.), Exclusive Governmental Liability for Space Accidents. 53 American Bar Association Journal 1967, pp. 831 ff.

Lay (S.H.), and Taubenfeld (H.J.), Liabilities and Space Activities: Causes, Objectives and Parties. 6 Virginia Journal of International Law, Vol. 6, 1966, pp. 252 ff.

Levitt (M.T.), Space Age Question: Who Owns a Fallen Satellite? Army-Navy-Air Force Register. The U.S. Military Review, 1959, No. 4102-4103.

Lipson (L.) and Katzenbach (N. de B.) The Law of Outer Space, Report to the National Aeronautics and Space Administration, 1960, in Legal Problems of Space Exploration, A Symposium, prepared for the Committee on Aeronautical and Space Sciences, U.S. Senate, Washington, 1961, pp. 779 ff.

Litvine (M.), Accord du 22 avril 1968 sur le sauvetage des astronautes, le retour des astronautes et la restitution des objets lancés dans l'espace extra-atmosphérique. 5 Revue belge de droit international, 1970, p. 528 ff.

Lovell (B.) and Margerison (T.), The Explosion of Science, The Physical Universe, London, 1967.

Lukin (P.I.), Pravo i kosmicheskaia radiosviaz (The Law and Space Radio-communications). Sovetskoe Gosudarstvo i Pravo, 1970, No. 7, pp. 83 ff.

McDougal (M.S.), Lasswell (H.D.), and Vlasic (I.A.), Law and Public Order in Space. New Haven, 1963.

Machowski (J.), The Legal Status of unmanned space vehicles. Proceedings of the 4th Colloquium of the IISL, New York, 1961, pp. 120 ff.

Selected Problems of National Sovereignty with Reference to the Law of Outer Space. 55 Proceedings of the A.S.I.L., 1961, pp. 161 ff.

– Legal Status of Meteors and Meteorites. 39 Annuaire de l'A.A.A., 1969, pp. 101 ff.

McMahon (J.F.), Legal Aspects of Outer Space. 38 B.Y.I.L., 1962, pp. 339 ff.

– Legal Aspects of Outer Space: Recent developments, 41 B. Y.I.L., 1965-1966, pp. 417 ff.

McNair, The Law of the Air, London, 1953.

Mankiewicz (R.H.), De l'ordre juridique dans l'espace extra-atmosphérique. 5 A.Fr.D.I., 1959, p. 103 ff.

– Some Thoughts on Law and Public Order in Space. 2 Canadian Yearbook of International Law, 1964, pp. 258 ff.

– Legal Status of Space Vehicles. Report of the 53rd ILA Conference, 1968, pp. 170 ff.

– Interventions with Respect to Permanent Stations on the Moon.

– Proceedings of the 11th Colloquium of the IISL, New York, 1968.

Mann (F.A.), The Doctrine of State Jurisdiction in International Law. 111 R.C.A.D.I., 1964: I, pp. 9 ff.

Mandl (V.), Das Weltraumrecht: Ein Problem der Raumfahrt. Berlin, 1932.

Markoff (M.G.), Lune et le droit international. 1964 R.G.D.I.P., p. 411 ff.

– Notion "d'utilisation pacifique" en droit international cosmique. 29 Revue générale de l'Air et de l'Espace, 1966, p. 413 ff.

– Régime juridique international de l'espace extra-atmosphérique. 25 Annuaire Suisse de Droit International, 1968, p. 41 ff.

– Délimitation de l'espace extra-atmosphérique. 32 Revue générale de l'Air et de l'Espace, 1969, p. 377 ff.

Mateesco (M.), Le Traité du 27 janvier 1967 et la réglementation des activités spatiales. 31 Revue Générale de l'Air et de l'Espace, 1968, p. 9 ff.

Mateesco Matte (N.), Aerospace Law. London-Toronto, 1969.

Meeker (L.C.), First Decade of Law in Space. 3 International Lawyer, January 1969, pp. 193 ff.

– Observation in Space, in "Law and Politics in Space". Edited by M. Cohen. Montreal, 1964.

Meyer (A.), Interpretation of the Term "peaceful" in the Light of the Space Treaty. 18 Zeitschrift f. Luftrecht und Weltraumrechtsfragen, 1969, pp. 28 ff.

– Legal Problems of Outer Space. 18 Zeitschrift f. Luftrecht und Weltraumrechtsfragen, 1969, pp. 10 ff.

Molodtsov (S.V.), Mezhdunarodno-pravovoi rezhim otkrytogo moria i kontynentalnogo shelfa (International Legal Regime of the High Seas and the Continental Shelf). Moscow, 1960.

Mouton (M.W.), The International Regime of the Polar Regions. 107 R.C.A.D.I., 1962: III, pp. 175 ff.

Murphy (R.T.), Air Sovereignty Considerations in Terms of Outer Space. 19 Alabama Lawyer, 1958, pp. 11 ff.

New Frontiers in Space Law. Ed. by E. McWhinney and M.A. Bradley, Leiden, 1969.

Nicolson (M.), The Environmental Revolution, London, 1970.

Oppenheim (L.) and Lauterpacht (H.), International Law, Vol. I. Peace. 8th edition. London, 1955.

Orr (J.M.), Treaty on Outer Space: An Evaluation of All Arms Control Provisions. 7 Columbia Journal of Transnational Law, 1968, p. 259.

Panhuys (H.F. van) and van Emde-Boas (M.J.), Legal Aspects of Pirate Broadcasting. 60 A.J.I.L., 1966, pp. 303 ff.

Patterson (E.W.), Law in a Scientific Age. New York, 1963.

Pépin (E.), Space penetration. 52 Proceedings of the A.S.I.L., 1958, pp. 229 ff.

– Les problèmes juridiques de l'espace. 13 Revue française de droit aérien, 1959, p. 307 ff.

Persin (J.), Will Space be Open to Piracy. 30 Telecommunication Journal, 1963, No. 3. pp. 113 ff.

Poulantzas (D.M.), International Law in View of Outer Space Activities. 35 Annuaire de l'A.A.A., 1965, pp. 171 ff.

– Some of the Potential Sources of the Law of Outer Space. 23 Revue Hellénique de Droit International, 1970, p. 377 ff.

Pradelle (A. de La), De l'origine de la maxime "cuius solum eius coelum". 1932 Revue Générale de Droit Aérien, p. 294 ff.

Probst (R.), Probleme des Raumflugs unter besonderer Berücksichtigung ihrer Bedeutung für den dauernd neutralen Staat. 19 Z.F.A.O.R.Vr., 1958, pp. 637 ff.

Quadri (R.), Droit international cosmique. 98 R.C.A.D.I., 1959: III, p. 505 ff.

Rajski (J.), Odpowiedzialnosc cywilna przewoznika lotniczego w prawie międznarodowym i krajowym (Civil Responsibility of the Air Carrier in International and Municipal Law). Warsaw, 1968.

– Responsabilité pour les dommages causés par des objets spatiaux, y compris l'observation météorologique par satellites. 24 Revue française de droit aérien, 1970, No. 1, p. 37 ff.

Rauchhaupt (W. von), A Light from the Past to Show up the Legal Problems of our Age of Space. Proceedings of the 1st Colloquium of the IISL, 1958, The Hague, pp. 1 ff.

Reintanz (G.), Weltraumrecht, Berlin, 1967.

Rivoire (J.), Design for a Law of Space. Proceedings of the 1st Colloquium of the IISL, The Hague, 1958, pp. 100 ff.

The Role of Science and Technology in Economic Development, UNESCO Report, Paris, 1968, 8 Science Policy Studies and Documents, pp. 11 ff.

Rozelear (A.J.W.), Extraterrestrial Mining. 15 Journal of the British Interplanetary Society, 1955, pp. 308 ff.

Rybakov (Iu.M.), Pravovaia reglamentatsiia otvetsvennosti za ushcherb v sviazi s deiatelnostiu gosudarstv v kosmose (Legal settlement of liability for national activities in outer space). 11 Pravovedenie 1967, No. 1, pp. 115 ff.

– Pravovaia reglamentatsiia spasaniia kosmonautov i kosmiches-kikh korablei (Legal problems of the rescue of astronauts and space vehicles). Sovetskoe Gosudarstvo i Pravo, 1966, No. 5, pp. 123 ff.

Sauer (A.), Die völkerrechtliche Bedeutung der Sputniks. 8 Jahrbuch f. Internationales Recht, 1959, pp. 37 ff.

Sauveplanne (J.G.), Freedom and Sovereignty in Air and Outer Space, 12 Netherlands International Law Review, 1965, pp. 228 ff.

Savatier (R.), Propriété de l'espace. 1965 Recueil Dalloz-Sirey, pp. 213 ff.

Schachter (O.), Legal Aspects of Space Travel. Journal of British Interplanetary Society, 1952, pp. 14 ff.

– Who owns the Universe? in "Across the Space Frontier". Ed. by Ch. Ryan, 1952.

– Scientific Advances and International Law. 55 California Law Review, 1967, No. 2, pp. 423 ff.

Schick (F.B.), Problems of Space Law in the United Nations. 13 I.C.L.Q., 1964, pp. 968 ff.

Schönborn (W.), La nature juridique du territoire. 30 R.C.A.D.I., 1929: V, p. 81 ff.

Schwarzenberger (G.), International Law as Applied by International Courts and Tribunals, Vol. 1. London, 1957.

Sissakian (N.M.), On the Way to the Inhabited Space. 15 Impact of Science on Society, 1965, No. 3.

Smedal (G.), Acquisition of Sovereignty over Polar Areas. Oslo, 1931.

Smirnoff (M.), Quelques idées sur les principes d'une convention internationale de l'espace. 14 Revue française de droit aérien, 1960, p. 359 ff.

– Philosophie du droit de l'espace. 23 Revue française de droit aérien, 1969, p. 151 ff.

– Régime juridique commun de l'espace aérien et cosmique comme la seule solution du problème de la délimitation de ces espaces. 25 Revue française de droit aérien, 1971, p. 27 ff.

Sontag (P.M.), Erwerb von Hoheitsbereichen im Weltraum und auf Himmelskörpern. 12 Jahrbuch f. Internationales Recht, 1965, pp. 272 ff.

– Der Weltraum in der Raumordnung des Völkerrechts. Köln-Berlin, 1966.

Szczepanski (J.), Zagadnienie zwickszenia efektywnosci wplywu nauki na rozwoj spoleczenstwa (Problems of Enhancing the Influence of Science on the Development of Society), 8 Problems of Science, v. 2, Warsaw, 1971, pp. 139 ff.

Tabibi (A.H.), The Right of Transit of Land-locked Countries. Kabul, 1968.

Taubenfeld (H.J.), Outer Space: The "territorial" limits of nations. 38 Fordham Law Review, October 1969, pp. 1 ff.

Taubenfeld (R. and F.), Some International Implications of Weather Modification Activities. 23 International Organization, 1969, pp. 808 ff.

Taylor (G.A.), The Doomsday Book, London, 1970.

Trooboff (P.D.), INTELSAT: Approaches to the renegotiation. 9 Harvard International Law Journal, Winter 1968, pp. 1 ff.

Tunkin (G.I.), Teoria mezhdunarodnogo Prava (Theory of International Law). Moscow, 1970.

Valladão (H.), The Law of Interplanetary Space. Proceedings of the 2nd Colloquium of the IISL, London, 1959, pp. 156 ff.

Vallat (F.), The Outer Space Treaty. 73 The Aeronautical Journal, 1969, pp. 754 ff.

Vasilevskaia (E.G.), Regulirovanie pravovogo polozheniia luny i drugikh nebeskykh tel (Settlement of the Legal Regime of Moon and Other Celestial Bodies). Sovetskoe Gosudarstvo i Pravo, 1968, No. 8, pp. 75 ff.

– Osvoenie luny: nekotorye perspektivy pravovogo regulirovaniia (Exploration of the Moon: Some Perspectives of the Legal Settlement). 1971 Sovetskoe Gosudarstvo i Pravo, No. 4, pp. 92 ff.

Vencatassin (J.L.), Problèmes économiques, juridiques et sociaux résultant de l'exploration et l'utilisation de l'espace extra-atmosphérique. 23 Revue française de droit aérien, 1969, p. 15 ff.

Verdon (C.) and Dalfen (C.M.), La Coopération régionale: nouvelle voie ou impasse dans le développement du droit des satellites de radiodiffusion directs? 8 Canadian Yearbook of International Law, 1970, pp. 39 ff.

Vereshchetin (V.S.), Pravovaia prirodo mezhdunarodnykh nauch-noteknicheskikh soglashenii po kosmosu (The Legal Character of International Scientific-technical agreements in the Field of Outer Space). Sovetskoe Gosudarstvo i Pravo, 1968, No. 5, pp. 86 ff.

– Pravoye formy mezhdunarodnogo sotrudnichestva SSR v mirnom osvoenii kosmicheskogo prostranstva (Legal forms of international cooperation of the USSR in the field of exploration of outer space). Sovetskoe Gosudarstvo i Pravo, 1967, No. 1, pp. 69 ff.

Verplaetse (J.G.), The Law of War and Neutrality in Outer Space. 39 Nordisk Tijdsskrift for International Ret, 1959, pp. 55 ff.

– International Law in Vertical Space. Air-Outer-Space-Ether. New York, 1960.

– On the Definition and the Legal Status of Spacecraft. 29 Journal of Air Law and Commerce, 1964, pp. 131 ff.

– Sur les sources du droit de l'espace extérieur. 20 Revue française de droit aérien, 1966, pp. 278 ff.

– Autour de l'Art. IV du Traité de droit cosmique du 27 janvier 1967. 31 Revue générale de l'Air et de l'Espace, 1968, p. 45 ff.

Wadegaonkar (D.), Legal Problems of Outer Space. 9 Indian Journal of International Law, 1969, pp. 47 ff.

Warkallo (W.), Energia atomowa a odpowiedzialnosc cywilna (Atomic Energy and liability in civil law). Mélanges K. Przybylowski, Warsaw, 1965, pp. 439 ff.

Wehringen (C.K.), Stations spatiales, la lune, la guerre. 33 Revue générale de l'Air et de l'Espace, 1970, p. 7 ff.

– Moon, Spaceports and Law. 36 Journal of Air Law and Commerce, Winter 1970, pp. 58 ff.

Wengler (W.), Völkerrecht. Berlin, 1964. 2 vol.

Wolczek (A.), Proceedings of the 1st Colloquium of the IISL, The Hague, 1958, pp. 115 ff.

Wolfke (K.), Custom in Present International Law. Wroclaw, 1964.

Zadorozhny (G.P.), Osnovnye problemy nauki kosmicheskogo prava (Basic Problems of Space Law) in "Kosmos i Mezhdunarodnoe Pravo. Ed. by E.A. Korovin. Moscow, 1962, pp. 23 ff.

Zemanek (K.), The United Nations and the Law of Outer Space. 1965 Yearbook of World Affairs, pp. 199 ff.

Zhukov (G.P.), OON i problema mirnogo ispolzovaniia kosmicheskogo prostranstva (U.N. and the Peaceful Use of Outer Space). Sovetskii Ezhegodnik Mezhdunarodnogo Prava, 1960, pp. 177 ff.

— Pravovoy rezhim kosmicheskogo prostranstva na sovremennom etape (The Present Stage of the Legal Regime of Outer Space), in "Kosmos i Mezhdunarodnoe Sotrudnichestvo", Moscow, 1963, pp. 10 ff.

– Problema Otvetstvennosti za uscherb v kosmiches kom prave (The Problem of Liability in Space Law). Sovetskoe Gosudarstvo i Pravo, 1965, No. 6, pp. 67 ff.

– Kosmicheskoe Pravo (Space Law). Moscow, 1966.

Zuckerman (Lord), Scientific Expectations, Times Literary Supplement, No. 3.635, 1971, p. 1 ff.

Zwicky (F.), Examples of Activities in Extraterrestrial Space. Paper Submitted to the Scientific-Legal Liaison Committee, International Academy of Astronautics.

– The Morphology of Justice in the Space Age and the Boundaries of Outer Space. 14 Acta Astronautica 1969, pp. 615 ff.

Zylicz (M.), Sur quelques problèmes de droit astronautique. 1958 R.G.D.I.P., pp. 655 ff.

Table of Cases Cited

Aves Island Case (1865). 2 Lapradelle et Politis, Recueil des Arbitrages Internationaux, p. 408 ff.

British Guiana–Venezuela Boundary Arbitration (1899). 92 British and Foreign State Papers, pp. 160 ff.
British Property in Spanish Morocco (1925). II U.N.R.I.A.A., pp. 615 ff.
Buchanan vs. Rucher (1808). 9, East, pp. 192 ff.
Bury v. Pope (1587), Cro. Eliz. 118.

Chicago and Southern Airlines vs. Waterman Steamship Corporation (1948). 333 U.S. 103
Clipperton Island Case (1931). II U.N.R.I.A.A., pp. 1105 ff.
Costa Rica Packet (1897). 5 Moore, International Arbitration, pp. 4592 ff.

Decisions of Claims Commission Mexico-United States. IV U.N.R.I.A.A., pp. 11 ff.

Grisbadarna Case (1909). XI U.N.R.I.A.A., pp. 147 ff.

Island of Palmas Case (1928). II U.N.R.I.A.A., pp. 829 ff.

Jamaica Case. British-United States Claims Commission 1798. Moore, International Adjudications. Modern Series, Vol. IV, pp. 489 ff.

"Lotus", Judgment No. 9, 1927. P.C.I.J., Series A, No. 10.

North Atlantic Fisheries Arbitration (1910). XI U.N.R.I.A.A., p. 198 ff.

Oregon Case (1846). 2 Lapradelle-Politis, Recueil des Arbitrages Internationaux, pp. 498 ff.

Rights of Nationals of the United States of America in Morocco, Judgment, I.C.J. Reports 1952, pp. 176 ff.

Schibsby vs. Westenholz (1870). L.R. 6, Q.B., pp. 155 ff.

Trail Smelter Arbitration: United States vs. Canada (1941). III U.N.R.I.A.A., pp. 105 ff.
Treaty of Neuilly, Art. 179, Annex, Par. 4 (Interpretation), Judgment No. 3, 1924, P.C.I.J., Series A, No. 3.

Index*

* Compiled by the Editors

About the International Institute of Space Law

The International Institute of Space Law (IISL) is an independent non-governmental organization that was founded by the International Astronautical Federation (IAF) in 1960. The IISL replaced the Permanent Committee on Space Law, which the IAF had created in 1958 under the chairmanship of Andrew G. Haley. The membership of the IISL is composed of individuals and institutions from more than forty countries who have been elected on the basis of their contributions to the field of space law or other social sciences related to space activities.

Since 1958 the IISL has held more than fifty Colloquia in many countries during which multiple panels address current issues in space law. These Annual Colloquia are held during the International Astronautical Congress (IAC) and the Colloquium Proceedings are published each year by the American Institute of Aeronautics and Astronautics (AIAA). In 2009, the *Nandasiri Jasentuliyana Keynote Lecture* was added to the Colloquium program. This lecture features a prominent speaker who addresses the members of the IISL and other IAC participants on a highly topical issue of broad interest. The second part of this session is dedicated to the development of future space lawyers and features young scholars who present papers on space law and policy. The IISL also organises a joint Scientific/Legal Roundtable session at the IAC each year with the International Academy of Astronautics (IAA) and regularly participates in Plenary Events at the IAC.

The purposes and objectives of the IISL include cooperation with appropriate international organizations and national institutions in the field of space law, the holding of meetings, colloquia and competitions on legal and social science aspects of space activities, the preparation or commissioning of studies and reports, and the publication of books and proceedings. Since 2001, the IISL has organized dedicated space law conferences in several countries, including Singapore, China, India and Thailand. It also organizes the annual *Eilene M. Galloway Symposium on Critical Issues in Space Law* in Washington, DC since 2006. In 2010, the first IISL-IAA symposium on *Space Policy and Law* was held in Washington, DC, as part of the 50th anniversary celebrations of both organizations. The IISL is also an officially recognized observer at sessions of the United Nations Committee on the Peaceful Uses of Outer Space, and its Scientific & Technical and Legal

Subcommittees. In cooperation with the European Centre for Space Law (ECSL), the IISL organizes an annual space law symposium for the delegates and staff attending the sessions of the UNCOPUOS Legal Subcommittee in Vienna, Austria. The programs deal with topical space law issues, and the papers presented are published in the IISL Proceedings.

The Manfred Lachs Space Law Moot Court Competition has been organized by the IISL each year since 1992 and hosts student teams from Europe, North America and the Asia Pacific region. The World Finals take place at the IAC and are judged each year by members of the International Court of Justice. In addition to the Manfred Lachs Trophy for the winning team, awards are given at the World Finals for the best memorials and the best oralist.

The IISL recognizes achievement in the field of space law by giving several awards, including the *Lifetime Achievement Award* and the *Diederiks-Verschoor Award and Prize* for the best Colloquium paper by a young scholar.

Further information regarding the IISL can be found at www.iislweb.org and www.spacemoot.org.

www.ingramcontent.com/pod-product-compliance
Lightning Source LLC
LaVergne TN
LVHW081515300926
849161LV00006B/1191
9789004186675